Coming into Their Own

About Search Institute

Search Institute is an independent, nonprofit, nonsectarian organization whose mission is to provide leadership, knowledge, and resources to promote healthy children, youth, and communities. The institute collaborates with others to promote long-term organizational and cultural change that supports its mission. For a free information packet, call 800-888-7828.

Search Institute's Healthy Communities • Healthy Youth initiative seeks to motivate and equip individuals, organizations, and their leaders to join together in nurturing competent, caring, and responsible children and adolescents. Major support for Search Institute's Healthy Communities • Healthy Youth (HC • HY) initiative is provided by Thrivent Financial for Lutherans Foundation.

About This Resource

Funding for the research for this resource was provided by the Donald W. Reynolds Foundation, a national philanthropic organization founded in 1954 by the late media entrepreneur for whom it is named. Reynolds was the founder and principal owner of the Donrey Media Group. Headquartered in Las Vegas, Nevada, it is one of the largest private foundations in the United States.

DONALD W. REYNOLDS
FOUNDATION

Peter C. Scales,

Arturo Sesma, Jr.,

and Brent Bolstrom

Search Institute • Minneapolis

Coming into

Their Own

How Developmental Assets

Promote Positive Growth

in Middle Childhood

Coming into Their Own:
How Developmental Assets Promote Positive Growth in Middle Childhood

Peter C. Scales, Arturo Sesma, Jr., and Brent Bolstrom
Copyright © 2004 by Search Institute

10   9   8   7   6   5   4   3

Printed in the United States of America on acid-free paper

Library of Congress Cataloging-in-Publication Data

Scales, Peter, 1949–
    Coming into their own : how developmental assets promote positive growth in middle childhood / Peter C. Scales, Arturo Sesma, and Brent Bolstrom.
       p.   cm.
    Includes bibliographical references and index.
    ISBN 1-57482-431-7
    1. Child psychology.   2. Preteens—Psychology.   I. Sesma, Arturo.   II. Bolstrom, Brent.   III. Title.
    BF721 .S347 2004
    155.42'4—dc22

                              2003022046

Search Institute, 615 First Ave. NE, Suite 125, Minneapolis, MN 55413
612-376-8955, 800-888-7828, www.search-institute.org

Credits
Editors: Susan Wootten, Kathryn (Kay) L. Hong, Mary Byers
Design: Diane Gleba Hall
Production: Mary Ellen Buscher

Contents

The Internal Assets

List of Tables

Acknowledgments

A book of this scope does not appear without the significant help of numerous people. We are grateful to them all for their contributions.

We cannot thank enough the Donald W. Reynolds Foundation for its generous support of Search Institute. That support enabled us to develop the Search Institute *Me and My World* survey, on which much of this book is based, as well as write the book itself. And those activities were just small parts of the wide-ranging impact the foundation's grant had on the development of statewide and community asset-building initiatives, especially in Arkansas, Nevada, and Oklahoma, and the creation and provision of numerous asset-building resources and trainings whose positive effects will be felt for many years. At Search Institute, we thank Director of Strategic Advancement Laura Lee Geraghty and Partner Services Manager Kristie Probst for their skilled management of the larger foundation grant and their support for the middle childhood work that this funding made possible.

The Reynolds Foundation grant enabled us to devote several years to developing the survey for children in grades 4 through 6. That work involved a pre-pilot in New Brighton, Minnesota, a suburb of St. Paul; two pilots in Oklahoma, one in Norman and one in Oklahoma City; and three field tests: one in Yucca Loma, California, one in Douglas County, Nevada, and one in Amherst, New York. Our deep appreciation goes to the pilot and field test survey coordinators and their teams in those sites: Amy Pucel (Minnesota); Sharon Rodine, Jan Miller, Sharon Heatly, Heather Horton, Camie Leal (Oklahoma); Mary-Diana

Pouli (New York); Valerie Smith (California); and Dori Draper (Nevada). They contributed more hours and effort than could ever be repaid or properly acknowledged, and illuminated the strengths and weaknesses of the survey along the way, both conceptually and administratively. They were indispensable colleagues in this effort.

We are indebted as well to the schools and districts that participated. Their administrators, teachers and other staff, and students and their parents all had a choice of whether to join us in this endeavor, and we cannot express our gratitude that they did. They allocated precious class time to helping us construct a survey that we hope will help them and thousands of schools and communities across the country better understand the developmental environment of their upper elementary children, and be even more effectively attentive to positively shaping that environment for all kids. We hope the survey and this book help them feel they made the right choice to participate.

The survey itself was composed mostly of items developed by the book's authors or adapted from items other Search Institute staff had created. Throughout the pilot process, we were joined in that item-generating process by former Search Institute senior scientist Nancy Leffert, Ph.D., now Dean of Psychology at Fielding Institute, Santa Barbara, California. Nancy was an integral member of the team that constructed the survey, and we deeply appreciate her wisdom and commitment to this project.

Former Search Institute Research Assistant Rene Vraa, now Field Research Project Coordinator with AGS Publishing, Circle Pines, Minnesota, worked tirelessly on the early gathering of scientific literature and provided helpful ideas on the initial development of survey items. Research Assistant Jennifer McGaffey also contributed valuable effort to the literature searching, particularly the search for relevant measures from other researchers, and skillfully managed the process of requesting and obtaining permission from other researchers to use or adapt their items in our survey.

We are thankful, too, for the permission these colleagues gave us to incorporate their work into this survey of developmental assets in middle childhood. Our deepest gratitude goes to Sharon E. Paulson, Gregory J. Marchant, and Barbara A. Rothlisberg, Ball State University (family support); Gregory L. Bowen and Natasha K. Bowen, University of North Carolina at Chapel Hill (parent involvement in schooling and learning engagement); Carol Midgely, University of Michigan (achievement motivation); Fred Beauvais, Ruth Edwards, and Eugene Oetting, Colorado State University (bonding to adults at school); Brenda Bryant, University of California at Davis (interpersonal competence—empathy); Beverly Cairns, University of North Carolina at Chapel Hill (interpersonal competence—friendship); Jude Cassidy, University of Maryland and

Steven Asher, Duke University (interpersonal competence—friendship); Laurence Steinberg, Temple University (coregulation); Shmuel Shulman and Inge Seiffge-Krenke, Bar-Ilan University, Israel (coping skills); and Scott Huebner, University of South Carolina (life satisfaction). We hope we have done justice to their work. The value the *Me and My World* survey may have for both basic research in positive human development and practical applications that improve children's lives is due in no small measure to the tremendous collegiality and commitment to the advancement of knowledge shown by these eminent researchers.

Our colleagues at Search Institute have been a bulwark of steadiness, brilliance, and dedication. We particularly appreciate and value the support of Search Institute President Peter Benson, Ph.D., and Director of Applied Research Marc Mannes, Ph.D. They believed in this project and consistently stood behind us in our effort to have as thorough a survey development process as possible and to take the time necessary to develop a book that would make a meaningful contribution to understanding positive development in middle childhood. They also engaged deeply in thinking about how best to conceptualize and measure the developmental assets in middle childhood. We are grateful for their leadership and support.

Throughout the survey development and testing, Survey Services Coordinator Deb Grillo and Administrative Manager of Applied Research Jean Wachs gave numerous critically important suggestions that consistently improved the survey. Deb also helped coordinate the prepilot in New Brighton, Minnesota, and Jean served as an internal reviewer for the book manuscript. Senior Data Analyst/Programmer Karen Bartig withstood with great humor and consistent high-quality work our avalanche of requests for data analyses always needed within thoroughly unreasonable time frames.

Throughout the writing of this book, we were gently nudged and vigorously challenged by Senior Editor Kay Hong. She provided conceptual insights and deftly managed the internal and external review of the preliminary manuscript, as well as the revision and production that followed. Sandy Longfellow, Manager of Search Institute's Information Resource Center, assisted mightily with the literature searching and acquisition of the hundreds of sources we needed to review. Our deep thanks as well to Susan Wootten for a wonderful early editing job. Her conscientious and involved reading of the manuscript resulted in numerous changes that significantly strengthened the book before it went out to reviewers. We are grateful for her insightful suggestions.

Our special thanks go to the internal and external reviewers of the preliminary manuscript. We hope that they see their plentiful suggestions, concerns, and questions attended to and answered in the final book. All authors need critical reviewers and skilled editors, but not all are fortunate enough to have them. We are grateful to ours for their significant shaping of the book. Reviewers from Search Institute included Senior Editor Kay Hong, Associate Editor Ruth Taswell, Associate Editor Becky Aldridge, Director of Publishing Kathleen Kimball-Baker, Administrative Manager of Applied Research Jean Wachs, and Director of Family and Congregation Initiatives Gene Roehlkepartain. External reviewers included Karen Vanderven, Ed.D., of the University of Pittsburgh; Michael Karcher, Ph.D., of the University of Texas-San Antonio; and Dan Hyson, Ph.D., school psychologist at Greenleaf Elementary School, Apple Valley, Minnesota. To a person, these reviewers pushed us further and demanded more of us, both in our scientific thinking and in our expression of ideas. Their multitude of thoughtful contributions cannot be neatly cataloged, so we simply offer our sincere thanks. We also are grateful for the early thinking of Michael Karcher and of Susan Hickman, graduate student at the University of Minnesota's Institute of Child Development. Their thoughtful contributions helped immensely in conceptualizing the asset framework for middle childhood.

Over these several years, we have immersed ourselves in this project and in middle childhood, extending the limits of love and tolerance for our families and friends, those closest to us. Invariably, despite our shortcomings or perhaps because of them, they have never failed to be there for us. No book can be born without the sacrifice of those who care the most about those who write it. Our love and gratitude to them are inexpressible.

Finally, we thank the children in our lives, who remind us that the reality of *their* lives is often not well captured by social science or well understood by most adults. We write a lot about trends and averages and patterns in this book, but children are not trends, averages, or patterns. Each is a unique gift, teaching us something about the truth of development in all its great variety and its resistance to being reduced to simple linear trends. It is to the wonder we feel in our appreciation of development in all its glory, and to those children who bring this wonder to our lives, that we offer our greatest thanks.

*Developmental assets are
the positive relationships,
opportunities, competencies,
values, and self-perceptions that
young people need to succeed.*

Introduction: The Developmental Assets Framework and Its Application to Middle Childhood

All stages of human development are inherently and infinitely fascinating. For parents, a child's birth and infancy are accompanied by both excitement and exhaustion. Toddlerhood brings with it the joy of curiosity and exploration. And the early childhood years are marked by that mixture of parental pride and letting go that comes with a child's first days of school, a rite of passage no less poignant than a child's first date in adolescence and, later, graduation from high school and college.

Middle childhood, which we define roughly as grades 4–6, holds its own special fascination and is the focus of this book. It is during these years, after all, that children approach the cusp of early adolescence. In many respects, children have one foot firmly planted in childhood, and with the other are gingerly reaching toward the vastly different world of adolescence. This transition will not be complete for a number of years, but for most children, the shift begins to declare itself during middle childhood. By the middle school years, most young people act and feel rather more like adolescents than they do children, but their childlike thoughts, behaviors, and qualities often still have a strong and unmistakable presence.

It is in middle childhood, however, that the first murmurs of the coming early adolescence begin to be heard and the first hints of the transition become apparent. Many children, though still clearly *children*, begin to occasionally act and feel in ways more characteristic of adolescents. Middle childhood is a time of great change, of enormous expansion of children's worlds and understandings of self and others, and a time when children's self-structures, values, beliefs, and aspirations are still malleable and relatively optimistic.

Children's risks and opportunities both increase in these years, and the changing landscape of risks, opportunities, and emerging capacities can lead to either developmental success or frustration, both in children's present and future. We have written this book because understanding the positive developmental experiences children need during middle childhood is critical for ensuring their well-being. Understanding what children need, and the individual, organizational, and community actions that emerge from that knowledge, can contribute to reducing children's risk behaviors, promoting their resilience, and enhancing their thriving during the upper elementary years, and to enabling them to effectively navigate the gradual transition between childhood and adolescence.

Here, we have tried to synthesize the scientific research on how a variety of "developmental assets" or building blocks of success (Benson, 1997) seem to "work" in middle childhood. This book provides some insights that can influence informal relationships among adults and young people, as well as formal programs and policies, so that preadolescents are on a path to a developmentally "rich" adolescence from which they ultimately "graduate" into successful adulthood.

The value of this explication of the asset framework in middle childhood lies both in deepening basic scientific understanding of the period and in helping to focus informal and formal applied efforts to improve children's lives. The overarching purpose of all this articulation is, as reflected in Search Institute's vision, *to create a world where all young people are valued and thrive.*

How can that vision be realized? At Search Institute, we believe there are five action strategies (as depicted in Figure 1), informed by an understanding of developmental assets in each age group from birth to 20, that can transform communities and society into more developmentally attentive places that foster more positive child development.

Five Action Strategies

- **Engage adults.** Engage adults from all walks of life to develop sustained, strength-building relationships with children and adolescents, both within families and in neighborhoods.
- **Mobilize young people.** Mobilize young people to use their power as asset builders and change agents.
- **Activate sectors.** Activate all sectors of the community—such as schools, congregations, youth, businesses, human services, and

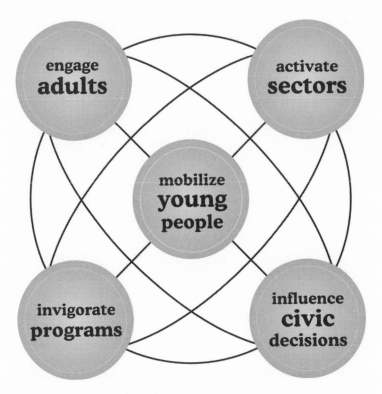

Figure 1. *Five Circles of Action Strategies*

health-care organizations—to create an asset-building culture and
to contribute fully to young people's healthy development.

- **Invigorate programs.** Invigorate, expand, and enhance programs
  to become more asset rich and to be accessible to all children and
  youth.
- **Influence civic decisions.** Influence decision makers and opinion
  leaders to leverage financial, media, and policy resources in support of this positive transformation of communities and society.

The developmental assets framework for middle childhood, like the foundational framework for adolescence from which it is derived and with which it
is fully aligned, is designed to provide a focus for those strategies. Collectively,
efforts to build young people's assets through those five action strategies are intended to have a powerful positive impact on young people's well-being, as well
as on families, schools and other organizations, programs, policies, neighborhoods, and a community's overall quality of life.

Risk Behaviors, Resilience, and Thriving Defined

Although *developmental* assets are the focus of this book, we occasionally refer to "risk behaviors," "resilience," and especially "thriving," or indicators of optimal development in middle childhood. Risk behaviors in middle childhood include alcohol, tobacco, and other illicit drug use; antisocial behavior; physical agression/violence; and frequent sadness. Resilience refers to children who function at adequate levels despite facing adversity and vulnerability; resilient children "overcome the odds" against them to function acceptably in their families, schools, peer groups, and community settings. Thriving, however, suggests a state of well-being that goes beyond the level of being "acceptable" or "adequate." Thriving suggests optimal development and that a child is on the path to a hopeful future.

Adolescents who report higher levels of developmental assets also report fewer risk behaviors, more resilience, and greater thriving outcomes, and we hypothesize the same relationships exist during middle childhood.

Thriving is a less commonly discussed topic than risk behaviors in the developmental literature, but we give it strong emphasis in this book. The following table presents the broad thriving dimensions that we include in the term "thriving" and that are measured in the *Me and My World* survey for children in grades 4–6.

Thriving Indicators, with Definitions

School success	Child gets mostly B's or good/above-average marks on report card.
Helps others	Child helps friends, neighbors, or others on one or more days per week.
Values diversity	Child's parents teach the importance of having friends and playing with peers who are different from the child.
Delays gratification	Child can wait for a larger reward later, rather than needing to obtain a smaller reward immediately.
Coregulation	Child often helps parents make decisions about things the child cares about.
Coping skills	Child regularly uses active coping skills to deal with problems.
Life satisfaction	Child is satisfied with her or his life.

The Framework of Developmental Assets

The lens we use to look at middle childhood is the developmental assets framework developed by Search Institute. Developmental assets are relationships, opportunities, values, and skills that are building blocks for young people's successful growth in the physical, social, emotional, moral, spiritual, cognitive, and psychological arenas. Since 1990, more than 1,000 communities have requested Search Institute to survey students in grades 6 through 12 (now totaling more than 1.5 million students) in order to understand their experience of these developmental assets and to stimulate strategies for enhancing the relationships, opportunities, values, and skills that young people need to "succeed." An adolescent succeeds developmentally if he or she meets three broad criteria:

- Engages minimally (if at all) in patterns of negative risk-taking behavior, such as alcohol and other drug use (some taking of "risks," is, of course, developmentally appropriate and necessary, such as risking honesty with a friend or risking embarrassment in trying out a new activity or skill);
- Is resilient in the face of challenges; and
- Engages in positive actions that suggest not just adequate development but optimal development or thriving, such as regularly helping others and valuing racial/ethnic diversity.

Our focus on middle childhood in this book arises from the conviction that *positive development in middle childhood keeps or puts children on a path to experiencing this kind of "successful" adolescence.*

Search Institute's original developmental assets framework emerged from analysis of the research literature on adolescent development, problem prevention, youth resilience, and related areas (see Benson, 1997; Benson, Leffert, Scales, & Blyth, 1998). The framework originally identified 30 assets, but was modified to encompass 40 assets in the mid-1990s on the basis of further literature review, focus group results, and analysis of surveys measuring students' experience of the assets. The 40 assets are grouped for ease of communication into internal and external asset areas, within each of which are four separate asset categories. *External assets* are those that adults (and, to a lesser extent, peers) provide for young people, including the categories of support, empowerment, boundaries and expectations, and constructive use of time. The *internal assets* are composed of the values, skills, and self-perceptions young people develop gradually in order to become self-regulating, and include the categories of commitment to learning, positive values, social competencies, and positive identity.

Our efforts to conceptualize the terrain of developmental strengths in young people have been strengthened by several findings of developmental scholars and practitioners that we summarize here and detail more fully elsewhere (Benson, Scales, & Mannes, 2003). First, research and evaluation studies have suggested that programmatic approaches narrowly aimed at reducing and/or preventing risk behaviors (the prevailing paradigm of youth research, policy, and services in the past several decades) are less effective than more comprehensive approaches rooted in meeting the broad developmental needs of young people (Roeser, 2001; Roth, Brooks-Gunn, Murray, & Foster, 1998; Schorr, 1993).

Second, a burgeoning number of studies show that context—specifically, the interactions and embeddedness of individuals within multiple, layered, and overlapping environments constituting the totality of their lives—creates complex and diverse developmental paths (Bronfenbrenner, 1979; Lerner, 1998). An important corollary to this ecological theory is that individuals (even infants) are influenced not simply by their environments but by actually having a hand in constructing those environments. An example of this reciprocal interaction is the effect of children's behavior on the parenting they receive, as well as the number and kind of other adults who may be attracted to children and offer them support and nurture (Mannes, 2001; Shonkoff & Phillips, 2000).

These learnings about developmental systems and the relative ineffectiveness of narrowly targeted problem-prevention strategies have led to increased debate about what constitute the markers of healthy development in young people (other than avoidance of harm and risk), and to an increased interest in the contributions that diverse contexts—family, school, peer, and community—make to development. These observations have led researchers and practitioners away from focusing primarily on problem prevention, and toward identifying and promoting the sources of positive development.

A variety of terms have been used over the past 75 years to name what children and youth require for positive development, including the execution of "developmental tasks," the resolving of "developmental crises," and the meeting of "developmental needs" (Masten & Curtis, 2000; Sroufe, 1979). For example, Sroufe (1979) characterized developmental tasks such as the management of tension and exploration and mastery as "organizational issues" in that patterns of adaptation are organized around these salient developmental issues. Regardless of terminology, these concepts have helped shape children's environments in various settings. Examples include the establishment of standards for "developmentally appropriate practice" in programs for young children (Bredekamp & Copple, 1997) and the creation of "developmentally responsive" middle-level schools for young adolescents (National Middle School Association, 2003).

Search Institute's developmental assets framework has emerged from a melding of these traditional and contemporary strands of both theory and empirical research in developmental psychology. In terms of the preceding discussion, developmental assets may be seen as the "nutrients" that permit the accomplishment of developmental tasks, resolution of developmental crises, and meeting of developmental needs.

Evidence of the validity of the framework's content for adolescents is provided in a comprehensive review and synthesis of more than 800 research studies (Scales & Leffert, 1999) that demonstrate the considerable degree to which the developmental importance of the asset constructs is broadly supported in the scientific literature. A series of studies involving large samples of students in grades 6 through 12 has also shown that the assets young people experience across multiple contexts of family, school, peers, and community are related to lowered high-risk behavior and increased youth "thriving" or optimal development (Benson, Scales, Leffert, & Roehlkepartain, 1999; Leffert, Benson, Scales, Sharma, Drake, & Blyth, 1998; Scales, Benson, Leffert, & Blyth, 2000). In short, the more assets adolescents report having—and the more they experience them across all parts of their lives—the less they engage in patterns of alcohol or other drug use, antisocial behavior, violence, and other high-risk behaviors. In addition, the more assets they have, the more they report succeeding at school, helping others, valuing diversity, and other indications that they are not merely avoiding problems but also thriving.

The research we discuss in this book strongly suggests that the same patterns extensively documented for adolescents pertain to children in middle childhood: The more developmental assets they experience, the better their odds of not just "doing okay" in their present and future but of thriving, of being the very best unique persons they can be. Thus, the developmental assets framework seems validly to describe a broad array of relationships, opportunities, values, and skills that promote a healthy middle childhood and increase the odds of a successful adolescence.

The general developmental assets framework also seems to have utility in describing positive development in early childhood (K–3). Although early childhood is not the focus of this book, it is important to understand the general stability of these positive developmental processes throughout the first two decades of life. Assets and the developmental issues we focus on do not simply appear in middle childhood, but rather emerge from accumulated experiences in the prior years. Thus, to set the stage for our presentation of the middle childhood assets framework, we first describe the mixture of developmental continuity and stage uniqueness that characterizes the years from early childhood through middle childhood and adolescence. We then briefly examine asset development in the early childhood period in order to lay the groundwork for considering middle childhood in more depth.

Continuity and Uniqueness:
Developmental Assets in the First Two Decades of Life

Human development is characterized by developmental continuity throughout life, as well as by developmental uniqueness. A given developmental asset
may reflect either or both attributes present during the first two decades of life.
We considered it important to determine how various assets reflected either
function as part of the process of deciding whether an asset included in the
adolescent framework should be retained for the middle childhood framework.
The asset framework we describe for middle childhood, presented in Table 1,
grows out of children's foundational experiences in early childhood and younger
ages, and contributes to their later experience of developmental assets during
adolescence.

The scientific literature we present here suggests that the assets included in
the adolescent framework are highly relevant for the middle childhood period,
reflecting developmental continuity. However, we also found that a number of
assets needed to be reframed somewhat to reflect the uniqueness of the middle
childhood stage of development and the maturity of children's capacities during that period. For example, sense of purpose may be a developmental asset for
both middle childhood and adolescence, but we would not expect children to
have as much insight into the purpose and meaning of their lives as we would
adolescents. We discuss those issues in depth in subsequent chapters.

We conceptualize these assets as developmentally relevant throughout at
least the first two decades of life, from birth to age 20. We retained the eight
asset categories from the original framework because they remain solidly valid
as broad domains of experience that children and youth at *all* ages need to experience positively in order to reduce their health risks, strengthen their resilience,
and promote their thriving.

The 40 assets placed within those eight categories also retain a remarkable
stability of their own across developmental stages. When in the first two decades of life is it unimportant for young people to feel loved and cared for in
their families, that other adults care about them, that people are expecting them
to do their best in life? When is it unimportant for young people to spend a reasonable portion of their "free" time in creative activities, organized youth programs, and spiritual pursuits? Is there any time throughout the first two decades
of life when it is unimportant that children are engaged in and enjoy learning;
are caring, honest, responsible people; are able to function well socially with all
sorts of others; can say no to unhealthy behaviors; and have a solid belief in their
own worth, capacities, and future?

To raise these questions is to answer them. The developmental assets framework does not include everything all children would ever need; no framework does. But it does offer a compellingly useful and consistently broad lens through which to understand development throughout at least the school-age years, and perhaps both earlier and beyond. The way we describe developmental assets during middle childhood is thus quite consistent with the way they have been described for adolescence.

The consistency of the view through this broad lens, however, does not imply that what one sees in looking more closely, more microscopically, never varies across ages and stages. *How* the broad asset dimensions manifest themselves—the categories of support, empowerment, boundaries and expectations, constructive use of time, commitment to learning, positive values, social competencies, and positive identity, and the 40 assets that comprise those categories—certainly varies across developmental periods. Later we will talk about some of the ways this variation in assets may express itself when comparing middle childhood with early childhood and with adolescence.

Our focus is to describe what the scientific research says about the developmental assets children may experience *before* adolescence, and consider how those positive experiences may contribute to children's developmental successes, both during the elementary school years and later, when those children enter adolescence. In addition to searching for general sources on middle childhood we focused our review by searching for studies using keywords associated with each of the eight developmental asset categories (e.g., for positive identity, we searched for identity, self-esteem, self-efficacy, purpose, optimism, and self-concept). We emphasized quantitative studies that involved 50 or more children and studies done since 1990, although we do refer to smaller, more qualitative studies and to research done prior to 1990. In all, we reviewed more than 1,000 studies and have cited more than 600 in this book. It is important to note, however, that middle childhood does not receive the same research attention as does early childhood and adolescence. This reality makes it difficult to summarize research and draw broad conclusions regarding some assets (e.g., homework, religious community, and sense of purpose).

We chose to focus particularly on the upper elementary school grades (4 through 6), a period we refer to as *middle childhood,* a time when most children accelerate their transition from childhood to early adolescence. We also touch, however, on issues relevant to early childhood in order to illustrate how the developmental assets of middle childhood may flow out of positive foundational experiences in families, schools, neighborhoods, and community settings.

Particular emphasis was given to grades 4 and 5, as these grades more fully reflect the middle childhood period for most children. We also emphasized grade 6, a transition year representing for most children the approximate end of middle childhood and the beginning of early adolescence (some children begin to experience physical and social aspects of adolescence even earlier, of course, in grades 5 and, sometimes, 4).

In the literature, age boundaries used to demarcate early childhood and middle childhood differ by author and discipline, with no single age range agreed upon by all. For example, researchers who also study adolescent development have variously defined middle childhood as comprising the years from 6 to 12 (Collins, Harris, & Susman, 1995), from 6 to 10 years (Eccles, 1999), and from as young as 5 to 8 years (Shiner, 1998). In contrast, the National Association for the Education of Young Children, a principal influence on the extent and quality of early child-care and education programs throughout the country, defines early childhood as encompassing the years from birth through age 8, or roughly through grade 3 (Bredekamp, 1986), with middle childhood obviously then beginning at grade 4.

Given this variation in age/stage definitions, it is helpful to provide a rough heuristic to guide our discussion. We defined several broad developmental stages from birth through adolescence:

- Infancy (approximately birth to age 2);
- Toddlerhood (approximately ages 2 to 3);
- Preschool (approximately ages 3 to 5);
- Early childhood (approximately kindergarten through grade 3);
- Middle childhood (approximately grades 4 through 6);
- Early adolescence (approximately grades 5 through 9); and
- Mid to late adolescence (approximately grade 9 to age 20).

Developmental Assets in the First Decade of Life

From 1990 to the mid-1990s, Search Institute introduced and refined the framework of developmental assets for adolescents. In the mid-1990s, we began to conceptualize the developmental assets framework as it applies to younger children, from birth through the elementary school years, in part by conducting an initial review of the scientific literature on child development in those periods (Leffert, Benson, & Roehlkepartain, 1997). In the report on this work, *Starting Out Right: Developmental Assets for Children,* we concluded that the underlying constructs reflected by the adolescent developmental assets framework also seemed relevant for children younger than about 12 years of age (approximately grade 6).

In 2000, Search Institute received a generous grant from the Donald W. Reynolds Foundation that enabled us to engage in extensive study of developmental assets present in the lives of preadolescent children. We conducted a more comprehensive literature search than we had done several years earlier and undertook an elaborate consideration of the nature of developmental assets in childhood. We also began a several-year effort to construct a survey—*Me and My World* (MMW)—that measures developmental assets that children experience in the middle childhood years.

As a result of this work, we have noted that what particular assets "look like" can be quite different for younger children when compared to the assets experienced by adolescents. For example, the setting and enforcing of clear rules and boundaries by adults for children is considered an asset for children of all ages. In an asset-rich environment for children, there would be very few exceptions to ensuring that children in the first few grades of early elementary school

Introduction to the *Me and My World* Survey

The developmental assets framework was originally devised as a conceptual and communications tool, and secondarily as a framework to suggest measurement of positive experiences in adolescence. As we developed the framework and measurements for middle childhood, we wanted to strike a more equal balance between those two purposes.

Preadolescents are, of course, not simply smaller versions of adolescents, but children who function in developmentally different worlds. To define and measure developmental assets for preadolescents, therefore, we could not merely reword items from the *Search Institute Profiles of Student Life: Attitudes and Behaviors* (A&B) adolescent survey to make them more readable for younger children. Instead, we had to reconsider each developmental asset, thriving indicator, risk behavior, and developmental deficit included on the adolescent survey in terms of its developmental appropriateness for younger children. We also had to identify constructs that were conceptually important and needed to be measured for younger children, but that were either not as conceptually critical for adolescents or not currently measured on the adolescent survey. The effort to more sharply define conceptually valid developmental assets for younger children was intertwined with the effort to measure those constructs at acceptable levels of reliability.

In addition, we hoped to develop a survey that, like the A&B survey, schools would not find burdensome and that could be self-administered within a sufficiently brief time. The literature suggests that although surveys are frequently read aloud to children below middle school age (grades 6–8), students in grades 4 and 5 routinely complete self-administered instruments

[sidebar *continued*]

investigating constructs similar to those to be included in this survey. It seemed likely that we could phrase survey questions for students in grades 4 and 5 in language they could comprehend and complete successfully on their own. We considered including 3rd graders, but concluded it would be much more difficult to achieve adequate readability. It also has been reported that younger children are more likely to provide extreme responses on Likert-type scales, especially to questions about subjective feelings, a bias that does not appear to be lessened by reducing the number of choices from which children must select responses (Chambers & Johnston, 2002).

In addition, on the A&B survey, students in grade 6 tend to omit survey items and fail to complete the survey in greater proportions than do older youth, suggesting either greater difficulty with the survey reading level, less ability to find the material relevant, or both. Search Institute's middle childhood survey—*Me and My World* (MMW)—is written at a grade 4 reading level and asks questions of 6th graders about issues that may be more relevant to them than are issues included in the adolescent survey. Thus, the data for students in grade 6 may be more valid than comparable grade 6 data from the adolescent survey. (Students for whom the MMW survey reading level is difficult may have the questions read aloud to them. In pilot testing, only a very small proportion of students, less than 5%, required that alternative.)

In developing the middle childhood framework and survey, we also wanted to strengthen some measurement aspects of the asset framework. For example, in the A&B survey, a number of assets are measured with only one item, or if measured with multiple items, do not reach the commonly accepted, minimum alpha reliability standard of .70. In addition, none of the thriving indicators are measured by more than one item. Thus, one of our goals in constructing the framework and survey for upper elementary children was to more fully conceptualize both the assets and thriving indicators and to measure them with commensurate operational depth, in hopes of strengthening the framework's content and construct validity, as well as improving the reliability of the measures (see Appendix). About one-quarter of the items were taken from or modified from other researchers' measures, with their permission. Please see the Acknowledgments for a listing of those researchers.

(kindergarten through grade 3) abide by rules and boundaries. In contrast, an occasional exception might be appropriate for the increasingly more cognitively and socially capable child in the later elementary school years.

By middle school and high school, fairly regular renegotiation of rules and boundaries between adolescents and adults could be considered a more appropriate norm, as adolescents are expected to assume a greater degree of self-regulation than are younger children. Moreover, family boundaries are likely to be more salient in the lives of children in the earliest grades, with school boundaries subsequently increasing in importance throughout the school-age years, and neighborhood boundaries becoming an increasingly important asset for children in the upper elementary grades, early adolescence (the middle school years), and adolescence (the high school years).

We have come to think of the developmental assets framework for middle childhood as having the same basic structure that we had previously defined and measured for adolescents, and broadly articulated for early childhood, but as being expressed in somewhat different ways in each of those age groups. To further provide a context for understanding the developmental assets framework for middle childhood, it also is helpful to briefly consider the nature of development *before* middle childhood, for the *early* childhood period provides foundational experiences that shape the assets in *middle* childhood.

The Transitional Nature of Early Childhood

The early childhood years (kindergarten through grade 3), ranging roughly from 5 to 8 years of age, are more properly characterized collectively as a transitional phase, rather than as a distinct developmental level. Years 5 through 6 seem to represent the end of early childhood, whereas years 7 through 8 signify the beginning of middle childhood (Sameroff & Haith, 1996). For example, the cognition of a child in kindergarten is more akin to the immature thinking of a preschooler than it is to that of a 7- or 8-year-old, who is more capable of symbolic reasoning and mental manipulation of objects (Bredekamp & Copple, 1997). The typical 5- to 6-year-old is capable of keeping one concept in mind at a time (what Piaget [1952] called centration).

Socially, the peer relations of 5- to 6-year-old children are based primarily on propinquity and shared activities; peer relationships of 7- to 8-year-olds are more frequently characterized by reciprocity and mutual support (Harter, 1996). To older children, it is not enough for their peers to be merely available and ready to play the same games. Older children begin to be concerned with the fairness and balance of "give and take" in a relationship, and with how the relationship makes them feel. Thus, the transitional nature of the kindergarten through grade 3 (K–3) period should be kept in mind as we discuss how assets in middle childhood might emerge from experiences in the earlier school years.

One of our goals is to build a comprehensive understanding of the positive experiences needed for healthy development throughout all the school years, which we define as comprising kindergarten through grade 12. Thus, throughout this book we ask how the developmental assets in middle childhood emerge from the positive experiences of children in the early elementary years, and also how they contribute to the assets experienced by young people when they become adolescents. There is great continuity between the three age groups, not only in the underlying structure of the assets (e.g., the family-support asset connotes high levels of love and support, regardless of developmental level), but also in how the assets are operationalized (e.g., one of the criteria for family support across these three developmental periods is how well the child and parent get along). Beyond these simple continuities, however, lie a number of differences corresponding to the varying capacities and skills of children in the developmental periods of early childhood, middle childhood, and adolescence.

We have attempted to highlight the similarities and differences between assets that are developing in the early elementary (early childhood) years and the developmental assets, especially the internal assets, that are more fully present in middle childhood and adolescence. We view the early elementary years not so much as a period when specific assets emerge, although for some young children, some assets may be quite well developed. Instead, we view it as a time when most children continue to have formative experiences that contribute to solidifying later asset development in middle childhood and adolescence. Thus, rather than fully posit a new asset framework for younger children in grades K–3, we have sought instead here to capture the essence and flavor of how specific assets in middle childhood and adolescence may evolve from earlier positive experiences.

In looking particularly at how the internal assets of middle childhood and adolescence may emerge and solidify, we also highlight the significance of the shared responsibilities that parents, family, and other adults have for nurturing all children. Clearly, parents are the most important primary influences in most children's lives, especially for younger children. But other adults in and outside the family may be said to have a "reasonable responsibility" to play a supportive role in promoting the positive development of all children and adolescents (Scales, 2003).

Shared responsibilities describe those adult-child relationships and relationship processes important in fostering positive development among younger children in *early childhood*, further laying and strengthening the groundwork for asset development in middle childhood. Our working assumption is that as the number of positive adult-child relationships increases, the greater the likelihood is of a child's optimal development. For example, it is good when a child enjoys a positive relationship with one parent; positive relationships shared with two parents are even better; and positive relationships with two parents and a teacher are better yet. The effect of these relationships is thus horizontally cumulative across all the contexts a child experiences, and reflects a basic principle of asset development: Adults from all contexts of a child's life (including home, school, neighborhood, friends' parents, and so on) can engage in positive, meaningful, and health-promoting interactions with that child.

Positive adult-child relationships involve three broad dimensions, such that they:

- Are warm and supportive (Sroufe, Egeland, & Carlson, 1999);
- Provide a degree of control for the child within boundaries and limit setting (Brazelton & Greenspan, 2000); and
- Are instructional and facilitative; the child and adult engage in joint activities of exploration, discovery, and learning (Ramey & Ramey, 2000).

Each dimension has deep theoretical and empirical foundations in developmental psychology; jointly, they describe a developmentally rich "relational ecology" in which children can flourish.

The concept of shared responsibilities applies particularly to our discussion of internal assets among young children. Search Institute's internal assets—those competencies and values that help children and youth make positive and healthy decisions—are critically important throughout the first two decades of life.

How these assets are *experienced and expressed* varies at different stages of life, especially in the consistency with which children may "have" some of the internal assets. For example, later we assert that most children in the upper elementary grades do not yet "have" the positive values. But that does not mean that most are not caring, honest, responsible people with integrity, who are striving to be healthy. Most children in middle childhood recognize these values as being among the ones they are supposed to live up to, and most try to do so.

We teach children to help others in need, tell the truth, understand and accept the consequences of their actions, say what they believe, and take care of their physical and mental health. But when they stray from being able to do so, they are, appropriately, held less accountable than middle and high school-age young people. Of course, we do hold preadolescent children responsible to some extent for their actions, for experiencing consequences is an important part of how they learn. But we do not expect from them the same consistency, self-awareness, and recognition of their impact on others as we do from early and older adolescents. It is in this sense that we mean that most children in middle childhood may not "have" the positive values or some of the other internal assets in quite the same way as older children do. Such internal assets are not absent by any means; they are continuously in development throughout the life span. But they are not as fully matured in middle childhood as among older children, and are even less developed, although still evident at times, in early childhood.

Thus, especially in discussing the foundational experiences in the K–3 years that contribute to later assets in middle childhood, we shift the focus away from thinking about various internal assets *possessed* by children in kindergarten through grade 3 and, instead, toward those conditions—found primarily in the context of relationships—that may *lead* to the kinds of personal asset traits more consistently evident in middle childhood and adolescence.

The Transitional Nature of Grade 6

Finally, 6th graders are intentionally included in both the adolescent and middle childhood developmental assets framework for conceptual and practical reasons. Considerable evidence suggests that the 6th-grade period, encompassing both a young person's dual transition from childhood to puberty and entrance into the middle school environment, can be particularly stressful and is associated with significant changes in self-perceptions and behavior (Graber & Brooks-Gunn, 1996). Many youth around grade 6 may function neither wholly as younger children nor as young adolescents. We must then ask, "Which asset framework provides the most appropriate conceptual reference point for understanding a 6th grader's developmental experience of self and environment?" By including grade 6 in both the middle childhood and adolescent frameworks and surveys, we will be able to build differing databases that can eventually offer researchers the opportunity to determine empirically the framework that best explains the developmental experiences and outcomes of children in grade 6.

Competence, Coregulation, and Coming into One's Own

No framework of human development is all-inclusive. It is only that, a frame, both a basic structure that supports additional details and a way of organizing and making meaning of information. All frames of reference emphasize some of life's experiences more than others. The asset framework attempts to be a reasonably broad and deep representation of development, yet relatively concise and graspable. All 40 of the assets are *important* at a certain level. It is unlikely, though, that all the assets are equally meaningful or salient, depending on the age group being considered.

On the basis of the research we present, the 40 assets in middle childhood may be thought of, fundamentally, as supporting children's competence and growing ability to regulate themselves with adult help (coregulation). Together with their continued development of self-identity, the middle childhood period may be said to be a time when children really begin coming into their own.

The developmental assets may play these roles in middle childhood because they support and respond to the following salient developmental changes that the research discussed here shows occur in this stage of life:

- **Increased cognitive abilities**, such as reasoning abstractly, understanding oneself as having both positive and negative components, taking the perspective of others, comparing oneself to peers, and reflecting on successes and disappointments;
- **A greater ability to plan and carry out activities and monitor oneself;**
- **An enhanced ability to function socially in a greatly expanded social world** consisting of peers and adults outside the family, especially in terms of understanding one's own and others' social roles, managing conflict, learning to cooperate with others, functioning well in groups, and contributing to the collective well-being (Collins et al., 1995; Eccles, 1999; Shiner, 1998).

Based on the literature reviewed here, a central theme around which we organized the prioritizing of constructs was that **development in middle childhood focuses heavily on the construction of various competencies that prepare young people for eventual personal responsibility or self-regulation.** Indeed, Lerner, Lerner, De Stefanis, and Apfel (2001) conclude that such "regulation by individuals of their relations with their complex and changing context is the *key* problem for successful development across life" (p. 10, emphasis added).

Obviously, this lifelong process of regulation—a "coming into one's own" that combines an increasingly defined self with increasing ability to successfully live life on one's own terms—begins at least at birth. The shock of birth and initial exploration of the world set in motion a balancing act between connection and individuation that continues throughout the life span. Long before middle childhood, most children have learned a degree of basic regulatory skills, such as feeding themselves, dressing themselves, and using the toilet, and have experienced informal (and, in the case of those attending preschool and other organized programs, formal) lessons about positive self-control, caring for others, sharing, and so on. They have had significant conflicts with parents (e.g., the "terrible twos"). They have gone to child care, preschool, and eventually kindergarten and full-day school, with the countless "on your own" moments those settings offer, even with adults' presence and guidance.

But to a significant degree, the changing cognitive, social, and self-monitoring abilities of children in middle childhood, manifested in a greatly expanding social world, reveal as never before children's multidimensional *coming into their own*. In middle childhood, we see a stronger linkage of competencies and coregulation with the developing self that will become more firmly constructed during the adolescence that waits on the developmental horizon.

Research on development in middle childhood indicates that this period is critical in the child's gradual movement toward self-regulation. It is during middle childhood that parents in well-functioning North American families begin to allow young people more input into the decisions that affect them, and children begin pushing for such input. While parental and adult regulation of children is developmentally appropriate in early childhood, and increasing evidence of *self-regulation* may be an appropriate indicator of developmental milestones reached in adolescence, a different standard of behavior regulation is appropriate in middle childhood.

This standard, *coregulation,* suggests that parents, other adults, and children increasingly make decisions together about how the child spends her or his time, rather than decisions being made and imposed unilaterally by adults only. The sense of gradually increasing the child's participation in such decisions should gain salience in the middle childhood years. In developmentally healthy children and families, we should see more and more evidence of children preparing, and being prepared, to take on greater responsibilities in life, indications that children are moving toward more autonomy, but with "appropriate influence and guidance during age-graded transitions" (Collins et al., 1995, p. 66). During middle childhood, what does the literature suggest are the best ways to determine whether a child is moving toward preparation for eventual responsibility? In trying to answer this broad question, we have arrived at a description of the asset framework's special relevance for middle childhood.

Several other theoretical formulations are consistent with and have guided our thinking. For example, Connell (1990) proposed a tripartite framework for understanding the relations among individuals and the social systems they occupy throughout the life span, not just in middle childhood. In that typology, competence, autonomy, and relatedness are seen as primary dimensions of development that reflect psychological needs throughout life; these needs may take different forms, depending on developmental stage and historic-cultural context.

Similar thinking has been advanced specifically about development in adolescence and early and middle childhood. For example, Barber and Olsen (1997) focused on adolescence, concluding that the literature supports a triumvirate of autonomy, regulation, and connection as fundamental dimensions of socialization for adolescents. Similarly, Masten and colleagues (1995) divided competence in childhood (including early and middle childhood) into three broad domains: academic competence (echoing Connell's competence and autonomy constructs, and Barber and Olsen's construct of autonomy), social competence (echoing the relatedness notion of Connell and the connection dimension of Barber and Olsen), and competence in behavior or conduct (echoing autonomy in Connell's framework and both autonomy and regulation in Barber and Olsen's work). Conduct issues often are reflected in academic and social competence. For example, the literature consistently shows that the behavior of young people in peer groups, especially at school, is strongly related to their academic performance (see Chapters 5 and 7).

Although we cover all eight asset categories in our review of the research, the issues raised in the foregoing discussion led us to place the greatest emphasis on those domains that seemed to reflect growing academic and social competence. We particularly stressed family functioning and the broadening middle childhood worlds of peer and other adult relationships. In sum, if children are developing successfully during middle childhood, they are coming into their own—expressing their unique selves through a significantly more complex array of competencies and regulatory negotiations with parents, other adults, and peers in their expanding environments.

The Framework of Developmental Assets for Middle Childhood

Table 1 presents the developmental assets framework we articulate for middle childhood and includes a definition of each asset.

The framework presented in Table 1, and elaborated in subsequent chapters, is consistent with Search Institute's familiar assets framework for adolescents, and with our earlier description of assets for preadolescent children in *Starting Out Right* (Leffert et al., 1997). The eight asset categories are the same, and the names of the 40 assets are essentially the same as those used in the earlier framework for younger children and in the adolescent framework.

What we introduce here are slightly modified definitions for some of the assets. For example, "school engagement" in the adolescent framework is, in the middle childhood framework, called "learning engagement" to emphasize the importance of children at this age developing an interest in learning regardless of where that learning occurs.

For some other assets, we also explicitly name in the definition components or elements that seem especially important to development in middle childhood. For example, interpersonal competence is an asset *throughout* the first two decades of life. But in middle childhood, we focus on the elements of empathy, friendship, and positive self-control. Of course, those components do not describe all of interpersonal competence, but the research we present suggests these are three particularly salient aspects of interpersonal competence during middle childhood.

Since the debut of the developmental assets framework in 1990, we have been immersed in studying and thinking about how it is best represented for different ages across the first two decades of life. And, of course, the results of innumerable research studies continue to be published that both confirm some aspects of that thinking and challenge other aspects. As a result, we retain some of our earlier ideas about assets in childhood and modify others. Inevitably, the pursuit of scientific understanding brings change in knowledge, and so there are some different *nuances* in the asset framework we present here for middle childhood, compared with the seminal framework for preadolescent children discussed in *Starting Out Right* (Leffert et al., 1997).

However, a close reading of both that foundational publication and this one underscores the wisdom of that earlier conceptualization. In this book, we elaborate, extend, and heighten the focus on particular aspects or components of the assets in middle childhood because of new research and the years of thinking that have passed between that earlier publication and this book. But there is nothing in that earlier volume and this book that is contradictory in our overall posing of these developmental assets as pivotal to the well-being of young people at all ages.

Table 1. The Framework of Developmental Assets for Middle Childhood, with Definitions

External Assets

Support

1. **Family support**—Family life provides high levels of love and support.

2. **Positive family communication**—Parent(s) and child communicate positively. Child feels comfortable seeking advice and counsel from parent(s).

3. **Other adult relationships**—Child receives support from adults other than her or his parent(s).

4. **Caring neighborhood**—Child experiences caring neighbors.

5. **Caring school climate**—Relationships with teachers and peers provide a caring, encouraging school environment.

6. **Parent involvement in schooling**—Parent(s) are actively involved in helping the child succeed in school.

Empowerment

7. **Community values children**—Child feels valued and appreciated by adults in the community.

8. **Children as resources**—Child is included in decisions at home and in the community.

9. **Service to others**—Child has opportunities to help others in the community.

10. **Safety**—Child feels safe at home, at school, and in her or his neighborhood.

Boundaries and Expectations

11. **Family boundaries**—Family has clear and consistent rules and consequences and monitors the child's whereabouts.

12. **School boundaries**—School provides clear rules and consequences.

13. **Neighborhood boundaries**—Neighbors take responsibility for monitoring the child's behavior.

14. **Adult role models**—Parent(s) and other adults in the child's family, as well as nonfamily adults, model positive, responsible behavior.

15. **Positive peer influence**—Child's closest friends model positive, responsible behavior.

16. **High expectations**—Parent(s) and teachers expect the child to do her or his best at school and in other activities.

Table 1. The Framework of Developmental Assets for Middle Childhood (cont.)

Constructive Use of Time

17. **Creative activities**—Child participates in music, art, drama, or creative writing two or more times per week.

18. **Child programs**—Child participates two or more times per week in cocurricular school activities or structured community programs for children.

19. **Religious community**—Child attends religious programs or services one or more times per week.

20. **Time at home**—Child spends some time most days both in high-quality interaction with parent(s) and doing things at home other than watching TV or playing video games.

Internal Assets

Commitment to Learning

21. **Achievement motivation**—Child is motivated and strives to do well in school.

22. **Learning engagement**—Child is responsive, attentive, and actively engaged in learning at school and enjoys participating in learning activities outside of school.

23. **Homework**—Child usually hands in homework on time.

24. **Bonding to adults at school**—Child cares about teachers and other adults at school.

25. **Reading for pleasure**—Child enjoys and engages in reading for fun most days of the week.

Positive Values

26. **Caring**—Parent(s) tell the child it is important to help other people.

27. **Equality and social justice**—Parent(s) tell the child it is important to speak up for equal rights for all people.

28. **Integrity**—Parent(s) tell the child it is important to stand up for one's beliefs.

29. **Honesty**—Parent(s) tell the child it is important to tell the truth.

30. **Responsibility**—Parent(s) tell the child it is important to accept personal responsibility for behavior.

31. **Healthy lifestyle**—Parent(s) tell the child it is important to have good health habits and an understanding of healthy sexuality.

Social Competencies

32. **Planning and decision making**—Child thinks about decisions and is usually happy with the results of her or his decisions.

Table 1. The Framework of Developmental Assets for Middle Childhood (cont.)
33. **Interpersonal competence**—Child cares about and is affected by other people's feelings, enjoys making friends, and, when frustrated or angry, tries to calm her- or himself.
34. **Cultural competence**—Child knows and is comfortable with people of different racial, ethnic, and cultural backgrounds and with her or his own cultural identity.
35. **Resistance skills**—Child can stay away from people who are likely to get her or him in trouble and is able to say no to doing wrong or dangerous things.
36. **Peaceful conflict resolution**—Child attempts to resolve conflict nonviolently.
Positive Identity
37. **Personal power**—Child feels he or she has some influence over things that happen in her or his life.
38. **Self-esteem**—Child likes and is proud to be the person he or she is.
39. **Sense of purpose**—Child sometimes thinks about what life means and whether there is a purpose for her or his life.
40. **Positive view of personal future**—Child is optimistic about her or his personal future.
This chart may be reproduced for educational, noncommercial uses only. Copyright © 2003 by Search Institute, 800-888-7828; www.search-institute.org.

Middle Childhood Modifications to the Adolescent Asset Framework

We define several of the 40 middle childhood assets somewhat differently from how they are defined in the asset framework for adolescents (see Benson et al., 1999). For the most part, these distinctions between how the asset is represented in one or the other age group are subtle, not sizable. They are intended to help the definition of the asset resonate better with what the literature seems to tell us is most developmentally salient at each life stage. In the chapters that follow, we explain how these particular assets may be subtly different in middle childhood compared to adolescence: time at home, the positive-values assets in general and healthy lifestyle in particular, resistance skills, and sense of purpose.

Three other slightly modified assets—*caring school climate, adult role models,* and *interpersonal competencies*—are broadly similar in middle childhood and adolescence, but we have explicitly identified especially important elements of these assets during middle childhood. Caring school climate includes caring experienced from both teachers and peers. Among adolescents, there are sufficient differences in the level of caring that students report from each of these sources

(Benson et al., 1999; *Developmental assets: A profile of your youth*, 2001) that it was desirable to identify and measure them separately for those in middle childhood, especially given the much increased importance of peers in middle childhood (see Chapter 5). The same is true for adult role models, with adolescents generally reporting much more positive parental role modeling than from other adults. With children in the upper elementary years experiencing rapidly expanding social worlds, it is important to know the kinds of positive modeling influences they are experiencing from adults outside their families (see Chapter 3).

The third of these assets is interpersonal competence (see Chapter 7). The literature suggests the developmentally critical importance of skills such as empathy, friend making, and positive self-control, and so we identify those elements in the definition. Positive self-control is not included in the adolescent framework, but we introduce it here as part of interpersonal competence in middle childhood for two reasons. One is that it reflects the child's movement toward fundamental competency and positive self-regulation. The other reason is that studies show that elementary-age children's positive self-control (their ability to recognize their own unproductive behavior and to try to calm themselves when angry or frustrated) is quite important. Positive self-control is associated with social acceptance and academic success, among other outcomes, particularly for boys (see Chapter 7).

During middle childhood, young people enlarge their peer-group interactions and encounter a more demanding school environment than they had experienced in earlier elementary years, both in terms of challenges posed by increased competition and social comparisons in the middle childhood years (Eccles, 1999). Thus, opportunities for making choices about how to deal with personal frustration and anger are perhaps as plentiful and critical to well-being in middle childhood as are the opportunities adolescents face in making choices regarding high-risk behavior.

Asset Prevalence and Relation to Developmental Outcomes in Middle Childhood

In each chapter, we show the proportion of the nearly 1,300 4th–6th graders participating in the three field tests of the *Me and My World* survey who say they experience these developmental assets. Generally speaking, more children than not say they do, although there are many assets reportedly experienced by only a minority of the field test participants. The proportion saying they do experience an asset tends to be higher than the proportion of adolescents who say they experience the same or comparable asset. As we elaborate throughout this book, these findings are consistent with previous research and supportive of developmental assets theory, in that studies consistently find preadolescents more likely than adolescents to have relationships and opportunities needed for positive development.

In addition, preliminary statistical analyses (not reported here) on the aggregated field test sample of 1,300 students in grades 4–6 show many of the same relationships between middle childhood developmental assets and developmental outcomes as have been reported among adolescents. Children with higher levels of the assets tend to report fewer risk behaviors and more indicators of thriving.

The low frequency of risk behaviors in this age group limits how strongly the effect of assets on risk behaviors in middle childhood can be shown. But even with this caveat, children with more assets report less engagement in antisocial behavior and violence, and possibly alcohol use (further analyses will be necessary to confirm the latter possibility). Tobacco use also may be differentiated between the children with the lowest level of assets, as compared to children even with average levels of assets. Sadness and marijuana use do not appear to be associated with asset levels, but this could well be mainly an anomaly of the field test sample. Additional research is needed to more fully understand these relationships.

In contrast, the only thriving indicator that does not appear related to asset levels is coregulation. Children with different levels of assets are not different in reporting how much they experience coregulation. It is possible that the sensitivity of our measure of coregulation is not sufficient to detect differences. However, successively higher levels of assets are associated with higher levels of all the other middle childhood thriving indicators: school success, helping others, valuing diversity, delaying gratification, coping skills, and life satisfaction. Overall, then, these field test findings offer suggestive evidence for the validity of the middle childhood asset framework. They substantially replicate the associations consistently found in samples of adolescents—and predicted by developmental assets theory to apply to younger children—between assets and positive developmental outcomes; namely, higher levels of assets are associated with fewer risk behaviors and more thriving.

Organization of This Book

In the following chapters, we examine, in detail, the developmental assets present during middle childhood by each of the eight asset categories. In each chapter, we:

- Discuss research studies that have helped shape our conceptualization of an asset framework for middle childhood;

- Describe similarities and differences between the conceptualization and measurement of each asset category for middle childhood and adolescence;
- Discuss briefly how positive experiences in the early childhood years (roughly grades K–3) may lay the foundation for the developmental assets of middle childhood and adolescence;
- Describe why the assets in a particular category are important to healthy functioning in young people;
- Explain the operational definitions of the assets within the specific asset category and how they were measured on the middle childhood survey during the survey field tests (it is important to note, however, that some items on the survey may have changed after this book went to press);
- Note the size of the research base and elaborate on what studies suggest about the correlates and effects of the particular asset category on the developmental outcomes of thriving, risk reduction, and resilience;
- Describe how the asset category might contribute to thriving, risk reduction, and resilience, and note variations in the experience or operation of those assets that studies might have reported by gender, grade, race/ethnicity, or other individual differences; and
- Mention, where appropriate, relevant preliminary findings from Search Institute's pilot and/or field test studies of children in the upper elementary years that may shed further light on how the developmental assets are experienced during middle childhood.

Conclusions:
The Role of Developmental Assets in Middle Childhood

In the final chapter, we will thematically summarize the key findings about developmental assets in middle childhood, both overall and in the context of the two classes of assets, external and internal. But to complete this introduction to our detailed discussion in subsequent chapters, we briefly list here, without commentary, the overall conclusions suggested by this review and synthesis of the scientific literature, themes we will elaborate on in the final chapter:

1. **The essence of the contribution made by developmental assets to children's healthy development in the middle childhood years appears to be the broad promotion of academic and social**

competencies and the shifting of regulatory processes toward a model of coregulation among child and caring adults.

2. The assets in middle childhood are interdependent.
3. Tremendous variability exists, both between and within individuals, in the importance of each asset in promoting particular developmental outcomes, both concurrently and longitudinally.
4. The research suggests that the middle childhood developmental assets reflect much of what children need for healthy growth across a variety of physical, cognitive, behavioral, social, emotional, and moral dimensions. However, the asset framework has some limitations; several key constructs identified in the literature are not represented among the 40 assets.
5. Nevertheless, the developmental assets framework generally has broad application to children in the upper-elementary years.
6. The developmental assets framework seems to have utility for describing and explaining developmental processes and outcomes among children across a wide range of diversities.
7. Despite utility across diversities, it is not likely that the developmental assets for middle childhood "work" equally well for all groups of children to explain developmental outcomes.
8. Our pilot and field test data on children's experience of these assets are limited, but early trends are consistent with what we know about adolescents.

This book is the first of several planned resources that elaborate the scientific foundation of developmental assets during middle childhood and build on our earlier description of developmental assets in younger children, *Starting Out Right* (Leffert et al., 1997). The *Me and My World* middle childhood assets survey referred to in this book has been fully developed and ready for use in communities in the United States and Canada. A companion survey of parents is also being developed for use in selected Search Institute research studies. In addition, we have begun to elaborate the developmental assets framework for preschool-age children and to consider how it may be integrated with the prevailing theories and practice of early child care and education.

We hope that this book, and related resources to come, will help make the developmental assets framework for younger children as useful a tool for engaging adults, mobilizing young people, activating sectors, invigorating programs, and influencing civic decisions as the framework for adolescents has been since 1990.

References

Barber, B. K., & Olsen, J. A. (1997). Socialization in context: Connection, regulation, and autonomy in the family, school, and neighborhood, and with peers. *Journal of Adolescent Research, 12,* 287–315.

Benson, P. L. (1997). *All kids are our kids: What communities must do to raise healthy and responsible children and adolescents.* San Francisco: Jossey-Bass.

Benson, P. L., Leffert, N., Scales, P. C., & Blyth, D. A. (1998). Beyond the "village" rhetoric: Creating healthy communities for children and adolescents. *Applied Developmental Science, 2,* 138–159.

Benson, P. L., Scales, P. C., Leffert, N., & Roehlkepartain, E. C. (1999). *A fragile foundation: The state of developmental assets among American youth.* Minneapolis: Search Institute.

Benson, P. L., Scales, P. C., & Mannes, M. (2003). Developmental strengths and their sources: Implications for the study and practice of community building. In R. M. Lerner, F. Jacobs, & D. Wertlieb (Eds.), *Handbook of applied developmental science: Vol. 1. Applying developmental science for youth and families: Historical and theoretical foundations* (pp. 369–406). Thousand Oaks, CA: Sage.

Brazelton, T. B., & Greenspan, S. I. (2000). *The irreducible needs of children.* Cambridge, MA: Perseus.

Bredekamp, D. (1986). *Developmentally appropriate practice.* Washington, DC: National Association for the Education of Young Children.

Bredekamp, S., & Copple, C. (1997). *Developmentally appropriate practice in early childhood programs.* Washington, DC: National Association for the Education of Young Children.

Bronfenbrenner, U. (1979). *The ecology of human development: Experiments by nature and design.* Cambridge, MA: Harvard University Press.

Chambers, C. T., & Johnston, C. (2002). Developmental differences in children's use of rating scales. *Journal of Pediatric Psychology, 27,* 27–36.

Collins, W. A., Harris, M. L., & Susman, A. (1995). Parenting during middle childhood. In M. H. Bornstein (Ed.), *Handbook of parenting: Vol. 1. Children and parenting* (pp. 65–89). Mahwah, NJ: Lawrence Erlbaum.

Connell, J. P. (1990). Context, self, and action: A motivational analysis of self-system processes across the life span. In D. Cicchetti & M. Beeghly (Eds.), *The self in transition: Infancy to childhood* (pp. 61–97). Chicago: University of Chicago Press.

Developmental assets: A profile of your youth (2001). Minneapolis: Search Institute (1999–2000 school year aggregate dataset).

Eccles, J. S. (1999). The development of children ages 6 to 14. *The Future of Children, 9,* 30–44.

Graber, J. A., & Brooks-Gunn, J. (1996). Transitions and turning points: Navigating the passage from childhood through adolescence. *Developmental Psychology, 32,* 768–776.

Harter, S. (1996). Developmental changes in self-understanding across the 5 to 7 shift. In A. J. Sameroff & M. M. Haith (Eds.), *The five to seven year shift: The age of reason and responsibility* (pp. 207–236). Chicago: University of Chicago Press.

Leffert, N., Benson, P. L., & Roehlkepartain, J. L. (1997). *Starting out right: Developmental assets for children.* Minneapolis: Search Institute.

Leffert, N., Benson, P. L., Scales, P. C., Sharma, A., Drake, D., & Blyth, D. A. (1998). Developmental assets: Measurement and prediction of risk behaviors among adolescents. *Applied Developmental Science, 2,* 209–230.

Lerner, R. M. (1998). Theories of human development: Contemporary perspectives. In

W. Damon (Series Ed.) & R. M. Lerner (Ed.), *Handbook of child psychology: Vol. 1. Theoretical models of human development* (5th ed., pp. 1–24). New York: Wiley.

Lerner, R. M., Lerner, J. V., De Stefanis, I., & Apfel, A. (2001). Understanding developmental systems in adolescence: Implications for methodological strategies, data analytic approaches, and training. *Journal of Adolescent Research, 16*, 9–27.

Mannes, M. (2001). Well-being and family-centered services: The value of the developmental assets framework. In E. Walton, P. Sandau-Beckler, & M. Mannes (Eds.), *Balancing family-centered services and child well-being: Exploring issues in policy, practice, theory, and research* (pp. 128–154). New York: Columbia University Press.

Masten, A. S., Coatsworth, J. D., Neemann, J., Gest, S. D., Tellegen, A., & Garmezy, N. (1995). The structure and coherence of competence from childhood through adolescence. *Child Development, 66*, 1635–1659.

Masten, A. S., & Curtis, W. J. (2000). Integrating competence and psychopathology: Pathways toward a comprehensive science of adaptation in development. *Development and Psychopathology, 12*, 529–550.

National Middle School Association. (2003). *This we believe: Successful schools for young adolescents.* Westerville, OH: Author.

Piaget, J. (1952). *The child's conception of number.* New York: Humanities Press.

Ramey, S. L., & Ramey, C. T. (2000). Early childhood experiences and developmental competence. In S. Danziger & J. Waldfogel (Eds.), *Securing the future: Investing in children from birth to college* (pp. 122–150). New York: Sage Foundation.

Roeser, R. W. (2001). To cultivate the positive . . . Introduction to the special issue on schooling and mental health issues. *Journal of School Psychology, 39*, 99–110.

Roth, J., Brooks-Gunn, J., Murray, L., & Foster, W. (1998). Promoting healthy adolescents: Synthesis of youth development program evaluations. *Journal of Research on Adolescence, 8*, 423–459.

Sameroff, A. J., & Haith, M. M. (Eds.). (1996). *The five to seven year shift: The age of reason and responsibility.* Chicago: University of Chicago Press.

Scales, P. C. (with Benson, P. L., Mannes, M., Hintz, N. R., Roehlkepartain, E. C., & Sullivan, T. K.). (2003). *Other people's kids: Social expectations and American adults' involvement with children and adolescents.* New York: Kluwer Academic/Plenum.

Scales, P. C., Benson, P. L., Leffert, N., & Blyth, D. A. (2000). Contribution of developmental assets to the prediction of thriving among adolescents. *Applied Developmental Science, 4*, 27–46.

Scales, P. C., & Leffert, N. (1999). *Developmental assets: A synthesis of the scientific research on adolescent development.* Minneapolis: Search Institute.

Schorr, L. B. (1993). Daring to learn from our successes. *Aspen Quarterly, 5*, 78–107.

Shiner, R. L. (1998). How shall we speak of children's personalities in middle childhood? A preliminary taxonomy. *Psychological Bulletin, 124*, 308–332.

Shonkoff, J. P., & Phillips, D. A. (Eds.). (2000). *From neurons to neighborhoods: The science of early childhood development.* Washington, DC: National Academies Press.

Sroufe, L. A. (1979). The coherence of individual development: Early care, attachment, and subsequent developmental issues. *American Psychologist, 34*, 834–841.

Sroufe, L. A., Egeland, B., & Carlson, E. A. (1999). One social world: The integrated development of parent-child and peer relationships. In W. A. Collins & B. Laursen (Eds.), *The Minnesota symposia on child development: Vol. 30. Relationships as developmental contexts* (pp. 241–261). Mahwah, NJ: Lawrence Erlbaum.

The External Assets

Supported young people know they can rely on positive, fulfilling relationships with many adults in their families, schools, and communities.

1

The Support Assets

Why Is Support Important?

Children need to have a sense that they are known and loved, cared about and cared for, and that these experiences of support are consistent and dependable. Support provided first by parents, and later by peers, teachers, and other adults, may provide children from infancy through adolescence with a fundamental environmental "nutrient" required for their well-being. Multiple experiences of support provide children "with the security they need to try new tasks, master new skills, and gain new confidence. Children without support are more apt to feel afraid, insecure, and isolated (Leffert, Benson, and Roehlkepartain, 1997, p. 29).

We chose six developmental assets across four contexts (family, school, neighborhood, and overlapping contexts) to represent the support needed by children for healthy development in middle childhood (grades 4–6):

- **Family**—Family support and positive family communication;
- **School**—Caring school climate (which includes both caring teachers and caring peers);
- **Neighborhood**—Caring neighborhood; and
- **Overlapping contexts**—Parent involvement in schooling and other adult relationships.

Each asset in the support category may be experienced separately by a child in unique parts of her or his world, but each also percolates through overlapping experiences and relationships that provide a warm, responsive environment for the child.

All six of the support assets were measured at acceptable levels of reliability (.70 or above) in the pilot and field tests of Search Institute's *Me and My World* survey. Thus, this is a psychometrically strong asset category (see Appendix).

Such strength of measurement is reassuring, because support may be the most foundational of all the asset categories necessary for the healthy development of children throughout the first two decades of life.

Table 2. The Support Assets	
Family support	Family life provides high levels of love and support.
Positive family communication	Parent(s) and child communicate positively. Child feels comfortable seeking advice and counsel from parent(s).
Other adult relationships	Child receives support from adults other than her or his parent(s).
Caring neighborhood	Child experiences caring neighbors.
Caring school climate	Relationships with teachers and peers provide a caring, encouraging school environment.
Parent involvement in schooling	Parent(s) are actively involved in helping the child succeed in school.

Summary of Research Findings: The Support Assets in Middle Childhood

We examined a large number of quantitative studies on the role of support in the lives of children. The studies reflect diversity in sample size, demographics, and sources of information. While parent and teacher reports were found in most of the studies we reviewed, a large portion of the research also relied on children's reports.

A consistent theme throughout much of the literature is the relationship between support (especially family support) and positive childhood outcomes, particularly higher academic achievement, healthy peer relationships, effective family communication, positive behavioral adjustment, and better mental health. In addition, many studies provide evidence that parent and caregiver involvement in schooling, as well as a caring school climate, play integral roles in shaping a more positive global environment conducive to healthy child development. Relatively few studies, however, address the influence of other adults (e.g., friends' parents and adult neighbors) in children's lives during middle childhood.

Family Support and Positive Family Communication

Family support, including such components as parenting style, family communication processes, and levels of parent-child attachment, has been linked to children's adjustment. Specifically, research indicates that family support is predictive of friendship quality, conflict resolution skills, behavioral adjustment at home and school, emotional competence, and academic performance. Communication dimensions within the family also play a significant role in promoting (or modeling) skills for resisting high-risk behaviors, effective problem-solving strategies, and social competence. Family support and positive family communication in middle childhood have been associated, directly or indirectly, with:

Academic Outcomes

- **Higher grades and standardized test scores** when parenting strategies include warmth, involvement, calm discussion, and proactive teaching (Granot & Mayseless, 2001; Pettit, Bates, & Dodge, 1997).

Mental and Behavioral Health Outcomes

- **Fewer child reports of loneliness** (Domitrovich & Bierman, 2001); **higher self-esteem** (Franco & Levitt, 1998); **greater ability to adapt under stress** (Bryant, 1994; Magnus, Cowen, Wyman, Fagen, & Work, 1999; Pettit et al., 1997); **less reported victimization by peers** (Domitrovich & Bierman, 2001); **less rejection by peers** (Granot & Mayseless, 2001 [secure attachment to mother]); **lower levels of internalizing behavioral problems in school** (Granot & Mayseless, 2001 [secure attachment to mother]); **more stable and higher levels of self-esteem,** especially when fathers routinely exhibit democratic problem-solving behaviors and value-affirming ways to show approval (e.g., verbal encouragement, physical affection, playing with child) (Kernis, Brown, & Brody, 2000); and **fewer maladaptive behaviors,** such as acting out, affiliation with deviant peers, moodiness, and difficulty following directions (Kaufmann et al., 2000 [authoritative parenting style]).

Social Outcomes

- **Better friendship quality** (Chase-Lansdale, Wakschlag, & Brooks-Gunn, 1995 [warm and caring parents]; Franco & Levitt, 1998); **lower levels of aggressive problem solving with peers** (Domitrovich &

Bierman, 2001; Krenichyn, Saegert, & Evans, 2001; Magnus et al., 1999); **higher levels of supportive and conflict-resolution aspects of friendship** (Domitrovich & Bierman, 2001; Franco & Levitt, 1998 [support from other adult relatives]); **greater friendship competence** (Freitag, Belsky, Grossman, Grossman, & Scheuerer-Englisch, 1996 [possibly mediated by positive family communication]; Granot & Mayseless, 2001 [secure attachment to mother]); **more prosocial behavior, lower levels of child aggression, and higher levels of prosocial problem solving** (Domitrovich & Bierman, 2001; Krenichyn et al., 2001; Magnus et al., 1999); **lower levels of externalizing behavioral problems in school** (Granot & Mayseless, 2001 [secure attachment to mother]; Magnus et al., 1999; Pettit et al., 1997); **fewer behavior problems and more responsible behavior at home** (Shumow, Vandell, & Posner, 1998 [firm parent responsiveness]); **greater cooperation by child in monitoring situations with caregivers** (Kerns, Aspelmeier, Gentzler, & Grabill, 2001 [secure attachment to parent]); **decreased level of social withdrawal and increased social self-restraint** for boys in grades 1–4 who experience a "pluralistic" family type (i.e., high level of communication and expression of ideas and opinions, but little pressure to conform to parental viewpoints) (Fitzpatrick, Marshall, Leutwiler, & Kremar, 1996); **higher levels of showing concern for others and greater ability to adapt under stress** (Kaufmann et al., 2000 [authoritative parenting style]); and **more prosocial behaviors with peers** when mothers gave direct responses to child requests for support (Bryant, 1994).

Researchers consistently report that a supportive parenting style, which is characterized by warmth, responsiveness, and firmness with flexibility and often called *authoritative* parenting—in contrast to rigid or *authoritarian* parenting and *permissive* parenting—is associated with many desirable youth outcomes, including greater engagement in positive behaviors indicative of developmental success and less child engagement in high-risk, antisocial, or maladaptive behaviors. These asset-related results are among the most positive in the scientific literature and have been found in a host of studies with adolescent samples (see review in Scales & Leffert, 1999), as well as in studies with younger children, as noted above. The support aspect of parenting style is a critical element in the relationship between parenting style and positive child outcomes; other elements of parenting style, including monitoring and discipline, are discussed under the boundaries-and-expectations asset category (see Chapter 3).

Some studies suggest that children living in dangerous neighborhoods may fare better when their parents set more boundaries for them, in part because this reduces their exposure to risk factors such as negative peer influence, violence, delinquency, and alcohol and other illegal drugs (e.g., Furstenberg, 1993). We should not then conclude, however, that rigid, authoritarian parenting is better for those children. Firm but flexible managing of children's environments can be done at the same time as being a warm and supportive parent who encourages children's psychological autonomy. Generally, research suggests that African American and Asian American children may be less harmed by authoritarian parenting than are white children, but that children across racial/ ethnic groups tend to fare better on most outcomes if parents are authoritative (Steinberg, 2001).

A parenting style characterized by affection, positive communication, and flexible supervision may be even more important in fostering positive outcomes than preventing negative ones. In one study of students in grades 1 through 5, Kaufmann and colleagues (2000) reported that such parenting style attributes accounted for twice as much variation in children's competence (degree of empathy and ability to handle pressure well) as they did for variation in children's maladaptive behaviors (moodiness and acting out).

A longitudinal study of children from kindergarten through grade 6 found that supportive parenting during a child's kindergarten year was not only related to the child's positive school adjustment at grade 6 (lower child behavior problems and greater levels of social skills and academic performance), but also mitigated the negative effects of family adversities, such as low socioeconomic status, single parenthood, and family stress, on school adjustment (Pettit et al., 1997). Children who have better relationships with their parents, reflected by family support and positive family communication, also seem to be better at forming close friendships with their peers, an association found across cultures (Freitag et al., 1996).

In a meta-analysis of more than 60 studies on parent-child attachment, Schneider, Atkinson, and Tardif (2001) reported that the closeness of the mother-child bond in infancy was related to children's later social competence with peers and close friends. The size of the relationship between parent-child bonding and later child competence was in the small-to-moderate range ("effect sizes" of .10s–.20s), but the impact of parent-child attachment across the 60 studies was consistent. The effects of close parent-child attachment on social competence were greater in studies of children in the middle childhood and adolescent years than for those in early childhood. Parents of children in the middle childhood years increasingly are challenged to "strike the delicate balance between assistance and respect for the autonomy of the child" (Krappmann, 1989, p. 102). Supportive parenting in these years typically requires that parents be mindful of minimizing interference in or attempts to control their children's expanding social worlds; at the same time, they must not withdraw their warm and responsive influence.

Pomerantz and Eaton (2000) reported that 5th graders, in comparison to 2nd graders, were more likely to view a parent's help, monitoring, and involvement in their decisions as indications of the children's incompetence, not as supportive actions. Children who felt excessively controlled and who also viewed parental efforts to help them not as supportive but as suggesting their incompetence also experienced lower self-esteem. However, this same sample of elementary-age children also tended to see parental control as having both negative and positive qualities, suggesting that neither the way in which parents express control, nor how children experience it, is monolithic in these years. Instead, "parental control" reflects both supportive and nonsupportive dimensions.

One determinant of how support is perceived by a child may be whether it is seen as a response to a child's expressed needs. Bryant (1994), for example, reported that maternal help, attention, and approval provided in direct response to a child's request for such support was related to a child's prosocial behavior with her or his siblings. On the other hand, maternal support provided when *not asked for* was unrelated to prosocial behavior among siblings. As a child grows older, a supportive parent may increasingly be one who allows the child to struggle and make mistakes, rather than one who intervenes quickly to provide help. The appropriate intervention point for a parent's help may vary depending on the task or issue involved, the child's mood, the setting, and whether the moment is private or public. Accepting and managing such ambiguity is one of the significant challenges of navigating middle childhood for both children and parents.

The social networks of children in the middle childhood years normally expand considerably, in contrast to the dominant influence parents may have exerted over their children in infancy and early childhood. The social world of children now includes more teachers, age-peers and classmates, neighbors of all ages, and adults and peers in community settings, such as child-care programs, religious organizations, and sports leagues. Although children's need for parental support remains relatively stable in these years, they also need *greater* contributions of support from all the other actors in their social networks, more so than when they were younger (Collins, Harris, & Susman, 1995).

In other words, the total accumulation of supportive influences needs to increase, and the distribution of that support may change. Perhaps as the relative contribution of nonparental support increases with development, the primacy of parental support of young children gradually gives way to a greater importance associated with nonfamilial sources of support. For example, a study of 5th and 6th graders suggested that the level of attachment children experienced with their best friends had a more significant association with their experiences of loneliness than did their level of attachment to either parent. In addition, the less connected these children felt to their school and neighborhood, the lonelier they reported being (Chipuer, 2001). Parental support, then, remains critical, but it must be complemented increasingly by support from others in the child's expanding world.

The impact of support assets on children may also differ by gender. In a study of Dutch children followed from age 7 months to 12 years, Van Aken and Riksen-Walraven (1992) reported that parental support for a child's autonomy was the *only* supportive action that influenced the early development of competence in boys. In contrast, a variety of supportive parenting behaviors were associated with early competence in girls, including less parental hostility and positive expressions of feelings for the child. These results suggest that young girls are more aware of and sensitive to a variety of parents' social cues, an explanation that would be consistent with research showing girls in middle childhood and adolescence, on average, also to be more socially competent than boys (see Chapter 7). The results also suggest children's sensitivity to gender-role stereotyping, with boys responding more to parents' promotion of independence, and girls to a greater variety of relationship dynamics such as warmth and expression of feelings.

This study also suggests the bidirectional, transactional nature of parent-child relationships. Not only was parental support associated with early competence; in turn, the competence (ego resiliency, or adapting successfully to the demands of a situation) of children at age 7 was related to the level of support parents provided at age 12, especially for boys. Competent children at age 7 enjoyed greater parental support later at age 12. Research rather consistently confirms this commonsense observation that parents (and other adults) do not simply "have a style" of interaction with children. Children's qualities and behaviors from the earliest ages influence parents' sense of competence and satisfaction as parents and affect parents' subsequent interactions with those children, and recursively on and on in the developmental dance of building the relationship. Indeed, parents and children "co-construct" children's development (Bornstein, 2003).

Relationships that children in middle childhood have with their mothers tend to differ from relationships they have with their fathers, although perhaps less so than traditional theories have described, even taking into consideration changes during the past two decades in how mothers and fathers in industrialized countries spend time with their children (Yeung, Sandberg, Davis-Kean, &

Hofferth, 2001). Children in middle childhood spend more time with their mothers, and mothers interact with their elementary-age children on a greater variety of topics and circumstances; fathers seem to spend more time with both sons and daughters in play or leisure activities. Generally, both genders report more closeness with mothers than fathers, a disparity that tends to increase as children experience puberty (Collins & Russell, 1991; Starrels, 1994).

Other Adult Relationships and Caring Neighborhood

Research suggests that a child's broad social network plays an important part in strengthening academic competence, prosocial behaviors and problem-solving skills in school, and overall psychological well-being, as well as providing meaningful support to parents. Children's strong informal and formal relationships with individuals outside the family, such as peers' parents, community members, neighbors, and mentors, have been associated, directly or indirectly, with:

Academic Outcomes

- **Higher achievement test scores, fewer externalized behavior problems, and more teacher-rated social competence,** especially for White children (Fletcher, Newsome, Nickerson, & Bazley, 2001).

Mental and Behavioral Health Outcomes

- **Fewer behavior problems** (such as hyperactivity and depression), **greater friendship skills, and lower degree of loneliness** (Marshall, Noonan, McCartney, Marx, & Keefe, 2001); **neighborhood viewed by parents as being safer** when child is more socially integrated and given greater opportunity for child-oriented activities within the neighborhood (O'Neil, Parke, & McDowell, 2001); **less affiliation with deviant peers** if parents and children reported individuals in the neighborhood would intervene if they saw children behaving mischievously (Brody et al., 2001); **lower levels of loneliness** when child reports high levels of activity, friendships, and safety within her or his neighborhood and school (Chipuer, 2001; O'Neil et al., 2001);and **higher perceived global self-worth, academic competence, peer acceptance, and behavioral conduct, and more internal locus of control** if child perceived her or his neighborhood as safe (Farver, Ghosh, & Garcia, 2000).

Social Outcomes

- **Higher social competence** if children were provided more resources within their neighborhood, and **more acceptance from**

peers if mothers perceived greater social involvement with neighborhood members (O'Neil et al., 2001); **higher grades and achievement test scores, fewer conduct problems in school, and higher levels of socioemotional adjustment** were associated with more socioeconomic resources and lower reported crime in the neighborhood (Shumow, Vandell, & Posner, 1999 [for 5th graders]).

Fewer studies address the impact on children of positive relationships formed with adults other than their parents, especially relationships with adults unrelated to them. Nevertheless, available studies clearly point to similar positive contributions generally made to children's development by those relationships—both informal, everyday interactions and more formal examples, such as mentoring or working as a volunteer with children (see reviews in Scales, 2003, and Scales & Leffert, 1999). For example, in an analysis of survey responses of more than 200,000 students in grades 6 through 12 in the 1999–2000 school year, Search Institute looked at the impact on adolescents of their experiences of 12 assets reflecting caring relationships with adults outside the child's family. Analyses of variance data showed that students experiencing these nonfamily adult assets at successively greater levels were significantly more likely to report fewer high-risk behavior patterns (such as antisocial behavior or violence) than were students at the next lower level. They were also more likely to report indicators of thriving, such as helping others and overcoming adversity (Scales, 2003). Youth "rich" in relationships with adults outside the family fared best, youth reporting above-average levels of those assets fared next best, and so on.

Using *Me and My World* (MMW) survey data from the pilot test in Norman, Oklahoma, we conducted a similar analysis of results for 4th through 6th graders. Perhaps because risk behaviors are so much less common among younger students than middle school (grades 6–8) and high school (grades 9–12) students, the level of children's nonfamily adult relationships was not significantly associated with risk behaviors such as alcohol or tobacco use, or violence. However, we found similar, though not quite as pervasive, analyses of variance results for these younger children when we looked at the relationship between engagement with nonfamily adults and *thriving* indicators, similar to results from examination of the same relation among older students. Students who experienced positive relationships with nonfamily adults, at successively greater levels, were correspondingly more likely to report experiencing the thriving indicators of helping others, valuing diversity, and coping skills (unpublished Search Institute data).

A significant and growing body of literature documents the positive effects that children experience from caring relationships with nonfamily adults, as well as from a caring neighborhood, although most of the research has been conducted with adolescents. In general, studies show that positive interactions with adults in the child's immediate neighborhood can make positive contributions to child well-being. There are exceptions, however. Shumow and colleagues (1999) showed that 5th graders (but not 3rd graders) turned in poorer academic performances if they had greater contact with neighbors *and* lived in high-risk neighborhoods with a high proportion of female-headed households, low income and educational levels, and high levels of violent crime. But children's experience of the caring-neighborhood asset may not always be independent of their parents' behaviors. The quantity and quality of parents' interactions with neighbors help create the climate in which children's relationships with neighbors may develop.

For example, perhaps the single greatest obstacle to the nurturing of children by caring adults outside their families is a dual belief that (1) nurturing young people is really the parents' responsibility, and (2) parents would oppose the significant involvement of unrelated adults in their children's lives (apart from the expected formal connections children have with teachers, child-care providers, religious leaders, and others). However, a study of U.S. adults by Search Institute found that parents were *more* supportive of children's engagement with adults outside the children's families than were nonparents. Parents and nonparents alike believed that such engagement was more important for the well-being of children ages 5 to 10 than for older children and adolescents (Scales, 2003). But if parents do not encourage these interactions of which they generally approve, then their children may experience less of a caring neighborhood than would otherwise be available to them.

A study of a racially and ethnically diverse sample of urban families with elementary-age schoolchildren (Marshall et al., 2001) showed how important for children the connection of parents to other adults in the neighborhood can be. Parents who themselves felt they had sources of emotional support in the neighborhood, who experienced a more heterogeneous network composed of greater proportions of unrelated neighbors and friends, and who saw their neighbors often were warmer and more responsive in their parenting. They also felt more effective as parents than did parents whose social networks were more heavily concentrated within their own families. In turn, the children of parents who felt more connected to their neighbors exhibited fewer behavior problems, such as hyperactivity and depression, and greater social competence as measured by friendship skills and degree of loneliness.

Similarly, a study of students in grade 4 found that, in general, children who established meaningful relationships with their friends' parents and whose parents also had meaningful relationships with the friends' parents (social network closure) had higher achievement test scores (but not grades), fewer externalized behavior problems, and, for White children only, higher teacher-rated social competence (Fletcher et al., 2001).

Not all studies report similar findings, however. For example, Pinderhughes, Nix, Foster, and Jones (2001) found that neither the frequency of informal neighborhood visiting nor the presence of community associations had an impact on parental warmth, discipline, or harsh interaction. The only neighborhood characteristics that significantly affected those parenting behaviors were the extent of poverty, dissatisfaction with public services, and perception of danger in the neighborhood, for which lower levels of all characteristics were related to better parenting practices. Neighborhoods in the Pinderhughes et al. study were chosen because of their particularly high-risk nature. Thus, that selection process may have limited the degree to which neighbors know and trust each other, and so also constrained the impact those variables could have had on parenting.

Caring School Climate

A safe, supportive, and caring school environment for children has been linked with overall classroom enjoyment, academic achievement, and social skills. Relationships with parents, adults at school (especially, but not limited to, teachers), and children's peers in the school setting are all connected to children's feelings about their school experiences. A caring school climate has been associated, directly or indirectly, with:

- **Higher levels of school satisfaction** (Baker, 1998; Griffith, 2000; Samdal, Nutbeam, Wold, & Kannas, 1998);
- **Better nonverbal communication skills** if children report close relationship to teachers (Davis, 2001);
- **Higher frustration tolerance, more task-orientation skills, and fewer externalizing behaviors** if children perceive positive affiliation with teachers, high levels of school bonding, low levels of dissatisfaction with teachers, and less school danger (Murray & Greenberg, 2001);
- **Higher reading and math standardized test scores** (Griffith, 2000; Johnson, Schwartz, Livingston, & Slate, 2000); and
- **Higher behavioral adjustment and achievement** if teachers are not emotionally distant and/or punitive (Wentzel, 2002).

Whether a child feels the climate of a school is caring is, of course, a matter of perception. Some children may be more fortunate in genuinely experiencing that positive condition. For example, the social skills children exhibit, which are influenced considerably by appropriate parental support, may in turn be an important contributor to whether young people attract caring from others, and thereby experience the support asset we call caring school climate. A number of studies have suggested that socially competent students are better liked by peers and teachers, and tend also to perform better academically (see review in Scales & Leffert, 1999). Thus, a caring school climate may contribute to further success, but may also be more likely to be an experience of students who are *already* socially competent and who have supportive parents.

Students need to experience a positive school climate. A number of studies have suggested that positive school climate is a significant contributor to elementary students' satisfaction with school, and that satisfaction with school is, in turn, related to better school adjustment and academic performance (Baker, 1998; Griffith, 2000; Johnson et al., 2000). Moreover, emerging research suggests there is a positive "pile up" effect when students experience assets across the multiple contexts of their lives (Benson, Scales, & Mannes, 2003). Consistent with these findings, a study of students in grades 5 and 6 (Paulson, Marchant, & Rothlisberg, 1998) found that the best achievement outcomes occurred among those children who perceived a *consistency and congruence* of authoritative styles among parents and teachers, accompanied by high parental involvement and a positive school "atmosphere." The definition of positive school atmosphere was consistent with our definition of a caring school climate, including whether students saw their school as warm, positive, nurturing, and safe.

Parent Involvement in Schooling

Not surprisingly, research reveals the importance of parent involvement in many areas of a child's education. Various aspects of parent involvement in education have been associated with positive outcomes, such as higher levels of academic performance, problem-solving ability, and achievement motivation, and lower levels of learning problems. Parents' involvement in their children's educational experiences in the classroom, as well as in the home, has been associated, directly or indirectly, with:

- **Reading achievement gains, higher standardized test scores** (for review, see Christenson, Rounds, & Gornery, 1992; Izzo, Weissberg, Kasprow, & Fendrich, 1999; Shumow et al., 1999 [parental involvement compensated for neighborhood risk]; Zellman & Waterman, 1998); and **math achievement gains** from grade 1 to grade 6 (Jimerson, Egeland, & Teo, 1999);
- **Higher grades and student self-evaluations of achievement** if parents took steps to develop children's own interests and if par-

ents attributed the child's achievement to the child's own efforts (Georgiou, 1999; Paulson et al., 1998);

- **Greater school engagement, better socioemotional adjustment, better attendance, and higher math problem-solving and reading comprehension standardized test scores** if teachers perceived good parent-teacher relationships (Izzo et al., 1999);
- **Fewer teacher-reported learning problems** (Zellman & Waterman, 1998);
- **Greater importance of grades, higher student perceptions of academic competence, and higher grade point average** if consistent positive messages were sent at home and in school (Paulson et al., 1998 [authoritative parenting and teaching styles, high parent involvement, and positive school climate]); and
- **Increased efficiency and motivation to learn** (Christenson et al., 1992).

Parent involvement in schooling may reflect and/or contribute both to a child's sense of broad support provided by parents and to her or his sense that school and family are consistent and supportive in caring about the child. In other words, parent involvement in schooling may not be completely independent of other support category assets. For example, in a study of students in grades 2 through 5 and their mothers, Zellman and Waterman (1998) reported—as have numerous other studies—that parent involvement was associated with positive child outcomes. In this case, higher parent involvement (helping with homework and visiting the school) predicted less "acting out" behavior among children and greater nonverbal skills, ability to solve new problems, and reading test scores. However, when measures of parent enthusiasm (how rewarding mother felt it was to be a parent) and parenting style (authoritative, authoritarian, and so on) were substituted for the parent involvement measure, the prediction of reading scores improved significantly over the prediction based on the parent involvement measure alone. Thus, the parent involvement dimension of support is clearly important, but may not be uniquely independent of other assets, such as family support and positive family communication.

The Support Assets
across the Early Childhood-Adolescence Life Span

Connell (1990) theorized that human beings have three fundamental psychological needs: competence, autonomy, and relatedness. A wealth of research suggests that feeling loved and cared for by certain key individuals—a feeling that Connell terms *relatedness* and we call *support*—may be a crucial contributor to the two other needs: competence, which Connell (p. 93) describes as attaining socially defined and valued outcomes, and autonomy, explained as experiencing oneself as the initiator of one's actions. Indeed, Bryant (1994, p. 24) argues, on the basis of Erikson's theory of psychosocial development, that relatedness and autonomy are hardly separable, for at every stage of development "is the vital resolution and constant work of achieving and maintaining a healthy balance between social connectedness and separateness." That balance may tilt in one direction more than the other, depending upon the stage of development and the circumstances of a child's life. Evidence suggests that in middle childhood, even though the child's striving for autonomy increases as an expected dimension of development, perhaps the healthiest "tilt" is toward more emphasis on the child's experience of greater relatedness (Freitag et al., 1996).

A child's initial experience of support, of course, comes from parents and other caregivers, and a broad, comprehensive literature attests to the impact of parental support on young people's development. For example, Maccoby's review (2000) suggests that parenting variables typically account for 20% to 50% of the variation in child and adolescent outcomes. Experiencing high-quality parenting as newborns and infants is critical for positive development, but consistently responsive (warm, accepting, and flexible) parenting may be even more critical. Children's cognitive and social development clearly needs both the "jump start" of early responsiveness parents provide in the first year of life and the long-term impact of responsive parenting sustained over childhood (Landry, Smith, Swank, Assel, & Vellet, 2001).

Family Support and Positive Family Communication

Family support and positive family communication, as well as other assets that describe family processes (e.g., parent involvement in schooling and family boundaries), may operate in slightly different ways for children in kindergarten through 3rd grade as compared to children in grades 4 through 6. At their core, however, they share a fundamental process: Children who experience these family assets are presumed to have parents who employ a child-centered parenting style—that is, their beliefs and attitudes about parenting create a healthy emotional climate for the parent-child relationship (Darling & Steinberg, 1993).

Child centeredness tends to be a consistent orientation of parents; if parents are child centered when children are toddlers, they also tend to be child centered when their children become adolescents. The *practices* parents employ as a result of their parenting style are sensitive to differences in the developmental stages of the child. However, although parenting behaviors may change depending on the age of the child, the underlying beliefs and attitudes toward the child remain the same. With this distinction between *style* and *practice* in mind, we turn now to what these family assets look like.

We envision the family-support and positive-family-communication assets as appearing fairly similar across the elementary school years (kindergarten through 6th grade). During both the K–3 and grades 4–6 periods, the existence of family support and positive family communication signifies that children are experiencing warmth and affection and are engaging in meaningful, democratic conversations in which their wishes and desires are solicited and negotiated.

Slight variations in children's experience of the assets occur, though, as both children and parents navigate these age periods. For example, family support for children in the early childhood period (grades K–3) is characterized by what Maccoby (1984) described as *other-regulation;* that is, where the parent is primarily responsible for, or has a large role in, assisting the child in her or his activities and in regulating emotions and behaviors. Support during this age period, then, is characterized by appropriate and sensitive parental responses to physical, emotional, and regulatory needs.

Gradually, over middle childhood, this dynamic shifts from *other-regulation* to *coregulation,* wherein parents and children negotiate together the roles and responsibilities commensurate with the child's abilities (Collins et al., 1995). For example, a characteristic of the family-support asset in middle childhood would be letting the child know that the parent is available for help and support when needed, rather than being primarily responsible for resolving any issues the child may have.

Likewise, with positive family communication, responsive and sensitive caregivers tailor their communication styles and demands to the child's ability level. Thus, parents of children at the beginning of the early childhood period (kindergarten and grade 1) are more likely to communicate with their children through commands, instructions, and explanations, as well as by labeling and identifying certain emotions and affective states for the child (Kochanska & Thompson, 1997). Because of the child's relatively immature cognitive abilities, such parental communication styles serve to better help children navigate their social world. In contrast, children at the end of early childhood (grades 2 and 3) and beyond are able and should be expected to engage in more sophisticated interactions.

Other Adult Relationships and Caring School Climate

The other-adult-relationships and caring-school-climate assets of middle childhood represent the redundancy of positive relational experiences described as "shared responsibilities," as discussed for kindergarteners through 3rd graders in the Introduction. In other words, the processes we propose for early childhood that correspond to the middle childhood caring-school-climate asset overlap substantially with those corresponding to the other-adult-relationships asset. Most nonfamily adult-child relationships in which children are likely to engage during the early elementary school years are with teachers (Pianta, 1997). One of our hypotheses is that to the extent that a child has these experiences repeated consistently across *multiple* relationships with adults, the greater the likelihood that the child will develop optimally.

Research on children's relationships with teachers shows that teacher-student relationships characterized by high levels of closeness and low levels of conflict and overdependency are related to better school adjustment, less grade retention, and fewer special education referrals (Birch & Ladd, 1998; Pianta, Steinberg, & Rollins, 1995). Future research is needed to clarify how variations in children's relationships with nonfamily adults other than teachers (e.g., other school staff, neighbors) may affect child outcomes, as well as to better understand the cumulative effects of multiple, high-quality adult relationships on children's development.

Kindergarten through 3rd-grade children's participation in peer interactions that are characterized by positive prosocial behaviors corresponds to the other aspect of the caring-school-climate asset for children in grades 4 through 6, their relationships with peers at school. Entrance into kindergarten and formal elementary school ushers in a new social context for children to negotiate. Whereas in preschool or child-care settings most children experience small groups with high adult-to-child ratios, elementary school settings are often characterized by fewer adults per child within physically larger classroom and school building spaces. Consequently, during the transition to kindergarten, children spend more time interacting with peers and vying for the attention of adults among greater numbers of peers (Ladd, 1996). This is an optimal time, then, for children to enter a peer group characterized by generosity, cooperation, and helpfulness, as peers can provide opportunities for children to acquire such prosocial behaviors (Eisenberg & Fabes, 1998). The process is likely to be cyclical, however, as children who already have prosocial tendencies when they enter peer groups are likely to be met with more positive behaviors by peers, which then reinforce their existing prosocial behaviors. Thus, the connection between peer group and prosocial behavior should not be viewed as a causal relation, but as a dynamic and recursive process of socialization and reinforcement (Eisenberg & Fabes, 1998).

Caring Neighborhood

That neighborhoods represent an important context for development is unquestioned; *how* neighborhoods affect development, however, has been less well explored. Certainly for younger children, the impact of the neighborhood seems to be indirect and may be mediated by parent perceptions, which then affect parental regulatory strategies (O'Neil et al., 2001). Further evidence of this indirect relation comes from a study by Richters and Martinez (1993), which reported that the level of community violence per se did not necessarily affect the level of children's behavioral problems; rather, the level of family violence—which was related to community violence—was inversely related to *child resilience:* Children who lived in violent neighborhoods could still be resilient if they did not also experience high levels of family violence. Thus, a "socially cohesive" or caring neighborhood refers to one in which there are shared bonds, connections, and common values among community members (Sampson, Raudenbush, & Earls, 1997), whose effect is mediated by the parent's influence on the child.

Parent Involvement in Schooling

Our conceptualization of the parent-involvement-in-schooling asset remains quite similar across early and middle childhood. We expect children with this asset to have parents who consistently monitor and assist in their children's schoolwork, when appropriate, and who participate in school activities, such as PTA meetings. In addition, the salience of the child-teacher relationship to positive developmental outcomes (Pianta, 1997) suggests that an important component of parent involvement is the parent's cultivation of a positive relationship with the teacher (Kohl, Weissberg, Reynolds, & Kasprow, 1994, cited in Kohl, Lengua, & McMahon, 2000). It is also similarly important for a teacher (or school) to create a warm and inviting atmosphere in which to foster a relationship with parents. Thus, both parent-initiated as well as teacher- and school-initiated behaviors are represented in our conceptualization of parent involvement in schooling for children in kindergarten through grade 3.

As is evident from this brief review, there are both consistency *and* change in the support assets from the early childhood to middle childhood periods. An important consideration, though, is that many of the nonfamilial-support assets may more directly affect older children than children in the early elementary grades. That is, at least for children in kindergarten and 1st grade, most of the effects of the support assets are presumed to be mediated by the parent. As children mature in the latter part of early childhood and on into middle childhood, the strength of family-mediating effects lessens somewhat, as children are able to more directly enter into situations or construct relationships without parental presence or assistance.

Measuring the Support Assets in Middle Childhood

What do Search Institute's data from the MMW suggest about children's experiences of the support assets? In Table 3, we present the proportion of 4th–6th graders in each of the three field test sites in California, Nevada, and New York who reported experiencing these assets. Because these data are from field tests, and the survey is undergoing further modification before being made widely available, they are suggestive, but not definitive. Despite these limitations, the data are reasonably consistent with the results of other researchers' studies noted in this chapter and elsewhere. (For details on the field test sites, see Appendix or the technical manual for MMW at www.search-institute.org.)

These data suggest that the great majority—approximately 90%—of students in grades 4 through 6 experience the family-support asset. Far fewer, only about 60%, seem to experience positive family communication or parent involvement in schooling. Far more children in middle childhood say they experience positive family communication than what adolescents report on our *Search Institute Profiles of Student Life: Attitudes and Behavior* (A&B) survey. But these figures still suggest a gap in these developmental strengths in family life—positive family communication and parent involvement in schooling—for a substantial proportion of 4th through 6th graders. Although most children report experiencing the support assets outside the family, substantial proportions do not.

Other Search Institute studies suggest that many children may have only a limited experience of the assets of other adult relationships and caring neighborhood. For example, Scales (2003) reported that only 15% of more than 200,000 6th through 12th graders in an aggregate 1999–2000 school year sample experi-

Assets	% Who Report Experiencing Asset		
	Nevada	California	New York
Family support	91	89	87
Positive family communication	60	64	52
Other adult relationships	63	59	63
Caring neighborhood	50	47	63
Caring school climate	62	57	62
Caring school climate—teachers items	71	68	71
Caring school climate—peers items	64	59	68
Parent involvement in schooling	65	56	45

Table 3. Proportion of Field Test 4th–6th Graders Who Report Experiencing the Support Assets

From field tests in 2003; N = 1,294.

enced a "rich" environment filled with at least 9 of 12 assets reflecting significant relationships with adults outside the family. Children in grade 6 reported significantly more of these experiences than did older children (6.6 of the 12 nonfamily-adult-relationship assets compared with 5.0 for students in grades 7–12; unpublished Search Institute data).

Despite the benefits that other adult relationships and a caring neighborhood can have for children, far too few children enjoy such positive developmental experiences. The aggregate 1996–1997 school year sample using the *Search Institute Profiles of Student Life: Attitudes and Behavior* survey (A&B) included nearly 10,000 6th graders. Only 41% of those 6th graders from across the United States said they experienced positive other adult relationships, and just 50% reported experiencing a caring neighborhood (Benson, Scales, Leffert, & Roehlkepartain, 1999). In a similar aggregate sample from the 1999–2000 school year that included more than 26,000 6th graders from across the country, comparable figures were reported: 47% experienced positive relationships with other adults and 52% experienced a caring neighborhood (*Developmental assets: A profile of your youth,* 2001). The likely explanation for our field test figures being somewhat higher is that younger children generally experience a more asset-rich environment, and the field tests include 4th and 5th graders as well as 6th graders.

Children may have an ambivalent experience of school as a caring place. In aggregate A&B survey samples, 38% (1996–1997) and 45% (1999–2000) of students in grade 6 reported the presence of the caring-school-climate asset. In those surveys, we combined into one measure students' feelings about their teachers and their peers as sources of caring. In each of the aggregate samples, students reported more "teacher caring" than "peer caring."

In the MMW survey for 4th through 6th graders, students' reports of contributions to a caring school climate provided by their teachers and peers are combined, but are also available as two distinct measures (see Introduction). Students in the MMW field test and pilot samples also reported much more teacher caring than peer caring, a gap that was substantial for each grade. Sixth graders, however, experienced significantly lower levels of a caring school climate from both teachers and peers than did 4th and 5th graders. This is possibly due to the fact that many are transitioning out of an elementary building into a middle or junior high school setting that is less developmentally responsive to them (National Middle School Association, 2003). The consistency of these results across five demographically different samples suggests the possibility that for most children in grades 4 through 6, students' relationships with teachers contribute much more positively to their perception of a caring school climate than do their relationships with peers.

In summary, these various sources of data suggest it is likely that 4th through 6th graders experience more support assets than do older adolescents. The data also suggest that children in middle childhood probably experience relatively more support assets within their families than outside their families, with peers' positive contribution to school climate the least likely component of support to be reported. Even for the most commonly experienced assets, however, considerable proportions of children (perhaps from one-third to one-half) say they do not "have" those positive developmental strengths. In their families, schools, neighborhoods, and community activities, and in their relationships with peers, children in the upper elementary school years of middle childhood need much more developmental attentiveness in order to provide them with the foundational support assets.

Overall, our conceptualization and measurement of support in middle childhood reflect the multiple social relationships children form in those years. Children who consistently experience support across family, school, peer, and neighborhood contexts are able to directly meet their relatedness needs; children may also contribute indirectly to meeting their own needs for competence and autonomy, which in middle childhood may be associated with children's social connectedness and the quality of their relationships.

References

Baker, J. A. (1998). The social context of school satisfaction among urban, low-income African-American students. *School Psychology Quarterly, 13,* 25–44.

Benson, P. L., Scales, P. C., Leffert, N., & Roehlkepartain, E. C. (1999). *A fragile foundation: The state of developmental assets among American youth.* Minneapolis: Search Institute.

Benson, P. L., Scales, P. C., & Mannes, M. (2003). Developmental strengths and their sources: Implications for the study and practice of community building. In R. M. Lerner, F. Jacobs, & D. Wertlieb (Eds.), *Handbook of applied developmental science: Vol. 1. Applying developmental science for youth and families: Historical and theoretical foundations* (pp. 369–406). Thousand Oaks, CA: Sage.

Birch, S., & Ladd, G. (1998). The teacher-child relationship and children's early school adjustment. *Developmental Psychology, 34,* 934–946.

Bornstein, M. H. (2003). Positive parenting and positive development in children. In R. M. Lerner, F. Jacobs, & D. Wertlieb (Eds.), *Handbook of applied developmental science: Vol. 1. Applying developmental science for youth and families: Historical and theoretical foundations* (pp. 187–210). Thousand Oaks, CA: Sage.

Brody, G., Ge, X., Conger, R., Gibbons, F. X., McBride Murray, V., Gerrard, M., & Simons, R. L. (2001). The influence of neighborhood disadvantage, collective socialization, and parenting on African American children's affiliation with deviant peers. *Child Development, 72,* 1231–1246.

Bryant, B. K. (1994). How does social support function in childhood? In F. Nestmann

& K. Hurrelmann (Eds.), *Social networks and social support in childhood and adolescence* (pp. 23–35). Berlin, Germany: Walter de Gruyter.

Chase-Lansdale, P. L., Wakschlag, L. S., & Brooks-Gunn, J. (1995). A psychological perspective on the development of caring in children and youth: The role of the family. *Journal of Adolescence, 18,* 515–556.

Chipuer, H. M. (2001). Dyadic attachment and community connectedness: Links with youths' loneliness experiences. *Journal of Community Psychology, 29,* 429–446.

Christenson, S. L., Rounds, T., & Gornery, D. (1992). Family factors and student achievement: An avenue to increase students' success. *School Psychology Quarterly, 7,* 178–206.

Collins, W. A., Harris, M. L., & Susman, A. (1995). Parenting during middle childhood. In M. H. Bornstein (Ed.), *Handbook of parenting, Vol. 1. Children and parenting* (pp. 65–89). Mahwah, NJ: Lawrence Erlbaum.

Collins, W. A., & Russell, G. (1991). Mother-child and father-child relationships in middle childhood and adolescence: A developmental analysis. *Developmental Review, 11,* 99–136.

Connell, J. P. (1990). Context, self, and action: A motivational analysis of self-system processes across the life span. In D. Cicchetti & M. Beeghly (Eds.), *The self in transition: Infancy to childhood* (pp. 61–97). Chicago: University of Chicago Press.

Darling, N., & Steinberg, L. (1993). Parenting style as context: An integrative model. *Psychological Bulletin, 113,* 487–496.

Davis, H. A. (2001). The quality and impact of relationships between elementary school students and teachers. *Contemporary Educational Psychology, 26,* 431–453.

Developmental assets: A profile of your youth. (2001). Minneapolis: Search Institute (1999–2000 school year aggregate dataset).

Domitrovich, C. E., & Bierman, K. L. (2001). Parenting practices and child social adjustment: Multiple pathways of influence. *Merrill-Palmer Quarterly, 47,* 235–263.

Eisenberg, N., & Fabes, R. A. (1998). Prosocial development. In W. Damon (Series Ed.) and N. Eisenberg (Vol. Ed.), *Handbook of child psychology, Vol. 3: Social, emotional, and personality development* (pp. 701–778). New York: John Wiley & Sons.

Farver, J. A. M., Ghosh, C., & Garcia, C. (2000). Children's perceptions of their neighborhoods. *Journal of Applied Developmental Psychology, 21,* 139–163.

Fitzpatrick, M. A., Marshall, L. J., Leutwiler, T. J., & Kremar, M. (1996). The effect of family communication environments on children's social behavior during middle childhood. *Communication Research, 23,* 379–406.

Fletcher, A. C., Newsome, D., Nickerson, P., & Bazley, R. (2001). Social network closure and child adjustment. *Merrill-Palmer Quarterly, 47,* 500–531.

Franco, N., & Levitt, M. J. (1998). The social ecology of middle childhood: Family support, friendship quality, and self-esteem. *Family Relations, 47,* 315–321.

Freitag, M. K., Belsky, J., Grossman, K., Grossman, K. E., & Scheuerer-Englisch, H. (1996). Continuity in parent-child relationships from infancy to middle childhood and relations with friendship competence. *Child Development, 67,* 1437–1454.

Furstenberg, F. F. (1993). How families manage risk and opportunity in dangerous neighborhoods. In W. J. Wilson (Ed.), *Sociology and the public agenda* (pp. 231–258). Newbury Park, CA: Sage.

Georgiou, S. N. (1999). Parental attributions as predictors of involvement and influences on child achievement. *British Journal of Educational Psychology, 69,* 409–429.

Granot, D., & Mayseless, O. (2001). Attachment security and adjustment to school in middle childhood. *International Journal of Behavioral Development, 25,* 530–541.

Griffith, J. (2000). School climate as group evaluation and group consensus: Student and parent perceptions of the elementary school environment. *Elementary School Journal, 101,* 35–61.

Izzo, C. V., Weissberg, R. P., Kasprow, W. J., & Fendrich, M. (1999). A longitudinal assessment of teacher perceptions of parent involvement in children's education and school performance. *American Journal of Community Psychology, 27,* 817–839.

Jimerson, S., Egeland, B., & Teo, A. (1999). A longitudinal study of achievement trajectories: Factors associated with change. *Journal of Educational Psychology, 91,* 116–126.

Johnson, J. P., Schwartz, R. A., Livingston, M., & Slate, J. R. (2000). What makes a good elementary school? A critical examination. *Journal of Educational Research, 93,* 339–348.

Kaufmann, D., Gesten, E., Santa Lucia, R. C., Salcedo, O., Rendina-Gobioff, G., & Gadd, R. (2000). The relationship between parenting style and children's adjustment: The parents' perspective. *Journal of Child and Family Studies, 9,* 231–245.

Kernis, M. H., Brown, A. C., & Brody, G. H. (2000). Fragile self-esteem in children and its associations with perceived patterns of parent-child communication. *Journal of Personality, 68,* 225–252.

Kerns, K. A., Aspelmeier, J. E., Gentzler, A. L., & Grabill, C. M. (2001). Parent-child attachment and monitoring in middle childhood. *Journal of Family Psychology, 15,* 69–81.

Kochanska, G. R., & Thompson, R. A. (1997). The emergence and development of conscience in toddlerhood and early childhood. In J. E. Grusec & L. Kuczynski (Eds.), *Parenting and children's internalization of values* (pp. 53–77). New York: John Wiley & Sons.

Kohl, G. O., Lengua, L. J., & McMahon, R. J. (2000). Parent involvement in school: Conceptualizing multiple dimensions and their relations with family and demographic risk factors. *Journal of School Psychology, 38,* 501–523.

Krappmann, L. (1989). Family relationships and peer relationships in middle childhood: An exploratory study of the associations between children's integration into the social network of peers and family development. In K. Kreppner & R. M. Lerner (Eds.), *Family systems and life-span development* (pp. 93–104). Hillsdale, NJ: Lawrence Erlbaum.

Krenichyn, K., Saegert, S., & Evans, G. W. (2001). Parents as moderators of psychological and physiological correlates of inner-city children's exposure to violence. *Journal of Applied Developmental Psychology, 22,* 581–602.

Ladd, G. (1996). Shifting ecologies during the 5 to 7 year period: Predicting children's adjustment during the transition to grade school. In A. J. Sameroff & M. M. Haith (Eds.), *The five to seven year shift: The age of reason and responsibility* (pp. 363–386). Chicago: University of Chicago Press.

Landry, S. H., Smith, K. E., Swank, P. R., Assel, M. A., & Vellet, S. (2001). Does early responsive parenting have a special importance for children's development or is consistency across early childhood necessary? *Developmental Psychology, 37,* 387–403.

Leffert, N., Benson, P. L., & Roehlkepartain, J. L. (1997). *Starting out right: Developmental assets for children.* Minneapolis: Search Institute.

Maccoby, E. E. (1984). Middle childhood in the context of the family. In W. A. Collins (Ed.), *Development during middle childhood: The years from six to twelve* (pp. 184–239). Washington, DC: National Academy of Sciences Press.

Maccoby, E. E. (2000). Parenting and its effects on children: On reading and misreading behavior genetics. *Annual Review of Psychology, 51,* 1–27.

Magnus, K. B., Cowen, E. L., Wyman, P. A., Fagen, D. B., & Work, W. W. C. (1999). Parent-child relationship qualities and child adjustment in highly stressed urban black and white families. *Journal of Community Psychology, 27*, 55–71.

Marshall, N. L., Noonan, A. E., McCartney, K., Marx, F., & Keefe, N. (2001). It takes an urban village: Parenting networks of urban families. *Journal of Family Issues, 22*, 163–182.

Murray, C., & Greenberg, M. T. (2001). Children's relationships with teachers and bonds with school: Social emotional adjustment correlates for children with and without disabilities. *Psychology in the Schools, 38*, 25–41.

National Middle School Association. (2003). *This we believe: Successful schools for young adolescents.* Columbus, OH: Author.

O'Neil, R., Parke, R. D., & McDowell, D. J. (2001). Objective and subjective features of children's neighborhoods: Relations to parental regulatory strategies and children's social competence. *Applied Developmental Psychology, 22*, 135–155.

Paulson, S. E., Marchant, G. J., & Rothlisberg, B. A. (1998). Early adolescents' perceptions of parenting, teaching, and school atmosphere: Implications for achievement. *Journal of Early Adolescence, 18*, 5–26.

Pettit, G. S., Bates, J. E., & Dodge, K. A. (1997). Supportive parenting, ecological context, and children's adjustment: A seven-year longitudinal study. *Child Development, 68*, 908–923.

Pianta, R. C. (1997). Adult-child relationship processes and early schooling. *Early Education and Development, 8*, 11–26.

Pianta, R. C., Steinberg, M., & Rollins, K. (1995). The first two years of school: Teacher-child relationships and deflections in children's classroom adjustment. *Development and Psychopathology, 7*, 295–312.

Pinderhughes, E. E., Nix, R., Foster, E. M., & Jones, D. (2001). Parenting in context: Impact of neighborhood poverty, residential stability, public services, social networks, and danger on parental behaviors. *Journal of Marriage and the Family, 63*, 941–953.

Pomerantz, E. M., & Eaton, M. M. (2000). Developmental differences in children's conceptions of parental control: "They love me, but they make me feel incompetent." *Merrill-Palmer Quarterly, 46*, 140–167.

Richters, J. E., & Martinez, P. E. (1993). The NIMH community violence project: I. Children as victims of and witnesses to violence. *Psychiatry, 56*, 7–21.

Samdal, O., Nutbeam, D., Wold, B., & Kannas, L. (1998). Achieving health and educational goals through schools: A study of the importance of the school climate and the students' satisfaction with school. *Health Education Research, 13*, 383–397.

Sampson, R., Raudenbush, S. W., & Earls, F. (1997). Neighborhoods and violent crime: A multilevel study of collective efficacy. *Science, 277*, 917–925.

Scales, P. C. (with Benson, P. L., Mannes, M., Roehlkepartain, E. C., Hintz, N. R., & Sullivan, T. K.). (2003). *Other people's kids: Social expectations and American adults' involvement with children and adolescents.* New York: Kluwer Academic/Plenum.

Scales, P. C., & Leffert, N. (1999). *Developmental assets: A synthesis of the scientific research on adolescent development.* Minneapolis: Search Institute.

Schneider, B. H., Atkinson, L., & Tardif, C. (2001). Child-parent attachment and children's peer relations: A quantitative review. *Developmental Psychology, 37*, 86–100.

Shumow, L., Vandell, D. L., & Posner, J. (1998). Harsh, firm, and permissive parenting in low-income families: Relations to children's academic achievement and behavioral adjustment. *Journal of Family Issues, 19*, 483–507.

Shumow, L., Vandell, D. L., & Posner, J. (1999). Risk and resilience in the urban neighborhood:

Predictors of academic performance among low-income elementary school children. *Merrill-Palmer Quarterly, 45,* 309–331.

Starrels, M. E. (1994). Gender differences in parent-child relations. *Journal of Family Issues, 15,* 148–165.

Steinberg, L. (2001). We know some things: Parent-adolescent relationships in retrospect and prospect. *Journal of Research on Adolescence, 11,* 1–19.

Van Aken, M. A. G., & Riksen-Walraven, M. (1992). Parental support and the development of competence in children. *International Journal of Behavioral Development, 15,* 101–123.

Wentzel, K. R. (2002). Are effective teachers like good parents? Teaching styles and student adjustment in early adolescence. *Child Development, 73,* 287–301.

Yeung, W. J., Sandberg, J. F., Davis-Kean, P. E., & Hofferth, S. H. (2001). Children's time with fathers in intact families. *Journal of Marriage and the Family, 63,* 136–154.

Zellman, G. L., & Waterman, J. M. (1998). Understanding the impact of parent school involvement on children's educational outcomes. *Journal of Educational Research, 91,* 370–380.

*Young people are empowered
to the extent that they are seen
by others as resources, make
contributions to society, and feel
free of threats to their safety.*

2

The Empowerment Assets

Why Is Empowerment Important?

Empowerment has been described in the context of child wellness as having the opportunity to gain access to resources that meet basic needs, to participate in and exercise self-determination, and to experience competence and self-efficacy that bring stability to one's life (Prilleltensky, Nelson, & Peirson, 2001). Ultimately, empowerment is experienced when people have sufficient power to meet their own needs and can also "work in concert with others to advance collective goals" (p. 145).

In the preceding chapter, we discussed how the support assets provide children with a strong sense both that they are loved and cared for and that there are numerous sources of nurturance and comfort available to them. The empowerment assets are related to the support assets, but also distinct from them.

For example, when children feel empowered, they first of all feel safe from harm. Even if they do not feel actively loved, children know at the very least that they will not be threatened and victimized in their homes, schools, or neighborhoods. Children who experience empowerment perceive that others value them for the talents and interests they contribute to their families, schools, and communities, and that they are provided chances to make those contributions. One could feel safe, valued, and appreciated in such a manner (that is, empowered), without necessarily feeling *loved* (an element of support).

This dimension of empowerment underscores what Cameron and Cadell (1999) describe as the "reciprocal" nature of empowerment, a "process based upon mutual respect" (p. 106). Children are empowered when they are valued as unique individuals and when they are provided with opportunities to build stronger, more cohesive relationships within their families, schools, and communities. Such opportunities may include active participation in group decision making in those settings, and being asked to contribute to a larger good through helping activities and volunteer service. Prosocial experiences may contribute to the development of a strong sense of personal power and efficacy, as well as an interest in broader civic engagement and participation as children grow.

The empowerment assets measured in Search Institute's *Me and My World* (MMW) survey reflect the conditions of feeling safe, valued, and useful across multiple settings. Four middle childhood empowerment assets were measured in five pilot studies and field tests of students in grades 4–6 (see Appendix). The community-values-children asset is measured at a strong level of internal consistency reliability. Service to others is measured by only one item; hence, reliability of that asset cannot be computed. The reliabilities of the safety and children-as-resources assets are low, but this is likely because three domains— home, school, and neighborhood—are measured together in the safety asset, and two domains—family and school roles—are measured together in the children-as-resources asset. Certainly there are young people who feel safe or useful in one of those arenas but not in the others.

Table 4. The Empowerment Assets	
Community values children	Child feels valued and appreciated by adults in the community.
Children as resources	Child is included in decisions at home and in the community.
Service to others	Child has opportunities to help others in the community.
Safety	Child feels safe at home, at school, and in her or his neighborhood.

Summary of Research Findings: The Empowerment Assets in Middle Childhood

Scales and Leffert (1999) concluded in their review of research on positive development in adolescence that empirical data on adolescents and empowerment was limited. We, too, found few quantitative studies indicating how children's experience of empowerment in the immediately preceding years of middle childhood (4th through 6th grades) might influence positive developmental outcomes. Instead, many references produced by our literature search described community or educational programs designed to allow children to be and feel responsible, valued, and cared for, through vehicles such as community service, service-learning, or other forms of experiential learning, and the references typically provided recommendations for parents, educators, and community members.

For example, Finn and Checkoway (1998) give detailed accounts of six community-based initiatives in the United States created to involve young people in community building. The report describes the impact of such initiatives on children in terms of general observations and is used by the authors to urge social policy makers and service providers to share "power in ways that enable young people to have a voice in the decisions that affect their lives" (p. 342).

Other literature (e.g., Blair, 1992) addresses the relative developmental importance of giving children useful roles within the family and school (e.g., assisting with chores and participating in decision-making processes). Rarely, however, were experimental designs used or empirical data produced in the studies we found in the empowerment literature. As Muscott (2000) stated in a review of the effects of service-learning on emotionally and behaviorally disturbed students, "Limitations in the research designs prevent anything more than guarded optimism regarding the effects of [service-related] participation on students' academic and cognitive, civic, social, and moral and/or personality development" (p. 346).

Nonetheless, positive implications derived particularly from research on the effects of service-learning and children's contributions to housework comprise a large portion of literature related to the community-values-youth and service-to-others assets. A recent report from the National Commission on Service-Learning (2001) summarized the weight of evidence from scientific studies. The commission noted that children who participated in volunteer activities, such as tutoring younger children, talking with senior citizens, and joining neighborhood revitalization projects, experienced an increased sense of civic engagement and the ability to make a difference, an enhanced motivation to learn, and a moral understanding of service. Similar conclusions about the value of young people's participation in community service and service-learning have been reported by Billig (2000) and Scales, Blyth, Berkas, and Kielsmeier (2000). In another study by Grusec, Goodnow, and Cohen (1996), the authors found that children who routinely participated in household work developed a greater concern for the welfare of others. Evidence from these two areas clearly shows that building a sense of agency or self-efficacy (see Chapter 8), coupled with a genuine appreciation for helping others, sets the stage for early prosocial development.

A larger body of literature exists with regard to the developmental impact of children's sense of safety in the school and community. Unfortunately, much of the research focuses on victimization and bullying, characterized by an emphasis on children feeling *un*safe. Research has consistently shown that children who are the continuous targets of verbal and physical aggression from peers experience an increased threat of psychosocial maladjustment, in the form of anxiety, loneliness, and depression (Hawker & Boulton, 2000).

Studies are also plentiful regarding the negative effects of children's witnessing or experiencing of violence in the family or community settings (see Margolin & Gordis, 2000; Errante, 1997). For example, Fitzpatrick and Boldizar (1993) examined the effects of community and neighborhood violence on healthy child development. In a sample of low-income African American youth, the authors found a significant relationship between youth who were victimized and who witnessed violence within the neighborhood and their subsequent reports of post-traumatic stress disorder symptoms. In addition, researchers such as Farver, Ghosh, and Garcia (2000) reported that elementary children who were exposed to high rates of neighborhood violence and who felt unsafe playing in their neighborhood had significantly lower perceived self-competence, global self-worth, and peer acceptance than peers residing in safer, less violent neighborhoods.

In contrast, few studies on childhood safety within the community address how perceptions of an environment that is relatively "free" from violence, abuse, and neglect, and that provides adequate resources and opportunities for play, may contribute to appropriate, healthy, psychosocial adjustment. Nevertheless, the consistent and substantial negative impact repeatedly reported when children experience or witness abuse or violence (that is, an absence of safety) demonstrates how important the experience of safety is to positive child development.

"Safety" is a broad concept, of course. We focus on the well-documented negative *direct* effects on children of experiencing a lack of personal safety in their relationships with others in their families, schools, and neighborhoods, not on other "safety" issues. For example, children exposed to disasters clearly experience threats to their safety, with research on children and disasters constituting a growing field, especially since the September 11, 2001, terrorist attacks on the United States (La Greca, Silverman, & Vernberg, 2002). An early national telephone poll of adults conducted within the first two months after those attacks suggested that at least one-third of their children had one or more symptoms of stress; nearly half of children were reported to be worried about their own safety or that of their loved ones (Schuster et al., 2001).

In addition, there are more indirect developmental "opportunity" costs that result to children when the relationships *among the adults in their environments* are of relatively less quality. For example, in a telephone poll of 1,000 parents in the United States, the YMCA of the USA and Search Institute found that parents who reported an "excellent" relationship with their spouse or partner were consistently more likely to do things that help children grow up in developmentally healthy ways than did parents who described their relationship as just "good," "okay," or "poor" (Roehlkepartain, Scales, Roehlkepartain, Gallo, & Rude, 2002). Children living with parents who have a poor-quality relationship might not literally be "unsafe," but clearly may experience less than ideal developmental nourishment, which is itself a threat to children's ability to thrive.

Community Values Youth and Service to Others

Providing children with opportunities to feel empowered and valued by others undoubtedly allows them to draw from a reservoir of positive experiences that foster prosocial development. Numerous studies demonstrate the benefits that middle school and high school youth experience when they engage in helping activities such as tutoring younger children, befriending the elderly, maintaining parks and other public spaces, and volunteering at food banks. Benefits include greater concern for others' social welfare; a sense of duty to help others; more civic involvement and greater commitment to school and community; higher school engagement, subject matter test scores, and grade point averages; and more communication with parents about school issues (see reviews in Scales & Leffert, 1999, and Scales et al., 2000). These positive outcomes seem especially likely when young people participate not just in community service but also in service-learning, in which community service is combined with intentional, systematic reflection on the meaning of the service activities and connects youth to larger worlds of learning in settings such as schools and religious congregations.

The primary goals and benefits of offering service-learning opportunities to youth appear to be to increase students' active connections to, and understanding of, their community, to address genuine community needs, and to encourage students to develop the values of caring and altruism (Billig, 2000). Emphasis on the potential academic benefits of service-learning, while less common, is rooted in the belief that many students, particularly vulnerable ones, may find the "real world" nature of service-learning more authentic and engaging than their usual classroom curriculum (Scales et al., 2000).

Most of the research has been conducted with middle school and high school students; very little research is available on the service or service-learning experiences of younger elementary-age students. In addition, religious congregations are as much a source of service activities as are schools (Independent Sector and Youth Service America, 2002), but little research has been conducted specifically on outcomes of young people's involvement in service-learning sponsored by congregations. One indication of the importance of this gap in research is that far more religiously active 6th–12th graders (in one large study, 58%) were found to contribute service to others than were inactive or nonreligious youth (34%) (Roehlkepartain, 2003, in an analysis of the data from Benson, Scales, Leffert, & Roehlkepartain, 1999). It is possible that similar differences would be seen among younger children as well.

Despite these research limitations, the available research suggests for elementary-age children, as it does for adolescents, that their participation in activities such as volunteering, household work, and service-learning is related to positive outcomes, including higher scholastic competence, greater prosocial behavior, and a heightened sense of responsibility. Children as resources—feeling valued and being given opportunities to provide service within the family, school, and community—has been associated, directly or indirectly, with:

Academic Outcomes

- **Higher levels of academic achievement and standardized test scores** (Billig, 2000; National Commission on Service-Learning, 2001).

Mental and Behavioral Health Outcomes

- **Ability to cope better with adversity** (Prilleltensky et al., 2001); **greater sense of personal responsibility, and self-efficacy** (Billig, 2000; Finn & Checkoway, 1998 [for children with learning and behavioral disabilities]; Muscott & O'Brien, 1999; Prilleltensky et al., 2001); and **reduced risk behaviors and fewer behavior problems** (Billig, 2000; National Commission on Service-Learning, 2001).

Social Outcomes

- **Greater concern for others and sense of empathy** (Brigman & Molina, 1999; Grusec et al., 1996; National Commission on Service-Learning, 2001); **increased sense of civic responsibility** (Billig, 2000; Finn & Checkoway, 1998; National Commission on Service-Learning, 2001; Ogden & Claus, 1997; O'Keefe, 1997); **more effective and closer parent-child relationships** (Blair, 1992; Gill, 1998) and **teacher-child relationships** (Swick, 2001); and **greater appreciation of diversity** (Billig, 2000; Muscott & O'Brien, 1999).

A National Center for Education Statistics report (1999) indicates that elementary schools are less likely to offer community service and service-learning opportunities to young people than are either middle schools or high schools.

Approximately 55% of elementary schools offer community service activities to their students, while 83% of high schools and 77% of middle schools do so. Similarly, only 25% of elementary schools provide service-learning options, compared with 46% of high schools and 38% of middle schools.

Despite such building-level incidence data, however, opportunities for individual children to experience service and its positive effects may actually be greater at the elementary level. Elementary schools that adopt service-learning appear to be more likely to make the project a schoolwide practice, rather than a special approach used only by selected teachers (Billig, 2000). A schoolwide service-learning approach means that more elementary than middle or high school students could potentially be exposed to a consistent value and experience that communicates adults' beliefs in children's usefulness, importance, and ability to make meaningful contributions toward bettering their schools and communities. Haynes and Comer (1997), for example, describe how service is a central part of the widely adopted Comer School Development Program. Service to the school or community is "integral to the 'life style' of the school" (p. 83) as a means of promoting altruism, civic responsibility, and good citizenship. Because the data are so limited, it is impossible to draw firm conclusions about how widespread this potential's realization is at the upper elementary school level (grades 4–6).

Even at the more widely researched middle-school level (grades 6–8), the service-learning programs tend to be brief. Extensive preparation for service and reflection afterward tends to be uncommon, according to both teacher and student reports (Scales et al., 2000; Melchior, 1997). Scales and colleagues (2000) found no significantly different grade-level effects of service-learning among middle school students (grades 6–8). Given the transitional nature of 6th grade, however, it is quite possible that a sample comparing 4th through 6th grade elementary school students would find that service-learning affects students differently by grade, regardless of school configuration.

Scales and colleagues (2000) did report that girls and boys may be affected differently by service-learning: Girls who experienced service-learning spoke significantly more with their parents about school than did girls in the control group or boys in either the service-learning or control groups in the study. However, service-learning activities examined in that study (e.g., collecting oral histories of town residents, making quilts for Women's History Month, befriending the elderly and younger children) tended to emphasize stereotypically gender-linked language and relationship skills, and so may have been biased toward girls.

Another study reported that, when compared to 4th graders, fewer 6th grade boys and girls said they would volunteer to visit elderly people in a nursing home, but the drop-off in volunteer interest was far more precipitous among boys than girls (*Weekly Reader* and Character Counts!, cited in National School Safety Center, 2001). Thus, additional research is needed on almost all grade and gender issues surrounding service and service-learning, especially in the upper elementary grades.

Children as Resources

Children benefit from being given useful roles across family and school environments. Allowing children to be active participants in processes such as decision making and conflict resolution with peers encourages healthy development and expression of thoughts and opinions. At the same time, children begin to build a sense of control and self-competence, two particularly salient indicators of well-being in middle childhood (Eccles, Roeser, Wigfield, & Freedman-Doan, 1999). This combination of meaningful participation with others and growing autonomy facilitates healthy ego development in adolescence (Allen, Hauser, Bell, & O'Connor, 1994).

Helwig and Kim (1999) examined the decision-making procedures of a grades 1–6 sample. They reported that children (especially older children) preferred consensus-based decision-making strategies in peer and family contexts (e.g., selecting a game to play, choosing the location of a family vacation), but relied on authority figures in the school context (e.g., making decisions about curriculum). These findings suggest not only that children have the capacity to distinguish between conceptions of personal jurisdiction and authority by the time they reach the upper elementary years, but also that they can recognize the importance of personal autonomy when making decisions that affect their lives.

In a longitudinal study on actual and preferred decision-making opportunities for students as they move from elementary to middle school, Midgley and Feldlaufer (1987) found that children expressed an increasing desire for input into classroom decision making as they got older. However, students actually felt they were afforded more decision-making opportunities in elementary school than in middle school. Organizational factors such as curriculum "departmentalization" or teachers' orientation toward more control and discipline in middle school may explain the incongruity between students' decision-making needs and their experiences as they get older.

Nevertheless, research provides some evidence that children in the middle childhood years do feel they are given significant opportunities to be involved and to be heard. Unfortunately, little research is available that investigates the types and/or effects of such opportunities in the middle childhood years. The work of Eccles and colleagues (Eccles et al., 1993; Eccles et al., 1999; Wigfield &

Eccles, 1994) may offer some indirect insight. Children's beliefs in their competence in domains such as math, writing, sports, and music have been found to decrease from elementary to middle school. Some of this decline may be due to increases in social comparisons that typically occur over that transition (Eccles, 1999). Children increasingly compare themselves to peers as they get older and thus accelerate a psychological focus on their perceived shortcomings compared to more adept classmates. But some of the decline in children's beliefs in their competence may also be due to a narrowing of the opportunities children have to assume useful roles and contribute to decisions in school.

One intriguing line of research does address the impact of children as resources, specifically through their involvement in the peer mediation process. Typically, peer mediation programs in schools entail teaching children basic skills necessary for positive, constructive conflict resolution. Students, rather than teachers or counselors, serve as primary negotiators between peers in conflict and employ various techniques to resolve disputes in peaceful and nonviolent manners. In their review of research on peer mediation programs, for example, Johnson and Johnson (1996) cited numerous studies linking children's direct participation in conflict resolution strategies with academic achievement, better school climate, and psychological well-being. These unique empowerment opportunities contribute to both an increasing sense of autonomy and self-perceptions of competence during middle childhood.

Providing children with opportunities to be and feel useful is associated, directly or indirectly, with:

Academic Outcomes

- **Intrinsic motivation for doing well in school** (Eccles et al., 1991); **competence beliefs** (Wigfield & Eccles, 1994 [decrease after transition to middle school]); **increased academic achievement, more positive school climate, higher self-esteem, and fewer discipline problems** (Johnson & Johnson, 1996); and **improved critical thinking and problem-solving skills** (Stomfay-Stitz, 1994).

Mental and Behavioral Health Outcomes

- **Greater sense of autonomy** (Helwig & Kim, 1999); and **greater self-responsibility and self-regulation** (Johnson & Johnson, 1994; Johnson & Johnson, 1996).

Social Outcomes

- **More prosocial behavior in school** (Johnson & Johnson, 1994).

Safety

A sizable body of research indicates that a lack of safety at home, at school, and in the neighborhood is related to more negative affect, greater psychosocial maladjustment, and increased behavior problems in youth. Boys in elementary school consistently report greater levels of victimization and witnessing violence across family, school, and community environments than do girls. The exception is sexual abuse, which is more commonly reported among girls (Fitzpatrick & Boldizar, 1993; Grills & Ollendick, 2002; Margolin & Gordis, 2000), as is the case among adolescents as well (Scales & Leffert, 1999).

Family   Children's experience of being victimized or feeling unsafe in the family has been associated, directly or indirectly, with:

Academic Outcomes

- **Increased risk for problems in cognitive functioning and physical complaints** (Green, 1993 [sexual abuse]; Kolbo, Blakely, & Engleman, 1996 [children who witness domestic violence]); and **less successful adjustment to school in abused children** (Cicchetti, Toth, & Rogosch, 2000).

Mental and Behavioral Health Outcomes

- **Higher levels of aggression,** (Cummings, Goeke-Morey, & Graham, 2002 [marital conflict]; Finzi, Ram, Har-Even, Shnit, & Weizman, 2001 [physical abuse]; Green, 1993; Knutson, 1995 [sexual abuse]); **more anxiety and depression** (Cummings et al., 2002 [marital conflict]; Green, 1993 [sexual abuse]); **higher rate of suicide attempts** if children have a history of family violence and/or substance abuse (Walrath et al., 2001); **increased incidence of post-traumatic stress disorder** (Green, 1993 [sexual abuse]; McCloskey & Walker, 2000); and **disturbances in the development of self** (Cicchetti et al., 2000).

Social Outcomes

- **Increased loneliness at school and difficulty with peers** (Green, 1993; Kolbo et al., 1996 [children who witness domestic violence]; McCloskey & Stuewig, 2001 [sexual abuse]; **peer rejection** (Bolger & Patterson, 2001 [chronic maltreatment]; Kolbo et al., 1996 [children who witness domestic violence]); and **ineffective peer relationships** (Cicchetti et al., 2000).

School   Children's experience of being victimized or feeling unsafe in school has been associated, directly or indirectly, with:

Academic Outcomes

- **Increased disruptiveness in class** (Hess & Atkins, 1998 [for victims of aggression]); and **attention difficulties** (Hanish & Guerra, 2002).

Mental and Behavioral Health Outcomes

- **Increased depression** (Goodman, Stormshak, & Dishion, 2001; for review, see Hawker & Boulton, 2000; for boys, Kochenderfer-Ladd & Skinner, 2002); **loneliness** (Hawker & Boulton, 2000; Kochenderfer-Ladd & Skinner, 2002); **levels of anxiety** (Craig, 1998; Grills & Ollendick, 2002 [for girls, mediated by global self-worth; for boys, moderated by global self-worth]; Hanish & Guerra, 2002; Hawker & Boulton, 2000); **avoidance** (Hess & Atkins, 1998 [for victims of aggression]; Kochenderfer-Ladd & Skinner, 2002 [for boys]); **more verbally and physically aggressive behaviors** (Craig, 1998; Hanish & Guerra, 2002; Hess & Atkins, 1998; Kochenderfer-Ladd & Skinner, 2002); and **lower perceived self-esteem** (Hawker & Boulton, 2000; Hess & Atkins, 1998 [for victims of aggression]).

Social Outcomes

- **More social problems and less social acceptance** (Hawker & Boulton, 2000; Kochenderfer-Ladd & Skinner, 2002); and **increased peer rejection** (Hess & Atkins, 1998).

Community/Neighborhood   Children's experience of being victimized or feeling unsafe in the community or neighborhood environment has been associated, directly or indirectly, with:

Academic Outcomes

- **Lower perceived academic competence** (Farver et al., 2000).

Mental and Behavioral Health Outcomes

- **Increased aggression and externalizing behaviors** (Farver et al., 2000; Margolin & Gordis, 2000); **higher levels of anxiety and depression** (Kliewer, Lepore, Oskin, & Johnson, 1998; Margolin & Gordis, 2000); **more intrusive thinking** (Errante, 1997 [intrusive thinking is defined as recurring memories or images of unpleasant events]; Kliewer et al., 1998) **and symptoms of post-traumatic stress disorder** for African American youth (Fitzpatrick & Boldizar, 1993; Margolin & Gordis, 2000); **lower perceived global self-worth** (Farver et al., 2000); and **less internal locus of control** (Farver et al., 2000).

Social Outcomes

- **Poorer peer relationships and social skills** (Errante, 1997; Margolin & Gordis, 2000); **less acceptance from peers** (Farver et al., 2000); and **more loneliness and social dissatisfaction** (O'Neil, Parke, & McDowell, 2001).

The importance of safety is underscored by the results of a study of a low-income, multiethnic sample of students in grades 4–5 (Ceballo, Dahl, Aretakis, & Ramirez, 2001). Children exposed to higher levels of personal victimization reported greater post-traumatic stress reactions such as safety concerns, sleeping difficulties, and loneliness, as well as more anxiety, withdrawal, aggression, hyperactivity, and delinquency. Higher levels of witnessing violence were also related to greater psychological distress, but were unrelated to internalizing or externalizing symptoms. Fear of crime per se was not directly related to any of the outcomes, but was indirectly linked to the results, since victimization and witnessing crime were associated with greater concerns over safety.

The connection of empowerment assets to the support assets (see Chapter 1) and boundaries-and-expectations assets (see Chapter 3) was also evident in this study: When mothers and children were in greater agreement about a child's *potential* level of exposure to violence, children reported less overall actual exposure. Researchers interpreted these results as suggesting that adequate parental monitoring of children's experiences, and communication about how to deal with violent surroundings, may have enabled children to minimize their personal exposure to violence.

The possible validity of this reasoning is strengthened by the findings from another study of low-income African American 8- to 12-year-olds and their parents (Kliewer et al., 1998). The authors reported that higher levels of exposure to violence were associated with anxiety, depression, and "intrusive thinking," in which images of the experienced or witnessed violence recurred regularly in children's thoughts. But, as suggested by the Ceballo and colleagues study above, children who report lower levels of parental support and higher levels of social strain are the most significantly affected by exposure to violence. "Social strain" assesses whether children feel they shouldn't talk about violence they have experienced or witnessed and typically measures children's perception of parental unwillingness to discuss violence.

Together, these studies suggest that when upper elementary-age children are exposed to violence, such experiences can contribute significantly to their worries over safety and negatively affect their psychological well-being. However, children who feel supported by parents and who can discuss with parents the violence they have seen or personally experienced may be protected from many of these deleterious effects. Fitzpatrick and Boldizar (1993) reported that among low-income African American children and youth, children of both genders who did not have a primary male living with them in their household experienced the severest post-traumatic stress disorder symptoms from being victimized or witnessing violence.

Most researchers agree there is a strong connection between being victimized, threatened, or abused and subsequent negative socioemotional development. But at least one comprehensive review of the literature suggests that this connection is difficult to determine. That difficulty may be due to methodological issues, such as poorly defined samples, a lack of consistency among definitions and criteria of maltreatment, or the controversy about whether a small but uncertain proportion of abused children might not experience highly negative long-term outcomes (Knutson, 1995).

The relationship between victimization and negative outcomes may differ among children, not only because of differing levels of parental/adult presence and support, but also because of differing wells of internal assets upon which children can draw. For example, Grills and Ollendick (2002) studied a largely White sample of middle-income 6th graders and found that victimized boys with higher levels of global self-worth reported fewer anxiety symptoms than did boys with lower levels of self-worth. Self-worth, then, moderated the effects of victimization. Among girls, however, self-worth was not a buffering asset, but instead appeared to mediate the relationship between victimization and anxiety. Being victimized seemed to promote more negative self-worth among girls, and those lower levels of self-worth helped explain their higher levels of anxiety, compared to less victimized girls.

Farver and colleagues (2000) studied an ethnically diverse sample of 7- to 11-year-old children and reported that their feelings of being unsafe, and not simply their experiences of being victimized, were important negative influences. Children living in high-violence neighborhoods felt unsafe playing outdoors, were more distrustful of police, reported lower perceptions of self-competence and greater external locus of control, and included more violent content in drawings depicting their neighborhoods than did children living in low-violence neighborhoods. In this study, children's simply *feeling* unsafe while playing in the neighborhood, regardless of the level of community violence, was related to their feeling less self-worthy, less scholastically competent, less accepted by peers, less physically attractive, and less athletically competent. They also behaved worse than children who felt safer and displayed more external locus of control rather than a psychologically healthier self-confidence. Thus, children who felt unsafe consistently displayed more negative socioemotional functioning, which may also have limited their ability to develop other important assets, such as positive peer relationships and other social competencies.

In their review of the research, Margolin and Gordis (2000) noted similar findings from other studies that suggested school-age children exposed to violence may have difficulty regulating their emotions, showing empathy, adapting appropriately to stress, being sensitive to social cues, and generating nonaggressive solutions to interpersonal problems. All these effects of violence can compromise children's social relations with peers and adults, and, as a consequence, a victimized child—one who *needs* even more social support than a child who is not victimized—may be less likely to *experience* that support. However, as Cicchetti and colleagues (2000) reported, maltreated children who experience *other* assets may show resilient adaptation: A sense of self-reliance, self-confidence, and positive expectations for the future (see Chapter 8) appear to be especially important in promoting resilience in those children.

The Empowerment Assets across the Early Childhood-Adolescence Life Span

As we shift course to consider the influences on children in grades K–3 that may lay the early groundwork for the middle childhood empowerment assets, it becomes harder to identify empirical sources for many of those assets. Little attention has been paid to issues such as service opportunities or how a community values its children, while most of the information on safety in school deals with negative behaviors, such as bullying and victimization. However, enough research exists that we can begin to sketch the form that the empowerment assets might take for those younger children.

Community Values Children

An appropriate index of the extent to which a community values its early elementary-age children is its shared vision and ethos of the importance of family and child well-being, evidenced by the "availability, accessibility, affordability, and quality" of several types of resources in a community (Leventhal & Brooks-Gunn, 2000, p. 322). They include recreational resources, high-quality child-care programs, excellent schools, and comprehensive medical facilities

(Carnegie Task Force on Meeting the Needs of Young Children, 1994; Leventhal & Brooks-Gunn, 2000). A U.S. Department of Education report (1999) also suggests that a coherent, well-coordinated delivery of this range of services is essential for child and family well-being.

Access to social and recreational activities, such as parks, community centers, and children's and youth groups, may be particularly important for bolstering children's social and physical development (Leventhal & Brooks-Gunn, 2000), especially if social and recreational opportunities result in high-quality adult-child interactions. Research suggests that children's perceptions of the available resources in their neighborhoods are linked to their social competence: O'Neil and colleagues (2001) reported that 3rd graders who perceived their neighborhoods to be rich in resources, such as parks, playgrounds, and recreation centers, reported less loneliness and social dissatisfaction than did children who perceived their neighborhoods to be deficient in those resources. The presence of a range of child and family supportive resources and services may imply that a community collectively values its youth; however, it tells us little about the degree to which *individual* children feel valued and important.

Children as Resources

Providing young children with opportunities to assume useful roles may be helpful in at least two ways. First, there may be direct, positive effects in simply engaging in these types of activities. Second, and perhaps more important, providing children with opportunities to experience useful roles may enable children to see themselves as resources and to learn that they have some control (or *agency*) over their environment.

A hypothesis of our work on developmental assets is that providing opportunities for meaningful engagement in tasks and discussions lays the foundation for acquiring decision-making skills later in childhood. However, research documenting this link for K–3 children is scant. Perhaps attention has been limited because of researchers' belief that young children lack the requisite cognitive, moral, and social competencies to benefit from such opportunities; hence, there may not be compelling felt need to study these dynamics. Indeed, Helwig and Kim (1999) reported that the decision-making processes of children ages 6 and younger are not cognitively sophisticated. Similarly, Pomerantz and Eaton (2000) reported that children in early elementary grades are more likely to report positive feelings and intents about parental control over them, while older children believe that greater parental control is indicative of parents' beliefs in their child's incompetence.

However, beliefs about the limits of young children's abilities to meaningfully participate are not necessarily due to any inherent limitations in this age group, but may instead be a sociocultural phenomenon. Rogoff (1996) has studied cultures in which the social organization of family roles and cultural expectations allows for children as young as 3 years old to assume significant family responsibilities. For example, in a sample of Guatemalan families, Rogoff reports that 3- to 5-year-olds show responsibility for a younger sibling by subordinating their own wishes and needs to those of the baby. According to Rogoff (1996), this behavior is tied to the culture's belief in the cooperative interdependence of community members, which impels the sacrifice of one's needs for others in greater need. Thus, even young children, given appropriate guidance, support, *and* opportunities, can meaningfully engage in activities that contribute to goals beyond satisfying individual needs, thus contributing to family and community building.

Service to Others

We conceptualize service to others for early elementary children as service and volunteer opportunities to help others that typically are provided to children by neighborhoods, congregations, schools, and parents. In addition, children whose parents engage in service and volunteer activities are more likely themselves to experience this asset. Research conducted among samples of older children and adolescents confirms that a strong predictor of young people's involvement in community service and volunteering is the degree to which their parents engage in those activities (Stukas, Switzer, Dew, Goycoolea, & Simmons, 1999). Interestingly, among adults surveyed in one national study (Scales, 2003), 55% reported that it is important to provide service opportunities for children ages 5 to 10 , while only 40% reported that it was important to do the same for adolescents ages 11 to 18. Perhaps adults feel a sense of obligation to assist young children in these endeavors, while at the same time believing that adolescents can engage in these types of activities without adult help.

A certain amount of structure is necessary for young children to participate fully in service-learning activities. This can be provided by neighborhood or community centers or religious congregations that encourage children and parents to volunteer, as well as school programs that explicitly link academic lessons with community involvement (Freeman & King, 2001). School-based service-learning is rapidly becoming an accepted pedagogy across the country (Billig, 2000; Schine, 1997). Freeman and King (2001) reported on a program for 4- to 5-year-olds, as well as 5th graders, called *Lunch Time Book Buddies—Pass It On,* which integrated curriculum content with volunteering at a senior center. The authors recount anecdotal evidence of the contributions this program made to children's literacy and socioemotional, physical, and cognitive abilities. There is evidence that community service involvement in adolescence is related to later community involvement when those adolescents become adults (Independent Sector and Youth Service America, 2002). However, more rigorous research designs are still needed to test the salutary effects of service-learning on young children, as well as testing the longitudinal hypothesis that service-learning activities in *childhood* can lead to greater civic involvement and responsibility in adolescence and adulthood.

Safety

At home   The home aspect of the safety asset for children in early childhood (grades K–3) is a function of two factors: Parents make the home a physically safe, organized environment, and they provide structure and routine in the daily rhythms of home life. Working with toddler-age children, Wachs (1979) reported that various types of cognitive functioning were positively related to "the degree to which the physical set-up of the home permits exploration, low level of noise and confusion, and temporal regularity" (p. 30). Equally important to cognitive functioning are the predictability and routine of the home environment, which are related to school interest and cooperative and compliant behaviors in children attending Head Start programs (Keltner, 1990). Unpredictability and chaos in the home suppress or undermine a child's sense of agency in the world, the sense that the child's own efforts can help bring about desired outcomes (Bronfenbrenner, 1999). These early childhood developmental "nutrients" of predictability and structure clearly continue to be important in promoting children's sense of safety in middle childhood.

At school   The school aspect of the safety asset comprises at least two levels: provision of a child's basic safety within the physical infrastructure of the school and attention to interpersonal safety regarding such issues as bullying and victimization. Guarantees of both levels of safety are necessary for children to experience a sense of safety within the school. The physical structure of the school should afford children a fundamental sense of safety and security. Strong anecdotal evidence exists of the deleterious effects of poor physical school conditions on children and attests to the importance of this dimension, which is often taken for granted when addressing school safety (Kozol, 1991). According to the National Center for Education Statistics (1999), nearly 11 million children are enrolled in schools with at least one on-site building that is deemed inadequate; of these children, 3.5 million were enrolled in schools that had at least one nonoperational building or a building in significantly poor condition.

The issue of bullying and victimization is more frequently discussed in the literature on school safety for elementary-age children, especially younger students. Olweus (1991) reported that about 12% of children in grades 2–6 experienced peer victimization, in contrast to approximately 5% of 7th through 9th graders. Kochenderfer and Ladd (1996) reported even higher rates for victimization of young children: 23% of the 5- to 6-year-olds in their study reported significant levels of peer victimization, including physical, verbal (direct and indirect), and general victimization experiences. These results are especially alarming, as research suggests that the earlier a child experiences victimization, the longer the effects of victimization tend to persist (Kochenderfer-Ladd & Wardrop, 2001). In fact, Kochenderfer-Ladd and Wardrop (2001) speculate that interventions focused on stopping or mitigating victimization experiences do not seem to be effective in altering the problematic developmental trajectories to which victimization contributes. This conclusion supports an argument for primary prevention approaches, whereby bullying and victimization experiences are halted before they begin. Forthcoming evaluations on comprehensive bullying prevention techniques from around the globe should shed light on promising intervention approaches for dealing with these issues (Smith & Brain, 2000).

In the neighborhood/community   For younger children, the neighborhood aspect of the safety asset overlaps considerably with the caring-neighborhood asset described in Chapter 1. Partly as a result of the indirect effects of neighborhoods on younger children (National Research Council, 2000), features of the neighborhood may not be as differentiated for younger children as they are for older children. The indicators of social cohesion that we hypothesize describe a caring neighborhood for kindergartners through 3rd graders implicitly suggest a *safe* neighborhood as well (e.g., parents know and trust their neighbors, people in the community are willing to help their neighbors, the child lives in a close-knit neighborhood). These indicators also reflect the indirect nature of neighborhood effects on younger children.

Measuring the Empowerment Assets in Middle Childhood

Our MMW field test data on children's experience of the empowerment assets suggest that 4th- through 6th-grade children are not likely to feel very valued by adults in their community. The data also support the commonsense notion that perceptions of safety vary widely depending on where children live (see Table 5).

Fewer than half, however, say they feel valued by their community, that they help make decisions in their families and schools, or that they are given chances to contribute to making their community a better place in which to live. The only notable difference in children's reports of empowerment assets among the three field test survey samples was that children in the less affluent California sample reported feeling less safe. Likewise, in the two earlier pilot studies of MMW, children in the more urban Oklahoma City sample (with a lower average socioeconomic level) also reported feeling less safe in their neighborhoods, but equally as safe as Norman, Oklahoma, children in their schools.

The safety asset (and, to a lesser extent, service to others) may be one of the few assets that increase as children get older. For example, Search Institute's data from large survey samples of adolescents show that high school students generally report experiencing lower levels of most of the assets than middle school students. And 6th–12th graders together generally experience lower levels than what our field tests suggest for students in grades 4 through 6. Among the empowerment assets, however, the service-to-others asset is slightly higher among adolescents (51%) than among the MMW field test samples of 4th through 6th graders, and the safety asset steadily increases from grade 6 to grade 12. Even in both of those cases, however, sizable proportions (from 40% to 50%) of students do not feel safe or contribute to making their community a better place.

Thus, the developmental snapshot that the field-test data provide may well suggest an undesirable developmental trajectory: The empowerment assets, which offer children the potential for positive growth and maturation, are underexperienced at both the middle childhood and adolescent developmental stages. Feeling valued by the community may become even less commonly experienced over time, and even the empowerment assets that increase do so fairly modestly, leaving far too many young people in both developmental stages experiencing far too little of these important assets.

Table 5. Proportion of Field Test 4th–6th Graders Who Report Experiencing the Empowerment Assets			
Empowerment Asset	**% Who Report Experiencing Asset**		
	Nevada	**California**	**New York**
Community values children	35	31	41
Children as resources	47	43	48
Service to others	38	37	38
Safety[a]	62	52	66

From field tests in 2003; N = 1,294.
[a] *Measured on school and neighborhood safety items; "home" added after field testing.*

References

Allen, J., Hauser, S., Bell, K., & O'Connor, T. (1994). Longitudinal assessment of autonomy and relatedness in adolescent-family interactions as predictors of adolescent ego development and self-esteem. *Child Development, 65,* 179–194.

Benson, P. L., Scales, P. C., Leffert, N., & Roehlkepartain, E. C. (1999). *A fragile foundation: The state of developmental assets among American youth.* Minneapolis: Search Institute.

Billig, S. H. (2000). Research on K–12 school-based service-learning: The evidence builds. *Phi Delta Kappan, 81,* 658–664.

Blair, S. L. (1992). Children's participation in household labor: Child socialization versus the need for household labor. *Journal of Youth and Adolescence, 21,* 241–258.

Bolger, K. E., & Patterson, C. J. (2001). Developmental pathways from child maltreatment to peer rejection. *Child Development, 72,* 549–568.

Brigman, G., & Molina, B. (1999). Developing social interest and enhancing school success skills: A service learning approach. *Journal of Individual Psychology, 55,* 342–354.

Bronfenbrenner, U. (1999). Environments in developmental perspective: Theoretical and operational models. In S. L. Friedman & T. D. Wachs (Eds.), *Measuring environment across the life span: Emerging methods and concepts* (pp. 3–28). Washington, DC: American Psychological Association.

Cameron, G., & Cadell, S. (1999). Fostering empowering participation in prevention programs for disadvantaged children and families: Lessons from ten demonstration sites. *Canadian Journal of Community Mental Health, 18,* 105–121.

Carnegie Task Force on Meeting the Needs of Young Children. (1994). *Starting points: Meeting the needs of our youngest children* (abridged version). New York, NY: Carnegie Corp.

Ceballo, R., Dahl, T. A., Aretakis, M. T., & Ramirez, C. (2001). Inner-city children's exposure to community violence: How much do parents know? *Journal of Marriage and the Family, 63,* 927–940.

Cicchetti, D., Toth, S. L., & Rogosch, F. A. (2000). The development of psychological wellness in maltreated children. In D. Cicchetti, J. Rappaport, I. Sandler, & R. P. Weissberg (Eds.), *The promotion of wellness in children and adolescents* (pp. 395–426). Washington, DC: Child Welfare League of America Press.

Craig, W. M. (1998). The relationship among bullying, victimization, depression, anxiety, and aggression in elementary school children. *Personality and Individual Differences, 24,* 123–130.

Cummings, E. M., Goeke-Morey, M. C., & Graham, M. A. (2002). Interparental relations as a dimension of parenting. In J. G. Borkowski, S. L. Ramey, & M. Bristol-Poewer (Eds.), *Parenting in the child's world* (pp. 251–263). Mahwah, NJ: Lawrence Erlbaum.

Eccles, J. S. (1999). The development of children ages 6 to 14. *The Future of Children: When School Is Out, 9,* 30–44.

Eccles, J. S., Miller Buchanan, C., Flanagan, C., Fuligni, A., Midgley, C., & Yee, D. (1991). Control versus autonomy during early adolescence. *Journal of Social Issues, 47,* 53–68.

Eccles, J. S., Roeser, R., Wigfield, A., & Freedman-Doan, C. (1999). Academic and motivational pathways through middle childhood. In L. Balter & C. S. Tamis-LeMonda (Eds.), *Child psychology: A handbook of contemporary issues* (pp. 287–317). New York: Psychology Press.

Eccles, J. S., Wigfield, A., Midgley, C., Reuman, D., Mac Iver, D., & Feldlaufer, H. (1993).

Negative effects of traditional middle schools on students' motivation. *Elementary School Journal, 93,* 553–574.

Errante, A. (1997). Close to home: Comparative perspectives on childhood and community violence. *American Journal of Education, 105,* 355–400.

Farver, J. M., Ghosh, C., & Garcia, C. (2000). Children's perceptions of their neighborhoods. *Journal of Applied Developmental Psychology, 21,* 139–163.

Finn, J. L., & Checkoway, B. (1998). Young people as competent community builders: A challenge to social work. *Social Work, 43,* 335–345.

Finzi, R., Ram, A., Har-Even, D., Shnit, D., & Weizman, A. (2001). Attachment styles and aggression in physically abused and neglected children. *Journal of Youth and Adolescence, 30,* 769–785.

Fitzpatrick, K. M., & Boldizar, J. P. (1993). The prevalence and consequences of exposure to violence among African-American youth. *Journal of the American Academy of Child and Adolescent Psychiatry, 32,* 424–430.

Freeman, N. K., & King, S. (2001). Service-learning in preschool: An intergenerational project involving five-year-olds, fifth graders, and senior citizens. *Early Childhood Educational Journal, 28,* 211–217.

Gill, G. K. (1998). The strategic involvement of children in housework: An Australian case of two-income families. *International Journal of Comparative Sociology, 39,* 301–315.

Goodman, M. R., Stormshak, E. A., & Dishion, T. J. (2001). The significance of peer victimization at two points in development. *Applied Developmental Psychology, 22,* 507–526.

Green, A. H. (1993). Child sexual abuse: Immediate and long-term effects and intervention. *Journal of the American Academy of Child and Adolescent Psychiatry, 32,* 890–893.

Grills, A. E., & Ollendick, T. H. (2002). Peer victimization, global self-worth, and anxiety in middle school children. *Journal of Clinical Child and Adolescent Psychology, 31,* 59–68.

Grusec, J. E., Goodnow, J. J., & Cohen, L. (1996). Household work and the development of concern for others. *Developmental Psychology, 32,* 999–1007.

Hanish, L. D., & Guerra, N. G. (2002). A longitudinal analysis of patterns of adjustment following peer victimization. *Development and Psychopathology, 14,* 69–89.

Hawker, D. S. J. & Boulton, M. J. (2000). Twenty years' research on peer victimization and psychosocial maladjustment: A meta-analytic review of cross-sectional studies. *Journal of Child Psychology and Psychiatry, 41,* 441–455.

Haynes, N. M., & Comer, J. P. (1997). Service learning in the Comer School Development Program. In J. Schine (Ed.), *Service learning: Ninety-sixth yearbook of the National Society for the Study of Education* (pp. 79–89). Chicago: University of Chicago Press.

Helwig, C. C., & Kim, S. (1999). Children's evaluations of decision-making procedures in peer, family, and school contexts. *Child Development, 70,* 502–512.

Hess, L. E., & Atkins, M. S. (1998). Victims and aggressors at school: Teacher, self, and peer perceptions of psychosocial functioning. *Applied Developmental Science, 2,* 75–89.

Independent Sector and Youth Service America. (2002). *Engaging youth in lifelong service: Findings and recommendations for encouraging a tradition of volunteering among America's youth.* Washington, DC: Author.

Johnson, D. W., & Johnson, R. T. (1994). Constructive conflict in the schools. *Journal of Social Issues, 50,* 117–138.

Johnson, D. W., & Johnson, R. T. (1996). Conflict resolution and peer mediation programs in elementary and secondary schools: A review of the research. *Review of Educational Research, 66,* 459–506.

Keltner, B. (1990). Family characteristics of preschool social competence among Black children in a Head Start program. *Child Psychiatry and Human Development, 21,* 95–108.

Kliewer, W., Lepore, S. J., Oskin, D., & Johnson, P. D. (1998). The role of social and cognitive processes in children's adjustment to community violence. *Journal of Consulting and Clinical Psychology, 66,* 199–209.

Knutson, J. F. (1995). Psychological characteristics of maltreated children: Putative risk factors and consequences. *Annual Review of Psychology, 46,* 401–432.

Kochenderfer, B. J., & Ladd, G. W. (1996). Peer victimization: Manifestations and relations to school adjustment in kindergarten. *Journal of School Psychology, 34,* 267–283.

Kochenderfer-Ladd, B., & Skinner, K. (2002). Children's coping strategies: Moderators of the effects of peer victimization. *Developmental Psychology, 38,* 267–278.

Kochenderfer-Ladd, B. J., & Wardrop, J. L. (2001). Chronicity and instability of children's peer victimization experiences as predictors of loneliness and social satisfaction trajectories. *Child Development, 72,* 134–151.

Kolbo, J. R., Blakely, E. H., & Engleman, D. (1996). Children who witness domestic violence: A review of empirical literature. *Journal of Interpersonal Violence, 11,* 281–293.

Kozol, J. (1991). *Savage inequalities: Children in America's schools.* New York: Crown.

La Greca, A. M., Silverman, W. K., & Vernberg, E. M. (2002). Children and disasters: Future directions for research and public policy. In A. M. La Greca & W. K. Silverman (Eds.), *Helping children cope with disasters and terrorism* (pp. 405–423). Washington, DC: American Psychological Association.

Leventhal, T., & Brooks-Gunn, J. (2000). The neighborhoods they live in: The effects of neighborhood residence upon child and adolescent outcomes. *Psychological Bulletin, 126,* 309–337.

Margolin, G., & Gordis, E. B. (2000). The effects of family and community violence on children. *Annual Review of Psychology, 54,* 455–479.

McCloskey, L. A., & Stuewig, J. (2001). The quality of peer relationships among children exposed to family violence. *Development and Psychopathology, 13,* 83–96.

McCloskey, L. A., & Walker, M. (2000). Posttraumatic stress in children exposed to family violence and single-event trauma. *Journal of the American Academy of Child and Adolescent Psychiatry, 39,* 108–115.

Melchior, A. (1997). *Interim report: National evaluation of Learn and Serve America school and community-based programs.* Washington, DC: Corporation for National Service.

Midgley, C., & Feldlaufer, H. (1987). Students' and teachers' decision-making fit before and after the transition to junior high school. *Journal of Early Adolescence, 7,* 225–241.

Muscott, H. S. (2000). A review and analysis of service-learning programs involving students with emotional/behavioral disorders. *Education and Treatment of Children, 23,* 346–368.

Muscott, H. S., & O'Brien, S. T. (1999). Teaching character education to students with behavioral and learning disabilities through mentoring relationships. *Education and Treatment of Children, 22,* 373–390.

National Center for Education Statistics. (1999). *Service-learning and community service in K–12 schools.* Washington, DC: U.S. Department of Education, Office of Educational Research and Improvement.

National Commission on Service-Learning. (2001). *Learning in deed: The power of service-learning for American schools.* Washington, DC: Author.

National Research Council. (2000). *From neurons to neighborhoods: The science of early childhood development.* Washington, DC: National Academy Press.

National School Safety Center. (2001). *NSSC review of school safety research.* Westlake Village, CA: Author.

Ogden, C., & Claus, J. (1997). Reflection as a natural element of service: Service learning for youth empowerment. *Equity and Excellence in Education, 30,* 72–80.

O'Keefe, J. M. (1997). Children and community service: Character education in action. *Journal of Education, 179,* 47–62.

Olweus, D. (1991). Bully/victim problems among schoolchildren: Basic facts and effects of a school-based intervention program. In D. Pepler & K. Rubin (Eds.), *The development and treatment of childhood aggression* (pp. 411–448). Hillsdale, NJ: Lawrence Erlbaum.

O'Neil, R., Parke, R. D., & McDowell, D. J. (2001). Objective and subjective features of children's neighborhoods: Relations to parental regulatory strategies and children's social competence. *Applied Developmental Psychology, 22,* 135–155.

Pomerantz, E. M., & Eaton, M. M. (2000). Developmental differences in children's conceptions of parental control: "They love me, but they make me feel incompetent." *Merrill-Palmer Quarterly, 46,* 140–167.

Prilleltensky, I., Nelson, G., & Peirson, L. (2001). The role of power and control in children's lives: An ecological analysis of pathways toward wellness, resilience and problems. *Journal of Community and Applied Social Psychology, 11,* 143–158.

Roehlkepartain, E. C. (2003). Building strengths, deepening faith: Understanding and enhancing youth development in Protestant congregations. In D. Wertlieb, F. Jacobs, & R. M. Lerner (Eds.), *Handbook of applied developmental science: Vol. 3. Promoting positive youth and family development—Community systems, citizenship, and civil society* (pp. 515–534). Thousand Oaks, CA: Sage.

Roehlkepartain, E. C., Scales, P. C., Roehlkepartain, J. L., Gallo, C., & Rude, S. P. (2002). *Building strong families: Highlights from a preliminary survey from YMCA of the USA and Search Institute on what parents need to succeed.* Chicago and Minneapolis: YMCA of the USA and Search Institute.

Rogoff, B. (1996). Developmental transitions in children's participation in sociocultural activities. In A. J. Sameroff & M. M. Haith (Eds.), *The five to seven year shift: The age of reason and responsibility* (pp. 274–294). Chicago: University of Chicago Press.

Scales, P. C. (with Benson, P. L., Mannes, M., Roehlkepartain, E. C., Hintz, N., & Sullivan, T. K.). (2003). *Other people's kids: Social expectations and American adults' involvement with children and adolescents.* New York: Kluwer Academic/Plenum.

Scales, P. C., Blyth, D. A., Berkas, T. H., & Kielsmeier, J. C. (2000). The effects of service-learning on middle school students' social responsibility and academic success. *Journal of Early Adolescence, 20,* 332–358.

Scales, P. C., & Leffert, N. (1999). *Developmental assets: A synthesis of the scientific research on adolescent development.* Minneapolis: Search Institute.

Schine, J. (Ed.). (1997). *Service learning: Ninety-sixth yearbook of the National Society for the Study of Education.* Chicago: University of Chicago Press.

Schuster, M. A., Stein, B. D., Jaycox, L. H., Collins, R. I., Marshall, G. N., Elliot, M. N., Zhou, A. J., Kanouse, D. E., Morrison, J. L., & Berry, S. H. (2001). A national survey of stress reactions after the September 11, 2001, terrorist attacks. *New England Journal of Medicine, 345,* 1507–1512.

Smith, P. K., & Brain, P. (2000). Bullying in schools: Lessons from two decades of research. *Aggressive Behavior, 26,* 1–9.

Stomfay-Stitz, A. M. (1994). Conflict resolution and peer mediation: Pathways to safer schools. *Childhood Education, 70,* 279–283.

Stukas, A. A. Jr., Switzer, G. E., Dew, M. A., Goycoolea, J. M., & Simmons, R. G. (1999). Parental helping models, gender, and service learning. *Journal of Prevention and Intervention in the Community, 18,* 5–18.

Swick, K. J. (2001). Service-learning in teacher education: Building learning communities. *The Clearing House, 74,* 261–269.

U.S. Department of Education. National Center for Education Statistics. (1999). *How old are America's public schools?* NCES 1999–048. Washington, DC: Office of Educational Research and Improvement.

Wachs, T. D. (1979). Proximal experience and early cognitive intellectual development: The physical environment. *Merrill-Palmer Quarterly, 25,* 3–42.

Walrath, C. M., Mandell, D. S., Liao, Q., Holden, E. W., De Carolis, G., Santiago, R. L., & Leaf, P. J. (2001). Suicide attempts in the "Comprehensive Community Mental Health Services for Children and Their Families" program. *Journal of the American Academy of Child and Adolescent Psychiatry, 40,* 1197–1205.

Wigfield, A., & Eccles, J. S. (1994). Children's competence beliefs, achievement values, and general self-esteem: Change across elementary and middle school. *Journal of Early Adolescence, 14,* 107–138.

Boundaries and expectations are the rules, standards, and norms in families, schools, neighborhoods, and communities that guide young people's choices and regulate their behavior.

3

The Boundaries-and-Expectations Assets

Why Are Boundaries and Expectations Important?

Boundaries and expectations reflect the rules, standards, and role modeling that children experience within the family, school, and neighborhood settings, and from their good friends. When children report experiencing these assets, it means they have rules set and enforced for them across these settings, are monitored by a variety of caring adults, and are exposed to positive examples of family, adult, and peer behavior. They also are experiencing consistently high expectations for behavior, in terms of school adjustment and academic achievement, alcohol and other drug use, and prosocial behaviors such as helping others. Collectively, these influences can support key developmental processes, such as the gradual evolution from parent and adult regulation of children to adult-child coregulation and eventually to self-regulation in later adolescence and young adulthood. Other developmental processes that can be positively affected by the boundaries-and-expectations assets include children's socialization regarding group norms, the development of motivation to achieve at school and in other arenas, and various aspects of friendship formation.

In many respects, boundaries and expectations should be considered in concert with support. It is the combination of the two broad themes of each—the love and caring provided through the support assets, and the firmness, standards, and limits provided through the boundaries-and-expectations assets—that defines the most effective socialization relationships in middle childhood.

An environment characterized by caring but without adequately defined boundaries may be too permissive. Similarly, limit setting without adequate caring may be perceived by children as too harsh. Neither socialization extreme by itself is developmentally advantageous, for children benefit most from an optimal balance of support *and* boundaries and expectations.

Assets in several other categories may be linked to assets in the boundaries-and-expectations category, as family boundaries and family support are in the construct of authoritative parenting discussed in Chapter 1. Moreover, those relations may undergo important changes across the middle childhood years. For example, Kerns and colleagues reported in a study of White, middle-class children in grades 3 and 6 that the more secure the attachment was between child and parent, the more parents subsequently monitored the child, and the more the child cooperated with parental monitoring by doing such things as checking in (Kerns, Aspelmeier, Gentzler, & Grabill, 2001). This relationship was significant for 6th graders and their parents, but was not apparent among 3rd graders and their parents. Kerns and colleagues hypothesized that the attachment-monitoring connection is more important among 6th graders and their parents because those families are negotiating autonomy issues more often than families of 3rd graders. It is also possible that families with younger children have more sources of information available to them to confirm their children's whereabouts, making monitoring easier, regardless of the quality of the child-parent relationship.

The Kerns et al. study demonstrates the importance of two dimensions of assets in the boundaries-and-expectations category: the context in which the assets are experienced and developmental processes that may be involved during middle childhood that affect how those assets contribute to healthy development. Similarly, O'Neil, Parke, and McDowell's study (2001) of a small sample of White and Latino families with 3rd graders showed that parental supervision and limit setting are often connected to parents' perceptions of neighborhood safety. In neighborhoods perceived as less safe, parents are likely to be more vigilant and restrictive. Those behaviors may have important developmental correlates, as children whose mothers limited their activities because of perceived neighborhood problems described themselves as lonelier than children whose neighborhood activities were not as restricted. The lonelier children, however, were also rated as more socially competent and accepted by their peers and teachers. It may be that the restrictive parents set children's activity limits within a parent-child relationship that was also warm and promoted children's *psychological* autonomy, the sense children have that their opinions matter and that they are encouraged to have and express ideas. If they did, then these results are not surprising. As we have discussed in earlier chapters, that authoritative parenting style is associated with a host of positive outcomes (Steinberg, 2001), including the kinds of social competence reported by O'Neil and colleagues (2001). These restricted children may have emotionally missed certain times with their peers, but if parents explained the reasons for their limit setting in ways that restricted children's behavioral but not psychological autonomy, these children may have felt more cared for and confident. They may also have experienced parents as models for communicating about difficult issues. All those developments would promote social competence.

In their study of a diverse sample of students in grades 3 and 4, Coley and Hoffman (1996) confirm these findings and offer a somewhat different perspective on the complex interactions among the qualities of individual children, their neighborhood environments, and parental supervision strategies. They reported that for most child outcomes, regardless of neighborhood quality, little difference existed between children who were closely supervised and children who were not supervised but were at least *monitored* (e.g., through rules concerned with safety, telephone check-ins, or leaving children unsupervised for less than one hour). Both supervised and monitored children generally fared better developmentally than children who were both unsupervised and unmonitored. However, children who lived in high-crime neighborhoods and were both unsupervised and unmonitored actually were rated as having *better* social skills and received higher language achievement scores. Yet the same children also had the highest external locus-of-control scores, reflecting low self-efficacy and lack of belief in their own abilities to control and direct their lives (see Chapter 8).

Coley and Hoffman (1996) explained these findings by suggesting that parental supervision strategies are not selected solely on the basis of neighborhood quality but also because of perceived child competencies. The most competent children, even in dangerous neighborhoods, were provided less supervision and monitoring. Although the increased autonomy was developmentally positive for children living in safe neighborhoods, thereby contributing to and reinforcing a high internal locus of control, such autonomy was developmentally disadvantageous for children in high-crime neighborhoods.

A study of about 3,600 high school students (Lamborn, Dornbusch, & Steinberg, 1996) offers another perspective on the impact parenting style may have on young people. Although the study did not include children in the upper elementary years, the results may well be relevant for middle childhood. Lamborn and colleagues reported that ethnicity and community context had complex effects on academic success, psychosocial development, and behaviors such as substance use, through their relations with parenting style. Specifically, adolescents of all ethnic backgrounds did better when they reported a "joint" decision-making style with their parents. However, joint parent-adolescent decision making was especially beneficial—and unilateral adolescent decision making especially detrimental—to Hispanic American youth living in ethnically mixed communities. In addition, African American adolescents benefited most from unilateral parental decision making (a more authoritarian style), and also suffered the most from unilateral adolescent decision making when they lived in predominantly White communities.

Lamborn and colleagues speculated that although African Americans living in mostly White communities may gain safety and economic advantages, their status as an ethnic minority group is heightened in those communities, creating greater risks that firm parental control, however, may help to mitigate. These relations may be affected more by the interaction of ethnicity, community context, and parenting style than by a child's age per se, and so may be quite relevant for thinking about how diversity impacts boundary-setting issues during middle childhood.

Search Institute's *Me and My World* field tests of students in grades 4–6 from selected schools in Nevada, California, and New York indicate that most of the assets in the boundaries-and-expectations category are measured at acceptable levels of internal consistency reliability, .70 or above (see Appendix). Two assets in this category, *positive peer influence* and *high expectations,* are measured at a promising level of reliability (in the .60s).

Table 6. The Boundaries-and-Expectations Assets	
Family boundaries	Family has clear and consistent rules and consequences and monitors the child's whereabouts.
School boundaries	School provides clear rules and consequences.
Neighborhood boundaries	Neighbors take responsibility for monitoring the child's behavior.
Adult role models	Parent(s) and other adults in the child's family, as well as nonfamily adults, model positive, responsible behavior.
Positive peer influence	Child's closest friends model positive, responsible behavior.
High expectations	Parent(s) and teachers expect the child to do her or his best at school and in other activities.

Summary of Research Findings: The Boundaries-and-Expectations Assets in Middle Childhood

Parenting styles have been widely researched in the area of family boundaries. Specifically, studies relating to an authoritative parenting style (characterized by a supportive family environment with clear limit setting, firm rules and consequences, and the promotion of open discussion and independence) make up a large portion of the family boundaries literature. Mattanah (2001) conducted a study on the parenting styles of families with 4th-grade children. He reported that children whose parents (especially fathers) exercised more effective limit setting, demonstrated warmth, and promoted psychological autonomy had greater academic achievement, fewer aggressive behaviors, and better mental health. Although limit setting, warmth, and autonomy promotion all were meaningful, a unique and important contribution to these outcomes was made by fathers who provided high levels of psychological autonomy (i.e., low levels of psychological control). This study of 4th graders and their families shows that children benefit most, not from tremendous amounts of parental control, but from a balance of control and autonomy that is optimal for healthy development at this age. Also salient to the discussion of family boundaries is the wealth of literature that investigates the impact of parental monitoring on childhood outcomes.

Neighborhood boundaries are often described in terms of broad social control. The roles neighborhood members play in socializing children through monitoring, communication with parents, and interacting directly with children (collective socialization) are vital to child well-being. Collective socialization practices, such as monitoring and supervision of children and youth within a neighborhood, have been linked to numerous community-level outcomes, such as decreased violence and increased social cohesion (see review in Leventhal & Brooks-Gunn, 2000). Although individual effects of neighborhood boundaries are less well understood, a recent study of 867 African American families, using a neighborhood-based design, provides evidence that the more collective socialization and nurturant or involved parenting in a neighborhood, the fewer deviant peer affiliations children had (Brody et al., 2001).

Because an expanding social world is a particularly pervasive developmental issue during the middle childhood years, the influence families, other adults, and peers exert on children has also been extensively examined. It is clear from the research that children are susceptible and, more important, vulnerable to negative pressure from others. A large-scale study conducted with nearly 2,000 children (in grades 4–6) and their parents found that children's associations with antisocial peers were strong predictors of their substance use (cigarette, alcohol, and marijuana) initiation (Oxford, Harachi, Catalano, & Abbott, 2000). However, family boundaries processes (i.e., firm rules, monitoring, and attachment to parent) mediated children's involvement with antisocial peers, thus decreasing the likelihood of children's alcohol and drug use.

Unfortunately, of the studies we identified, only a minority examined the direct effects of modeling on childhood prosocial development (Eisenberg & Fabes,

1998). Most of the studies were conducted in the laboratory using strangers as role models, thus making it difficult to draw firm conclusions about the impact of children's real-world experiences on subsequent behaviors. Nonetheless, a fair amount of research suggests that children do learn positive behaviors indirectly from others, as illustrated by the many evaluation studies on mentoring programs showing the benefits children experience by having such positive role models in their lives. For example, Thompson and Kelly-Vance (2001) found that boys deemed at risk for problem behaviors who were paired with mentors subsequently made significantly greater academic gains over a nine-month period than did boys at similar risk who did not have mentors. The existing research in the areas of parental relationship qualities, parent involvement, and school climate also shows that parents and teachers serve as positive role models for youth development.

When children receive consistent messages from adults about high expectations for their growth and appropriate behavior, their well-being is enhanced. A study by Paulson, Marchant, and Rothlisberg (1998) of 230 5th and 6th grade students highlights the importance of consistency across contexts for children's academic performances. These researchers found that when students perceived congruent positive parenting and teaching styles, along with high parental involvement *and* a positive school climate, they experienced higher achievement outcomes than students who did not enjoy those positive experiences. High and appropriate expectations, then, embodied by adults' support and involvement in students' school-related issues and activities, may well evolve into a sense of commitment to learning in these children.

Family Boundaries

A number of studies report that a home environment rich in consistent structure and limit setting has a positive impact on children's academic and social lives. Similarly, children of parents who provide appropriate levels of supervision and monitoring have also been shown to be more psychologically resilient and better adjusted. Family boundaries have been associated, directly or indirectly, with:

Academic Outcomes

- **Academic success** (Christenson, Rounds, & Gornery, 1992; Crouter, MacDermid, McHale, & Perry-Jenkins, 1990; Mattanah, 2001; Okagaki & French, 1998 [for European American children if parents place importance on monitoring]); and **higher achievement scores** if a strong relationship exists between children and their friends' parents, and among parents whose children are friends (Fletcher, Newsome, Nickerson, & Bazley, 2001).

Mental and Behavioral Health Outcomes

- **Fewer externalizing and internalizing behaviors** via an increased sense of self-regulation (Brody, Dorsey, Forehand, & Armistead, 2002; Mattanah, 2001); **lower levels of externalizing behaviors** among European American children if a strong relationship exists between children and their friends' parents, and among parents whose children are friends (Fletcher et al., 2001); **fewer symptoms of depression and anxiety** (Mattanah, 2001); **lower levels of aggression** in children with chronic illness (Garstein, Noll, & Vannatta, 2000) and **fewer delinquency problems** (Pettit, Laird, Dodge, Bates, & Criss, 2001; Vitaro, Brengden, & Tremblay, 2001); **reduction and/or delayed onset of drug use** in urban youth (Chilcoat & Anthony, 1996; Oxford et al., 2000); **reduced risk of smoking in adolescent years** if authoritative parenting style is present in middle childhood years (Jackson, Bee-Gates, & Henriksen, 1994); and **less engagement in sexual activity among 9- to 15-year-olds** if parents monitor child's whereabouts (Romer et al., 1994).

Social Outcomes

- **Increased positive peer relationships** if the child is initially rejected (Sandstrom & Coie, 1999) and **social competence** if there is greater supervision and limitation of activities in the context of a perceived unsafe neighborhood (O'Neil et al., 2001; Fletcher et al., 2001 [among European American children]); and **decreased involvement with antisocial peers** (Oxford et al., 2000).

Other contextual variables beyond the parent-child relationship can affect parents' ability to monitor their children. In a study of 181 dual-wage-earning couples with multiple children in the elementary grades (including at least one in grade 4 or 5), Bumpus, Crouter, and McHale (1999) reported complex interactions among parents' workloads, perceived marital quality, and family composition that affected parental monitoring. Families that reported having a younger elementary-age son in addition to their 4th- or 5th-grade child and also reported an unhappy marriage knew less about their children's whereabouts and experiences than did other parents when fathers also specifically reported heavy work demands. The younger child's gender and the parents' marital quality did *not* predict parental knowledge except in families in which the father worked long hours at a demanding job.

In addition to positive short-term effects, parental supervision and monitoring may also affect long-term outcomes through their impact on important developmental processes. For example, a small study of fewer than 100 children examined an intervention program offered to highly disruptive elementary school boys, ages 7 to 9 years, in grades 2 and 3 in Montreal, and to their parents. The program focused on improving parenting skills, including supervision of the child's activities. The intervention program directly lessened the boys' disruptiveness, improved parental supervision of the boys when they reached age 11, and contributed to less initiation of delinquency by age 13, in comparison to the control group (Vitaro et al., 2001). The improved parental supervision, in turn, directly predicted less delinquency and indirectly contributed to that positive outcome through the effect that supervision had on children's associations with delinquent peers. In fact, the effect of the family-boundaries asset on the developmental process of friendship formation was the *strongest observed* among the elements leading eventually to a reduced likelihood of delinquency at age 13. Although the sample size was less than 100 children, the results are provocative in suggesting that parental supervision contributes to a chain of events that, years later, can result in highly desirable developmental outcomes for children.

The broader community context in which parenting occurs also plays a role in the relationship between family boundary setting and child outcomes. For example, Simons and colleagues (2002) conducted a large study of African American families with 10- to 12-year-olds who lived in towns and small cities in Georgia and Iowa. They found that parental supervision and control helped prevent antisocial behavior regardless of other community characteristics, but also found that the beneficial effect of parental/caregiver control on prevention of children's antisocial behavior lessened as the level of community crime increased and parents' perception of neighborhood safety decreased.

In addition, if parents used corporal punishment as discipline, effects differed depending on community setting. In communities where the use of physical punishment was rare, higher use of corporal punishment was related to higher levels of child misconduct. However, in communities where physical punishment was common, there was no effect on child misconduct. This finding suggests that the normative climate of a community affects the impact that various parenting practices can have on child outcomes.

School Boundaries

Research on school discipline, teaching styles, and school climate comprises a large portion of the literature describing the school-boundaries asset. Effective school boundaries have been associated, directly or indirectly, with:

Academic Outcomes

- **More positive attitudes toward math and higher math achievement scores** in Singaporean classrooms where teachers express leadership, helpfulness/friendliness, and understanding behaviors (Goh & Fraser, 2000).

Mental and Behavioral Health Outcomes

- **Fewer externalizing and internalizing behaviors** via an increased sense of self-regulation (Brody et al., 2002); **fewer school office discipline referrals** (Sprague et al., 2001).

Social Outcomes

- **Improved self-discipline, prosocial behavior, and social competence** (Bear, 1998 [authoritative teaching style]).

For decades, research has shown that students at all levels of K–12 education do better socially and academically in schools that are orderly and safe and in which rule enforcement is perceived to be done fairly (National Education Goals Panel, 1998). Speedy and certain punishment of students for less serious infractions of school rules (such as using profanity or disturbing the class) may also help reduce the incidence of serious offenses (such as possessing alcohol, other drugs, or weapons); such dependable boundary enforcement appears to be more common in schools with younger, elementary-age students than in middle schools (Anderman & Kimweli, 1997).

School practices that maintain order and safety are especially important, not only because they protect students' basic physical well-being, but also because they strengthen students' bonding with adults at school, in itself an important developmental asset (see Chapter 5). For example, researchers have found that students as young as 5 or 6 years of age who have been picked on or bullied at school—victimization experiences that schools with strong rule-setting and enforcement practices can help limit—are significantly less likely to like school and more likely to stay home from school (Ladd, Kochenderfer, & Coleman, 1997).

As is the case for effective families, successful schools also need to balance opportunities for student input into decisions—a practice that can help empower students—with firm adult decision making that is in the best interests of all students. For example, research has found that students making the transition from elementary to junior high schools feel they are less involved in school decision making than they were as younger students (Midgley & Feldlaufer, 1987). However, in grades 1 through 6, students apparently prefer adult decision making rather than consensus decision making when it comes to certain issues, such as school curriculum decisions (Helwig & Kim, 1999).

Another important parallel between schools at all grade levels and families is that boundary setting and enforcement most effectively contribute to positive child development when done within a broader environment of caring and support. In the case of schools, the purpose of boundary setting is not the arbitrary exercise of adult authority but rather the creation and maintenance of an environment that supports learning. When children notice that rules are clear, fair, and consistently enforced, they experience a dependable climate in which they can focus with less distraction on the challenges and joys of learning. In that more orderly and predictable environment, norms and expectations promoting achievement can be strengthened, student motivation and engagement can increase, and student attendance and study habits can improve. All these effects have been found to be related to academic success (Starkman, Scales, & Roberts, 1999).

Neighborhood Boundaries

We found few studies that examined the impact of neighborhood boundaries in middle childhood; most of those we did locate were conducted with children living in distressed urban communities. Outcomes such as safer neighborhoods and social and academic competence have been linked to neighborhood boundaries. In general, research reflects the notion that a collective effort by neighborhood members to monitor and supervise children promotes positive child development. Neighborhood boundaries have been associated, directly or indirectly, with:

Academic Outcomes

- **Higher achievement scores** if there is a strong relationship between children and their friend's parents and among parents whose children are friends (Fletcher et al., 2001).

Mental and Behavioral Health Outcomes

- **Lower levels of externalizing behaviors** if there is a strong relationship between children and their friend's parents and among parents whose children are friends (Fletcher et al., 2001).

Social Outcomes

- **Decreased affiliations with deviant peers,** especially among children in more disadvantaged neighborhoods (Brody et al., 2001); **increased social competence and fewer behavior problems** (Marshall, Noonan, McCartney, Marx, & Keefe, 2001 [via improved parenting]); **less neighborhood violence** (Sampson, Raudenbush, & Earls, 1997 [collective efficacy]); and **improved rates of prosocial behavior and having conventional friends** in a sample of children and adolescents ages 10-18 (Elliot et al., 1996).

Research suggests that one way neighborhoods affect children is through the collective socializing behavior of residents. For example, Sampson and colleagues (1997) found in a study of Chicago neighborhoods that when residents said they would intervene if they saw adolescents breaking the law or violating neighborhood values or norms ("informal social control"), both the actual crime levels and neighbors' perceptions of crime levels were lower than actual and perceived crime levels in neighborhoods in which residents declined to intervene. The higher the collective efficacy of the neighborhood, in other words, the safer the residents in the neighborhood felt and actually were. Neighborhoods with higher socioeconomic status and greater residential stability typically have been found to contribute to better child and adolescent outcomes (especially for boys), a result that is partly explained by the lower levels of social trust, cohesion, and collective efficacy often found in low-income neighborhoods (Leventhal & Brooks-Gunn, 2000).

In their comprehensive review, Leventhal and Brooks-Gunn (2000) noted that most effects of neighborhood characteristics on child outcomes, including boundary setting, socioeconomic status, and residential instability, seem to be quite modest, adding from 1% to 5% to the ability of researchers to explain a given child outcome. In part, these apparently small contributions may be due to the mediating and moderating roles that family and, for older youth, peer variables have on neighborhood effects. Younger children's susceptibility to neighborhood effects may especially be affected by parent and family variables, such as parents' mental health, parents' ability to construct social support systems, or specific parenting practices such as the greater use of parental control and supervision strategies in high-risk neighborhoods.

To illustrate, a study of nearly 900 African American families with 5th graders—drawn from a variety of metropolitan and nonmetropolitan settings in Iowa and Georgia—provides insights about how parenting, neighborhood disadvantage, and neighborhood boundaries may interact to affect child development

(Brody et al., 2001). In the study, children who experienced harsh and inconsistent parenting and those who experienced low levels of collective socialization from adults in their neighborhoods were more likely to affiliate with deviant peers. In addition, the protective effects of nurturing and involved parenting and high levels of collective socialization by neighborhood adults were greatest for children in the neighborhoods that were the most disadvantaged.

Another important finding from this study was that children and parents perceive their neighborhoods differently. The effects described above were based largely on 5th grade children's reports of neighborhood disadvantage and collective socialization, not on parents' reports. Although Brody and colleagues (2001) did find overlap in children's and parents' reports about the neighborhood, considerable differences were found as well. Similarly, in a study of 186 African American families in 18 urban neighborhoods, Burton and Price-Spratlen (1999) found that in 56% of the cases, children and parents could not agree on the boundaries that defined their neighborhood. Preadolescent children tended to identify a smaller geographical area defined by their friendship ties, and parents tended to describe a larger area defined by their perceptions of how far their children could navigate on their own. Moreover, in these urban neighborhoods, one-third of the children experienced family patterns in which they essentially resided simultaneously in many different neighborhoods, spending significant time with grandparents, extended kin, and other relatives. Both developmentally and structurally then, parents may understand only part of the neighborhood world their upper-elementary or older children experience.

Neighborhoods in which children have plentiful opportunities for activities and friendships with their age-peers and adults and there is a collective effort to provide adequate resources for play and a sense of safety, may provide more adequate boundaries than neighborhoods without those qualities. Chipuer's (2001) study on community connectedness and loneliness among 5th and 6th graders in Australia suggests that such activities, relationships, and resources significantly predict less neighborhood loneliness. The presence of such neighborhood assets likely strengthens neighborhood safety, as well as making parents more willing to allow children greater exposure to neighborhood influences.

Parent, Family, and Nonfamily Adult Role Models

Research shows that parents and other adults serve as socializing agents for children through direct influence (e.g., instructing/teaching, stating expectations) as well as through modeling and connecting children with other positive sources of social influence, such as responsible peers and adults. While there has been a greater amount of attention given in research to the impact of negative adult influence on childhood behaviors, positive influence experienced through mentoring, parental involvement in schooling, and high-quality parent-child relationships also has been associated, directly or indirectly, with:

Academic Outcomes

- **Increased academic gains** (Paulson et al., 1998; Thompson & Kelly-Vance, 2001); **reading achievement and interest in literature** (Christenson et al., 1992); **fewer behavior problems** (Bradley, Corwyn, McAdoo, & Coll, 2001) and **better academic performance** if parents provide enriching learning experiences in the home (Izzo, Weissberg, Kasprow, & Fendrich, 1999; Shumow, Vandell, & Posner, 1999); and **improved occupational aspirations and expectations** for inner-city boys (Cook et al., 1996).

Mental and Behavioral Health Outcomes

- **Lower fat-eating patterns and higher consumption of fruits and vegetables** in African American children whose parents model healthful dietary behavior (Tibbs et al., 2001); **self-efficacy** for African American boys who perceive parents as efficacious (Whitbeck, 1987); **lower levels of aggression, inattention, and impulsivity** in children who do not have a family history of substance abuse (Martin et al., 1994); and **fewer externalizing and internalizing behaviors** (Brody, Stoneman, & Flor, 1996).

Social Outcomes

- **Positive aspects of friendship for girls (e.g., helping behavior, resolution of conflict, and validation)** when fathers possessed similar positive friendship qualities (Simpkins & Parke, 2001).

Perhaps because much of the role-modeling research tends to focus on how adults influence young people's risk-taking behaviors, such as sexual intercourse or alcohol and other drug use, the majority of such studies involve adolescents rather than elementary-age children. A wealth of research shows that adult behaviors strongly influence similar youth behaviors, such that parents who smoke, drink, or give birth to children at a young age tend to have adolescents who repeat those same behaviors (see review in Scales & Leffert, 1999).

Some studies suggest that adult modeling of such negative behaviors may influence elementary-age children as well. For example, in a study of rural, White students in grades 1 through 6, Smith, Miller, Kroll, Simmons, and Gallen (1996) reported that 27% had consumed alcohol, and that for 3rd through

6th graders, who tended to accurately describe their parents as drinkers or nondrinkers, there was a strong association between their perceptions of parental drinking and their own drinking status. In fact, 64% of children's previous drinking experience had occurred *with* their parents, and 13% had occurred with other adults. A longitudinal study of a large sample of children in New Zealand reported similar findings about the direct role played by many parents in their children's substance use behaviors. Among 11-year-olds who had smoked, 38% said their most recent instance of smoking had taken place in the presence of a parent, and 25% reported they had been given the cigarette by the parent (Stanton & Silva, 1992).

Simpkins and Parke (2001) conducted a study of 125 students in grade 4 and their parents that suggests the adult role-modeling process may differ depending on the child's gender and on whether the behavior is modeled by the father or mother. In looking at how the qualities parents exhibited in their friendships affected elements of children's friendships, the researchers found that positive qualities of girls' friendships, such as helping and conflict resolution behaviors, were significantly related to the positive qualities present in their father's friendships. In contrast, the negative elements of girls' friendships were related to the negative qualities present in their mother's friendships. Overall, the qualities present in parents' friendships were more strongly related to qualities present in girls' friendships than they were to qualities present in boys' friendships.

The researchers interpreted these findings as supporting fathers' important roles in helping children develop socioemotional capacities, and supporting gender-linked differences in the size of boys' and girls' friendship groups and play patterns. Simpkins and Parke (2001) reasoned that because boys seem to spend more time playing away from home and in larger groups than girls, perhaps parents' relationship influences are less meaningful to boys than they are to girls, who observe parents more and whose friendship groups typically are smaller and more personal. It is unclear whether these effects occur because of direct parental teaching or demonstration of friendship skills, or whether parents' friendships affect their well-being and contribute to the effectiveness of their parenting styles, thereby indirectly influencing children's friendships. Whitbeck (1987) also reported gender differences in a small sample of 9- to 15-year-olds. Parents' self-efficacy seemed to have a stronger modeling impact on boys' levels of self-efficacy, whereas parents' positive relationships with girls, reflected by effective levels of support and control, seemed to more strongly affect girls' self-efficacy.

Clearly, whether and how the modeling process occurs is influenced by a number of contextual variations, and indirect paths from parent behaviors to child outcomes may be more likely than direct ones. For example, in a small sample of rural African American 9- to 12-year-olds and their parents, Brody and colleagues (1996) studied how parents' formal religiousness affected children's competence. They found that church attendance and the importance of religion to the family did not directly contribute to youth levels of self-regulation. However, religiousness was linked to improved family relationships and norms (e.g., love, forgiveness, and concern for the needs of others) that in turn lower the likelihood that young people will experience problems and increase their competence at regulating themselves. Religiousness had an especially strong link to fathers' reports of interparental conflict, such that more religious fathers reported less conflict with their spouses. That lessened conflict and increased family cohesion may have had as much to do with children's positive social adjustment outcomes as any direct effect of the parents' religious practices.

Similarly, Tibbs and colleagues (2001) reported that parents who say they frequently model healthful, low-fat diets to their children reported, as one would expect, that they themselves ate a diet lower in fat and higher in fruits and vegetables than parents who did not model healthful eating behaviors. In other words, parents' reports of modeling were consistent with how they described their *own* diets. Children's eating patterns were not assessed, so it is unclear whether the parents' modeling had an impact on the children. However, because the parents were recruited from a national parent education program for parents of young children, it is likely that their personal dietary choices had a healthful impact on the food they served their children. Parents concerned with their children's diets may help children maintain their own healthful diets as they grow up, perhaps less because of modeling in the strictest sense and more because of parental control of basic dietary resources.

In an unusual study conducted in the late 1960s, Mahoney and Magnusson (2001) studied the relationship between Swedish parents' level of community involvement when their children were 10 years old, and the children's subsequent criminal records up to 30 years later. The extent of parents' involvement (particularly the father's) in community and neighborhood groups when children were young was a strong preventive influence that lowered the incidence of children's later criminality. The positive effects of community involvement were most pronounced for children who performed poorly at school and who had multiple indicators of social and academic disadvantage. The researchers speculated, but could not conclude, that one mechanism for these relations might have been that involved parents were more skilled at managing and directing their children toward out-of-home leisure opportunities. Thus, although role modeling per se may have contributed to children's positive outcomes, involved parents may simply have been more effective in their overall parenting styles and more directive in shaping their children's use of time.

Another example of the complexity of the effects of role modeling on youth development is that the availability of positive role models may be less important than who models the behavior. For example, Cook and colleagues (1996) compared occupational expectations and aspirations of low-income African American boys in grades 2, 4, 6, and 8 to middle-income White boys in the same grades. The poor African American boys actually listed more adult role models from family, neighborhood, school, church, and television than did the White boys. A higher number of reported role models was positively related to both higher educational and occupational expectations. However, the poor African American boys held lower educational and occupational expectations for themselves than did their more affluent White peers, and reported bigger gaps between their expectations and aspirations, in part because the African American boys were also significantly less likely to have a biological father present in the home. Cook and colleagues speculated that the particularly conscientious role-modeling and mentoring influence biological fathers can exert may be more important to young people than the sheer number of available positive role models. More research is needed with poor White children (who were not included in this sample) and middle-income African-American children (also not in the Cook et al. study) to better understand the role-modeling influence of biological fathers compared to other positive role models.

Perhaps the most common source of data on the role-modeling contributions of adults to youth development (other than parents) is found in the literature on the evaluation of mentoring programs. DuBois, Holloway, Valentine, and Cooper (2002) conducted an extensive meta-analysis of 55 such evaluations and reported a tendency toward more positive mentoring effects on children in middle childhood than on adolescents. However, positive effects disappeared when the researchers controlled for a number of "best practices" for mentoring programs, such as efforts to promote parental involvement, supervision and training of mentors, and the provision of structured activities for the mentor and child. The results suggested that mentoring programs for younger children currently include more of these best practices than do programs for older children. The researchers also suggested that various aspects of the mentoring relationship, such as frequency of contact, length of the relationship, and emotional closeness, might all be partly responsible for the positive effects of role modeling on youth. However, specific measures of these relationship dimensions are rarely included in mentoring evaluations, so the degree to which they contribute to the positive effects remains unclear.

Positive Peer Influence

Peers also supply children with abundant modeling opportunities. Again, studies in this area are much more likely to focus on negative peer influences, in the form of negative peer pressure. Risk behaviors, such as substance use and early sexual activity, are less common in middle childhood than in adolescence (Centers for Disease Control and Prevention, 2002; Ianotti, Bush, & Weinfurt, 1996). But a handful of studies indicate that peers do influence substance use initiation and antisocial behavior in the later childhood years. On the other hand, the positive aspects of friendships and peer groups (e.g., positive peer pressure and role modeling) have also been associated with multiple positive outcomes. Research shows that *positive* peer influence in middle childhood has been associated, directly or indirectly, with:

Academic Outcomes

- **Greater classroom motivation** (Kindermann, 1993; Sage & Kindermann, 1999); **better academic performance** (Bagwell, Schmidt, Newcomb, & Bukowski, 2001); and **better grade point average** when peer norms support academic excellence (Kurdek, Fine, & Sinclair, 1995).

Mental and Behavioral Health Outcomes

- **Less aggression tolerance,** compared to peers reporting negative peer influence (Newcomb, Bukowski, & Bagwell, 1999); **better social and romantic competence in adulthood** (Bagwell et al., 2001); and **greater disapproval of drinking** (Gillmore et al., 1998).

Research shows that *negative* peer influence in middle childhood has been associated, directly or indirectly, with these mental and behavioral health outcomes:

- **Early intent to use and actual use of cigarettes, alcohol, and marijuana** (Coombs, Paulson, & Richardson, 1991 [for Anglo and Hispanic youths, ages 9–17]; Dielman, Campanelli, Shope & Butchart, 1987; Oxford et al., 2000) and **substance use in adolescent years** if children had associated with deviant peers in middle childhood (Dishion, Capaldi, & Yoerger, 1999 [marijuana and alcohol use]); and **smoking initiation** (Stanton & Silva, 1992);
- **Increased early sexual behavior** in African American girls, ages 9 to 15 years old (Romer et al., 1994);
- **Antisocial behavior** (Dishion, Patterson, & Griesler, 1994); and
- **Fewer positive expectations for the future** among inner-city 6th through 8th graders (Dubow, Arnett, Smith, & Ippolito, 2001).

Peer influence can be experienced in a number of ways. Children may be subject to direct influence, in the usual sense of peer "pressure" (direct coercion or encouragement); to normative influence (complying to gain group approval); and to modeling (identification or wanting to be like a particular friend). The latter may be especially important in the developmental process of identity formation (West & Mitchell, 1999). In middle childhood, friendship groups often form on the basis of gender and racial similarity, and on the basis of particularly strong dimensions of biosocial or behavioral similarity, such as attractiveness and personal appearance, aggressive behavior, popularity, or academic achievement (Cairns, Xie, & Leung, 1998). Simply sharing interests and activities may also be a basis for friendship formation (Sage & Kindermann, 1999).

Peer influence is typically thought of as a negative force, such as peer pressure to experiment with risk-taking behavior. However, Sage and Kindermann's small observational study (1999) of 5th graders and their classroom engagement suggested that, overall, members of a given student's peer network had a more positive than negative influence on the student's classroom behavior. Highly motivated students were given peer approval both for being on task academically (e.g., paying attention to the teacher, participating in class discussions) *and* for behaviors that were off task, such as telling jokes or making faces. In contrast, low-motivation students were given peer approval only for behaviors that were off task. The result seemed to be a reinforcement of motivation in students already so inclined, and somewhat of a discouragement for those already low in motivation.

Newcomb and colleagues (1999), in a study of more than 300 students followed through the fall and spring of grade 6, reported a similar pattern showing how positive peer pressure can affect the trajectory of psychosocial development by reinforcing a student's existing positive attitudes and behaviors. In the fall, each child was paired statistically with a second child who had scored similarly on a measure of aggression tolerance, but whose best friend's aggression tolerance score differed by at least one standard deviation from the score of the first child's best friend. By spring, children with aggressive best friends had much higher tolerance for aggression, whereas the aggression tolerance scores of children with nonaggressive best friends did not change.

In a similar demonstration of how peers can support or reinforce other positive elements of children's lives, Kurdek and colleagues (1995) reported on a study of 6th graders, finding that peer norms for academic excellence predicted grade point average (GPA), but only when parental acceptance was high during childrearing. Peer norms supporting school success did not uniquely predict GPA once race, gender, the number of times parents had been divorced or remarried, and other family climate variables were controlled, but peer norms did reinforce the positive effects of authoritative parenting on students' grades.

Positive peer influence is not only evident over the relatively brief term of one school year. In an 18-year follow-up of adults first studied when they were in grade 5, Bagwell and colleagues (2001) reported that children who had a best friend in grade 5 (each named the other as best friend in both fall and spring), when compared to those who were "chumless," had numerous better outcomes as young adults. These included better school performance at ages 23 and 28, better relationships with their parents and siblings, a more active social and romantic life at age 23, and better ability to avoid depression at both adult ages. Bagwell and colleagues also found that chumless children were more likely to be in trouble with the law at age 23, although at age 28, it was the "friended" children who were more likely to be in trouble with the law. This anomalous finding led the researchers to speculate that at least some of the friend pairs represented relationships between students who had each been previously re-jected by other peers, raising the likelihood of their being "trained" in deviancy. The findings at age 28 may have reflected behaviors of those who didn't simply experiment with delinquency, but actually persisted in it over the life course. Overall, though, in the Bagwell et al. study, children with best friends in grade 5 had many more positive outcomes than negative ones.

Rodkin, Farmer, Pearl, and Van Acker (2000) reported that among 4th-through 6th-grade boys, there appear to be two kinds of popular boys: prosocial and antisocial (or "tough"). Highly aggressive boys, then, may be as socially con-nected as the prosocial, model boys, but presumably have more deviant peers.

In an attempt to explain how friendships might influence antisocial be-havior, Dishion and colleagues (1994) proposed a "confluence model," based on acceptance, friendship selection, and friendship interaction. In their longi-tudinal study of antisocial boys between the ages of 9 and 14, the researchers found that deviant boys maintained many positive qualities of friendships (e.g., compliments, support, laughter), but they expressed interests and histories that differed from their nondeviant peers, most notably their favorable attitudes toward rule breaking. Moreover, antisocial children sought out, or "shopped" for, children of a similar deviant disposition. Consequently, these peers served to reinforce preexisting negative behavioral patterns. This study illustrates the notion that peer influence does not simply "happen" to a young person; rather, young people have a hand in constructing their own peer worlds by virtue of whom they choose to befriend.

Similar to the gender differences we described when we examined the influ-ence on young people of adult role models, positive peer influence may also op-erate somewhat differently in its effects on boys and girls. For example, Erdley, Nangle, Newman, and Carpenter (2001) studied nearly 200 students in grades 3 through 6, almost all of whom were European American. For boys, the degree of peer acceptance (how much peers liked playing with the child), the number of best friendships (a maximum of three), and the number of total friendships (best friends and good friends) all emerged as unique factors in predictions of loneliness, whereas only the total number of friendships served as a factor in predicting loneliness in girls. Lack of peer acceptance also uniquely predicted depression in boys, but not in girls. This finding suggested to the researchers that group acceptance may be more important to the psychological well-being of boys than girls. Girls' specific, close friendships may buffer them against the negative effects of rejection by a larger group.

High Expectations

Relatively few studies on high and appropriate expectations for growth rely on children's perceptions of parent and teacher expectations. Rather, a number of studies involve parent reports about what they expect of their children, particularly academically (in terms of grades and level of schooling). High and appropriate expectations for growth have been associated, directly or indirectly, with:

Academic Outcomes

- **Intrinsic motivation and academic achievement** (Christenson et al., 1992; Ginsburg & Bronstein, 1993 [parental encouragement in response to grades]); Georgiou, 1999 [parental behavior that promotes children's interests]); **reading and math achievement** for low-income African American 6th graders (Reynolds & Gill, 1994); **higher grades** (Halle, Kurtz-Costes, & Mahoney, 1997; Okagaki & French, 1998; Wentzel, 2002); **higher self-expectations for learning** (Kuklinski & Weinstein, 2001); and **students' classroom goals and interests and mastery motivation** (Wentzel, 2002).

Social Outcomes

- **Higher teacher-rated social adjustment and competence scores** (Reynolds & Gill, 1994).

Parents' expectations for their children's achievement exert a strong influence on actual achievement outcomes, although which specific parental beliefs are salient may differ according to parents' racial and ethnic backgrounds. For example, Okagaki and French (1998) studied a sample of more than 200 families that included a 4th or 5th grade child and that represented substantial proportions of Latinos, Asian Americans, and European Americans. They reported that European American parents' expectations of the number of years of schooling their children would eventually complete, as well as their dissatisfaction with low grades and emphasis on monitoring their children and creating an academically rich home environment, were all positively related to children's actual grades. Among Latinos, only parental dissatisfaction with low grades predicted children's grades, and among Asian Americans, only the number of years of schooling parents expected their children to complete was related to children's grades. In a small study of low-income African American 3rd and 4th graders and their parents, Halle, Kurtz-Costes, and Mahoney (1997) reported that parents' expectations for the years of schooling their child would complete were positively related to both the child's math and reading grades.

Weinstein, Marshall, Sharp, and Botkin (1987) studied 579 children in grades 1, 3, and 5 and reported that teacher expectations significantly influenced students' self-expectations. Although 1st and 3rd graders were not as accurate in describing teacher expectations, they were aware that teachers treated high and low achievers differently. By 5th grade, children more accurately described teacher expectations and mirrored teacher expectations in their own self-expectations. In other words, if children felt teachers expected high achievement from them, then high achievement was also what the children expected of themselves.

Wentzel (2002) studied 452 suburban 6th graders, of whom half were White and half were African American. The research found that certain dimensions of parenting behavior, such as nurturance, control, and maturity demands, can be generalized to the school setting to describe teacher behavior and predict student outcomes. Consistent with the literature on high expectations, a construct Wentzel used as a measure of maturity demands, she reported that teachers' high expectations for students were a significant predictor of students' classroom goals, interest in class, and mastery motivation, as well as classroom grades. The results also suggested, however, that grades were predicted more by students' desire to be responsible in class and do what teachers expected of them than by their interest in the class content per se. Therefore, for children in late middle childhood, academic achievement may be explained as much or more by the way teachers' high expectations affect students' *social* goals as by the manner in which such expectations affect their academic motivation.

In a related study, Kuklinski and Weinstein (2001) looked at teacher expectancy effects in a sample of 376 urban 1st- through 5th-grade students and found that teacher expectations of student future performance and academic achievement were moderated both by classroom environment and developmental differences among students. Teacher expectations had the greatest effect on the achievement of students in grade 1, accounting for 9% to 12% of achievement across different classrooms. However, the effect of teacher expectations was only half as explanatory of the student achievement of 5th graders for whom the effects of their own self-expectations equaled that of their teachers, together explaining 9% of the variance in self-expectations for academic success. Importantly, if the classroom was one in which students perceived that they were being treated differently on the basis of their achievement (i.e., low achievers felt they were not expected to succeed), these effects were stronger in grades 3 (for achievement) and 5 (for self-expectations). This study suggests that performance messages from teachers are indeed important, but that both classroom and developmental context affect how students attend to those messages and which outcomes of interest are most affected.

More indirect routes by which expectations may affect student performance are suggested by Goddard's study (2001) of 452 teachers in 47 urban elementary schools. He examined differences in mathematics and reading achievement scores by schools as a function of the collective efficacy felt by teachers in each school (i.e., by the presence of a collective belief and social norm that teachers in a given school could successfully teach students). As predicted, students in elementary schools with higher mean levels of collective teacher efficacy earned significantly higher achievement scores in both reading and mathematics. Interestingly, the degree of teacher consensus about their level of collective efficacy did not predict achievement—only the actual mean level of collective efficacy did. This study suggests that one way to increase students' academic success may be to raise the level of teacher beliefs in their own ability to succeed. In turn, teachers who feel efficacious may set higher and more equitable expectations for their students, encouraging children's sense of connection to school and motivation to achieve.

The Boundaries-and-Expectations Assets across the Early Childhood-Adolescence Life Span

Family Boundaries

The way in which boundaries are established reflects a central issue in the developmental progression of family boundaries from the early elementary grades through middle childhood. For children in early middle childhood, effective boundaries and standards of behavior are established by explanations, rationales, and the child's experience of the consequences of her or his behavior (Kuczynski, Marshall, & Schell, 1997). This process, called induction, is thought to promote the child's internalization of values and standards of behavior, rather than merely promoting compliance with values. The distinction between the two processes reflects the difference between internal and external guides for behavior: Internalization refers to a process whereby the child uses internal cues—rules and values—to govern behavior, whereas compliance refers to a process whereby external cues—parents' or other adults' exercise of power—moderate the child's behavior (Kochanska & Thompson, 1997). In short, over the course of middle childhood, some values may begin to become the child's own, part of her or his unique self-structure (i.e., psychological makeup or identity), while others remain standards set by parents or other adults and not yet "owned" by the child.

Another important aspect of family boundaries is the degree to which parents monitor not only the child's whereabouts (Patterson, Reid, & Dishion, 1992), but also other activities in which the child engages, such as watching television (Bradley, 1999). For example, Patterson and his colleagues (Dishion & McMahon, 1998; Patterson, DeBaryshe, & Ramsey, 1989) demonstrated that parental monitoring is a significant factor in protecting children from engaging in antisocial behavior.

However, recent studies of monitoring indicate that the most important element in effective monitoring may not be parents' active solicitation of information from children. Rather, it is voluntary disclosure on the child's part that may be what accounts for much of the relation between parental monitoring and child outcome (Stattin & Kerr, 2000). This research, although conducted with young adolescents, points to an important facet of parental monitoring: Effective monitoring goes beyond parents' active efforts to find out about their child's whereabouts and activities; it must also include the active role of the child (Crouter, Helms-Erikson, Updegraff, & McHale, 1999).

Parental supervisory or monitoring practices, although generally found to be important for positive child development, do not always have a simple relation to child developmental outcomes. For example, Colder, Mott, Levy, and Flay (2000) studied more than 700 African American 5th graders in an inner-city setting. They reported that the more children perceived their neighborhood as unsafe, the more children believed aggression was an appropriate behavior and the more aggressively they behaved. Restrictive parental discipline, monitoring, and involvement did not change that relation. However, children of parents who used very strict discipline methods had stronger positive beliefs about the appropriateness of aggression. Children who were poorly monitored also reported higher beliefs in aggression as acceptable behavior. Similarly, Pettit, Bates, Dodge, and Meece (1999) found, in a study of more than 400 6th and 7th graders, that low parental monitoring of children in grade 6 predicted behavior problems in grade 7. The risk for problem behavior was greatest, however, for children who experienced lower levels of boundaries-and-expectations assets across several parts of their environment, including low parental monitoring, unsupervised time with peers, and living in relatively unsafe neighborhoods.

School Boundaries

In addition to the important relationship experiences children have in schools with teachers, peers, and other adults, other structural school factors can also play a role in healthy child and youth development. For example, Eccles and Wigfield (2000) identify a number of factors, including classroom orderliness and predictability, classroom authority structure, and teaching practices that emphasize self-evaluation and motivation. Collectively, these dimensions of classroom structural factors represent a child-centered, emotionally positive classroom environment, which has been shown to be related to both better academic outcomes and positive behaviors (Eccles & Wigfield, 2000; Pianta, La Paro, Payne, Cox, & Bradley, 2002). An intriguing question for future study is whether these structural factors have invariant effects across the elementary grades, or whether a developmental trajectory exists for school-level factors that makes them more important to children at some ages than at others.

Neighborhood Boundaries

Leventhal and Brooks-Gunn (2000) describe three mechanisms through which neighborhoods are presumed to influence youth development: available institutional resources, youth and adult relationships, and existing neighborhood norms and collective efficacy. The first two are addressed in our discussion of the caring-neighborhood and other-adult-relationships support assets in Chapter 1. The third mechanism—norms and collective efficacy—refers to a shared ethos of the neighborhood, a collective sense of responsibilities and of what behavior is acceptable within that community (Leventhal & Brooks-Gunn, 2000). Embedded in this definition is the notion of *informal social control* (Sampson et al., 1997), which refers to the degree to which residents of a community would be willing to intervene if they saw something untoward occur in their neighborhood.

Recent research has begun to examine the outcomes of collective efficacy processes with adolescents (e.g., Brody et al., 2001, described above), but the relevance of a shared ethos for younger children has yet to be examined in that depth. Consistent with our earlier view of neighborhood consequences, the primary effect of the benefits that may accrue from having a neighborhood steeped in a shared vision of and response to acceptable child behaviors may be on parents, whose behaviors, influenced by those neighborhood norms, may then have a salutary secondary effect on children's development (Shonkoff & Phillips, 2000).

Parent, Family, and Nonfamily Adult Role Models

Although the research is far from ideal, multiple lines of inquiry, including both laboratory and correlational research designs, converge on the finding that children do model their parents' prosocial behaviors (Eisenberg & Fabes, 1997). How this happens is unclear, although research indicates that the process is *not* simply a matter of the child's imitating the parent (or other salient adult figures). Children actively select and organize whom and what to imitate in their social environment (Kuczynski et al., 1997), and this active involvement has been shown to occur in children as young as 2 and 3 years old (Kuczynski, Zahn-Waxler, & Radke-Yarrow, 1987). For children in the early elementary grades, a variety of adults with whom the child has a close relationship can act as effective role models of positive behavior.

However, when we say children "actively select" role models at this age or even middle childhood, we do not mean that they have in place a firm value system that guides such choices. We mean only that all children, from infancy onward, "choose" the adults whom they like. Infants smile at some people and not others. Grade school children initiate play with some adults and not others. Gradually and increasingly, children do develop an internal value system that shapes such choices. But in childhood, and especially in the K–3 years and earlier, those choices are often based on nothing more profound than a single physical feature of an adult or a shared activity the child and adult enjoy.

Positive Peer Influence

Children's early childhood peer relationships help socialize them and provide them with support and opportunities to experience and become adept at the give-and-take of effective relationships (Bredekamp & Copple, 1997). Children learn relational skills such as cooperation, turn taking, and conflict resolution strategies within the peer group (Hartup, 1992). Additionally, the presence of a reciprocal friend has been shown to facilitate a child's adjustment to kindergarten: Ladd (1996) describes how kindergarten children who saw their friends as sources of validation and support were more likely to form good impressions of their other classmates as well as to express positive attitudes toward school. Thus, the positive peer influence asset for children in kindergarten through grade 3 reflects both the socialization and supportive aspects of peer relations.

Parents can also actively influence not only the kinds of activities in which their children engage with peers but also the quality of those interactions. In a departure from the way peer influences operate in middle childhood and adolescence, a heightened degree of importance is attached to the way in which parents actively involve themselves in their children's early childhood peer experiences (Rubin, Bukowski, & Parker, 1998). Parents do so by providing opportunities for their child to be with other children, monitoring their children's peer interactions, and coaching their children to deal competently with their peers. Research on effective, active parenting efforts on behalf of children's peer experiences indicates that children generally benefit in the peer group from such parental involvement (Parke & Ladd, 1992).

High Expectations

Most people would agree that expressing high expectations for a young child's academic competence and achievements has significant and important effects on the child. Much research, however, focuses on expectations for the educational attainment of older children (i.e., late elementary and above). This gap in the literature is important because it is not empirically clear what the developmental implications are of expressing high academic expectations to children: Do high expectations for student achievement function similarly across all periods of childhood?

In one of the few studies explicitly addressing the developmental course of the importance of high expectations, Kuklinski and Weinstein (2001) suggested that adult expectations regarding children's academic achievement do have differential effects, depending on the age of the child. The authors reported that for younger students (grades 1 and 3), high teacher expectations had a direct effect on academic achievement scores, but did not affect the children's self-expectations regarding ability. This indirect pathway leading from teacher expectations to child self-expectations and subsequently to achievement outcomes was seen only for older (grade 5) children. The implication is that teacher expectations, although important to children in the early grades, function differently across developmental periods.

Overall, scant empirical attention has been given in the middle childhood literature to the importance of adult expectations, not only for academic functioning, but also for other areas of development. Nevertheless, even though pathways of influence may differ, research does indicate that high expectations play important positive roles for children of all ages. Thus, all adults in the child's life can play a role in expressing to the child a belief and a confidence in the child's current and future competent functioning.

Measuring the Boundaries-and-Expectations Assets in Middle Childhood

Results of the *Me and My World* field tests, conducted among approximately 1,300 4th through 6th graders in Nevada, California, and New York, show that each boundaries-and-expectation asset except neighborhood boundaries was reportedly experienced by a majority of children. The largest proportion in each community reported they experienced school boundaries, positive peer influence, and high expectations. This positive result suggests that during

Table 7. Proportion of Field Test 4th–6th Graders Who Report Experiencing the Boundaries-and-Expectations Assets			
Asset	**% Who Report Experiencing Asset**		
	Nevada	**California**	**New York**
Family boundaries	60	58	57
School boundaries	87	90	82
Neighborhood boundaries	56	58	61
Adult role models	59	62	51
Parent/family measures	72	68	61
Nonfamily adult measures	51	58	48
Positive peer influence	88	87	94
High expectations	89	89	93
From field tests in 2003; N = 1,294.			

middle childhood, the majority of children may experience adequate levels of supervision, monitoring, standard setting, role modeling, and expectations that help guide their behavior in healthy ways. In each field test community, however, neighborhood boundaries was the least commonly reported asset in the boundaries-and-expectations category.

A considerably higher proportion of students in each field test sample reported experiencing more family boundaries, adult role models, and high expectations than did 6th graders in Search Institute's 1999-2000 aggregate survey sample of youth in more than 300 U.S. communities. Yet that trend is consistent with the institute's data for 6th through 12th graders, documenting that the boundaries-and-expectations assets are reported successively less often by students in the higher grades. These results are also consistent with the developmental research cited throughout this book on the developmental stage of middle childhood as compared to adolescence. As young people mature, they increasingly negotiate new rules and expectations in accord with their gradually increasing ability to self-regulate. Because the field test samples included younger children in the grades 4 and 5, the survey theoretically should have yielded, and did yield, larger proportions of responses from children who said they experienced the regulatory strategies of family and nonfamily members alike, as well as the positive influence of their peers.

References

Anderman, E. M., & Kimweli, D. M. S. (1997). Victimization and safety in schools serving young adolescents. *Journal of Early Adolescence, 17,* 408–438.

Bagwell, C. L., Schmidt, M. E., Newcomb, A. F., & Bukowski, W. M. (2001). Friendship and peer rejection as predictors of adult adjustment. *New Directions for Child and Adolescent Development, no. 91,* 25–49.

Bear, G. G. (1998). School discipline in the United States: Prevention, correction and long term social development. *Educational and Child Psychology, 15,* 15–39.

Bradley, R. H. (1999). The home environment. In S. L. Friedman & T. D. Wachs (Eds.), *Measuring environment across the life span* (pp. 31–58). Washington, DC: American Psychological Association.

Bradley, R. H., Corwyn, R. F., McAdoo, H. P., & Coll, C. G. (2001). The home environments of children in the United States: Part 1. Variations by age, ethnicity, and poverty status. *Child Development, 72,* 1844–1867.

Bredekamp, S., & Copple, C. (1997). *Developmentally appropriate practice in early childhood programs.* Washington, DC: National Association for the Education of Young Children.

Brody, G. H., Dorsey, S., Forehand, R., & Armistead, L. (2002). Unique and protective contributions of parenting and classroom processes to the adjustment of African American children living in single-parent families. *Child Development, 73,* 274–286.

Brody, G. H., Ge, X., Conger, R., Gibbons, F. X., Murry, V. M., Gerrard, M., & Simons, R. L. (2001). The influence of neighborhood disadvantage, collective socialization, and parenting on African American children's affiliation with deviant peers. *Child Development, 72,* 1231–1246.

Brody, G. H., Stoneman, Z., & Flor, D. (1996). Parental religiosity, family processes, and youth competence in rural, two-parent African American families. *Developmental Psychology, 32,* 696–706.

Bumpus, M. F., Crouter, A. C., & McHale, S. M. (1999). Work demands of dual-earner couples: Implications for parents' knowledge about children's daily lives in middle childhood. *Journal of Marriage and the Family, 61,* 465–475.

Burton, L. M., & Price-Spratlen, T. (1999). Through the eyes of children: An ethnographic perspective on neighborhoods and child development. In A. S. Masten (Ed.), *The Minnesota symposia on child psychology: Vol. 29. Cultural processes in child development* (pp. 77–96). Mahwah, NJ: Lawrence Erlbaum.

Cairns, R., Xie, H., & Leung, M. (1998). The popularity of friendship and the neglect of social networks: Toward a new balance. In W. M. Bukowski & A. H. Cillessen (Eds.), *Sociometry then and now: Building on six decades of measuring children's experiences with the peer group* (pp. 25–53). *New Directions for Child and Adolescent Development, no. 80.* San Francisco: Jossey-Bass.

Centers for Disease Control and Prevention. (2002). *Surveillance Summaries* (MMWR Publication No. SS-4). Atlanta: U.S. Government Printing Office.

Chilcoat, H. D., & Anthony, J. C. (1996). Impact of parent monitoring on initiation of drug use through late childhood. *Journal of the American Academy of Child and Adolescent Psychiatry, 35,* 91–100.

Chipuer, H. M. (2001). Dyadic attachments and community connectedness: Links with youths' loneliness experiences. *Journal of Community Psychology, 29,* 429–446.

Christenson, S. L., Rounds, T., & Gornery, D. (1992). Family factors and student achievement: An avenue to increase students' success. *School Psychology Quarterly, 7,* 178–206.

Colder, C. R., Mott, J., Levy, S., & Flay, B. (2000). The relation of perceived neighborhood danger to childhood aggression: A test of mediating mechanisms. *American Journal of Community Psychology, 28,* 83–103.

Coley, R. L., & Hoffman, L. W. (1996). Relations of parental supervision and monitoring to children's functioning in various contexts: Moderating effects of families and neighborhoods. *Journal of Applied Developmental Psychology, 17*, 51–68.

Cook, T. D., Church, M. B., Ajanaku, S., Shadish, W. R., Kim, J. R., & Cohen, R. (1996). The development of occupational aspirations and expectations among inner-city boys. *Child Development, 67*, 3368–3385.

Coombs, R. H., Paulson, M. J., & Richardson, M. A. (1991). Peer vs. parental influence in substance use among Hispanic and Anglo children and adolescents. *Journal of Youth and Adolescence, 20*, 73–88.

Crouter, A. C., Helms-Erikson, H., Updegraff, K., & McHale, S. M. (1999). Conditions underlying parents' knowledge about children's daily lives in middle childhood: Between- and within-family comparisons. *Child Development, 70*, 246–259.

Crouter, A. C., MacDermid, S. M., McHale, S. M., & Perry-Jenkins, M. (1990). Parental monitoring and perceptions of children's school performance and conduct in dual- and single-earner families. *Developmental Psychology, 26*, 649–657.

Dielman, T. E., Campanelli, P. C., Shope, J. T., & Butchart, A. T. (1987). Susceptibility to peer pressure, self-esteem, and health locus of control as correlates of adolescent substance abuse. *Health Education Quarterly, 14*, 207–221.

Dishion, T. J., Capaldi, D. M., & Yoerger, K. (1999). Middle childhood antecedents to progressions in male adolescent substance use: An ecological analysis of risk and protection. *Journal of Adolescence, 14*, 175–205.

Dishion, T. J., & McMahon, R. J. (1998). Parental monitoring and the prevention of child and adolescent problem behavior: A conceptual and empirical foundation. *Clinical Child and Family Psychology Review, 1*, 61–75.

Dishion, T. J., Patterson, G. R., & Griesler, P. C. (1994). Peer adaptations in the development of antisocial behavior. In L. R. Huesmann (Ed.), *Aggressive behavior: Current perspectives* (pp. 61–95). New York: Plenum Press.

DuBois, D. L., Holloway, B. E., Valentine, J. C., & Cooper, H. (2002). Effectiveness of mentoring programs for youth: A meta-analytic review. *American Journal of Community Psychology, 30*, 157–197.

Dubow, E. R., Arnett, M., Smith, K., & Ippolito, M. F. (2001). Predictors of future expectations of inner-city children: A 9-month prospective study. *Journal of Early Adolescence, 21*, 5–28.

Eccles, J. S., & Wigfield, A. (2000). Schooling influences on motivation and achievement. In S. Danziger & J. Waldfogel (Eds.), *Securing the future: Investing in children from birth to college* (pp. 153–181). New York: Sage Foundation.

Eisenberg, N., & Fabes, R. A. (1998). Prosocial development. In W. Damon & N. Eisenberg (Eds.), *Handbook of child psychology* (pp. 703–778). New York: John Wiley & Sons.

Elliot, D. S., Wilson, W. J., Huizinga, D., Sampson, R. J., Elliot, A., & Rankin, B. (1996). The effects of neighborhood disadvantage on adolescent development. *Journal of Research in Crime and Delinquency, 33*, 389–426.

Erdley, C. A., Nangle, D. W., Newman, J. E., & Carpenter, E. M. (2001). Children's friendship experiences and psychological adjustment: Theory and research. *New Directions in Child and Adolescent Development, no. 91*, 5–24.

Fletcher, A. C., Newsome, D., Nickerson, P., & Bazley, R. (2001). Social network closure and child adjustment. *Merrill-Palmer Quarterly, 47*, 500–531.

Garstein, M. A., Noll, R. B., & Vannatta, K. (2000). Childhood aggression and chronic illness: Possible protective mechanisms. *Journal of Applied Developmental Psychology, 21,* 315–333.

Georgiou, S. N. (1999). Parental attributions as predictors of involvement and influences on child achievement. *British Journal of Educational Psychology, 69,* 409–429.

Gillmore, M. R., Wells, E. A., Simpson, E. E., Morrison, D. M., Hoppe, M. J., & Wilson, A. (1998). Children's beliefs about drinking. *American Journal of Drug and Alcohol Abuse, 24,* 131–151.

Ginsburg, G. S., & Bronstein, P. (1993). Family factors related to children's intrinsic/extrinsic motivational orientation and academic performance. *Child Development, 64,* 1461–1474.

Goddard, R. D. (2001). Collective efficacy: A neglected construct in the study of schools and student achievement. *Journal of Educational Psychology, 93,* 467–476.

Goh, S. C., & Fraser, B. J. (2000). Teacher interpersonal behavior and elementary students' outcomes. *Journal of Research in Childhood Education, 14,* 216–231.

Halle, T. G., Kurtz-Costes, B., & Mahoney, J. L. (1997). Family influences on school achievement in low-income, African American children. *Journal of Educational Psychology, 89,* 527–537.

Hartup, W. W. (1992). Friendships and their developmental significance. In H. McGurk (Ed.), *Childhood social development* (pp. 175–205). Hove, UK: Lawrence Erlbaum.

Helwig C. C., & Kim, S. (1999). Children's evaluations of decision-making procedures in peer, family, and school contexts. *Child Development, 70,* 502–512.

Ianotti, R. J., Bush, P. J., & Weinfurt, K. P. (1996). Perception of friends' use of alcohol, cigarettes, and marijuana among urban schoolchildren: A longitudinal analysis. *Addictive Behaviors, 21,* 615–632.

Izzo, C. V., Weissberg, R. P., Kasprow, W. J., & Fendrich, M. (1999). A longitudinal assessment of teacher perceptions of parent involvement in children's education and school performance. *American Journal of Community Psychology, 27,* 817–839.

Jackson, C., Bee-Gates, D. J., & Henriksen, L. (1994). Authoritative parenting, child competencies, and initiation of cigarette smoking. *Health Education Quarterly, 21,* 103–116.

Kerns, K. A., Aspelmeier, J. E., Gentzler, A. L., & Grabill, C. M. (2001). Parent-child attachment and monitoring in middle childhood. *Journal of Family Psychology, 15,* 69–81.

Kindermann, T. A. (1993). Natural peer groups as contexts for individual development: The case of children's motivation in school. *Developmental Psychology, 29,* 970–977.

Kochanska, G. R., & Thompson, R. A. (1997). The emergence and development of conscience in toddlerhood and early childhood. In J. E. Grusec & L. Kuczynski (Eds.), *Parenting and children's internalization of values* (pp. 53–77). New York: John Wiley & Sons.

Kuczynski, L., Marshall, S., & Schell, K. (1997). Value socialization in a bidirectional context. In J. E. Grusec and L. Kuczynski (Eds.), *Parenting and the internalization of values: A handbook of contemporary theory* (pp. 23–50). New York: John Wiley & Sons.

Kuczynski, L., Zahn-Waxler, C., & Radke-Yarrow, M. (1987). Development and content of imitation in the second and third year of life: A socialization perspective. *Developmental Psychology, 23,* 276–282.

Kuklinski, M. R., & Weinstein, R. S. (2001). Classroom and developmental differences in a path model of teacher expectancy effects. *Child Development, 72,* 1554–1578.

Kurdek, L. A., Fine, M. A., & Sinclair, R. J. (1995). School adjustment in sixth graders: Parenting transitions, family climate, and peer norm effects. *Child Development, 65,* 430–445.

Ladd, G. W. (1996). Shifting ecologies during the 5 to 7 year period: Predicting children's adjustment during the transition to grade school. In A. J. Sameroff & M. M. Haith (Eds.),

The five to seven year shift: The age of reason and responsibility (pp. 363–386). Chicago: University of Chicago Press.

Ladd, G. W., Kochenderfer, B. J., & Coleman, C. C. (1997). Classroom peer acceptance, friendships, and victimization: Distinct relational systems that contribute uniquely to children's school adjustment? *Child Development, 68,* 1181–1197.

Lamborn, S. D., Dornbusch, S. M., & Steinberg, L. (1996). Ethnicity and community context as moderators of the relations between family decision making and adolescent adjustment. *Child Development, 67,* 283–301.

Leventhal, T., & Brooks-Gunn, J. (2000). The neighborhoods they live in: The effects of neighborhood residence on child and adolescent outcomes. *Psychological Bulletin, 126,* 309–337.

Mahoney, J. L., & Magnusson, D. (2001). Parent participation in community activities and the persistence of criminality. *Development and Psychopathology, 13,* 125–141.

Marshall, N. L., Noonan, A. E., McCartney, K., Marx, F., & Keefe, N. (2001). It takes an urban village: Parenting networks of urban families. *Journal of Family Issues, 22,* 163–182.

Martin, C. S., Earleywine, M., Blackson, T. C., Vanyukov, M. M., Moss, H. B., & Tarter, R. E. (1994). Aggressivity, inattention, hyperactivity, and impulsivity in boys at high and low risk for substance abuse. *Journal of Abnormal Child Psychology, 22,* 177–203.

Mattanah, J. F. (2001). Parental psychological autonomy and children's academic competence and behavioral adjustment in late childhood: More than just limit-setting and warmth. *Merrill-Palmer Quarterly, 47,* 355–376.

Midgley, C., & Feldlaufer, H. (1987). Students' and teachers' decision-making fit before and after the transition to junior high school. *Journal of Early Adolescence, 7,* 225–241.

National Education Goals Panel. (1998). *National education goals report: Building a nation of learners.* Washington, DC: Author.

Newcomb, A. F., Bukowski, W. M., & Bagwell, C. L. (1999). Knowing the sounds: Friendship as a developmental context. In W. A. Collins & B. Laursen (Eds.), *The Minnesota symposia on child psychology: Vol. 30. Relationships as developmental contexts* (pp. 63–84). Mahwah, NJ: Lawrence Erlbaum.

Okagaki, L., & French, P. A. (1998). Parenting and children's school achievement: A multiethnic perspective. *American Educational Research Journal, 35,* 123–144.

O'Neil, R., Parke, R. D., & McDowell, D. J. (2001). Objective and subjective features of children's neighborhoods: Relations to parental regulatory strategies and children's social competence. *Applied Developmental Psychology, 22,* 135–155.

Oxford, M. L., Harachi, T. W., Catalano, R. F., & Abbott, R. D. (2000). Preadolescent predictors of substance initiation: A test of both the direct and mediated effect of family social control factors on deviant peer associations and substance initiation. *American Journal of Drug and Alcohol Abuse, 27,* 599–616.

Parke, R. D., & Ladd, G. W. (1992). *Family-peer relationships: Modes of linkage.* Hillsdale, NJ: Lawrence Erlbaum.

Patterson, G. R., DeBaryshe, B. D., & Ramsey, E. (1989). A developmental perspective on antisocial behavior. *American Psychologist, 44,* 329–335.

Patterson, G. R., Reid, J. B., & Dishion, T. J. (1992). *Antisocial boys.* Eugene, OR: Castalia.

Paulson, S. E., Marchant, G. J., & Rothlisberg, B. A. (1998). Early adolescents' perceptions of patterns of parenting, teaching, and school atmosphere: Implications for achievement. *Journal of Early Adolescence, 18,* 5–26.

Pettit, G. S., Bates, J. E., Dodge, K. A., & Meece, D. W. (1999). The impact of after-school peer contact on early adolescent externalizing problems is moderated by parental monitoring, perceived neighborhood safety, and prior adjustment. *Child Development, 70,* 768–778.

Pettit, G. S., Laird, R. D., Dodge, K. A., Bates, J. E., & Criss, M. M. (2001). Antecedents and behavior-problem outcomes of parental monitoring and psychological control in early adolescence. *Child Development, 72,* 583–598.

Pianta, R. C., La Paro, K. M., Payne, C., Cox, M. J., & Bradley, R. (2002). The relation of kindergarten classroom environment to teacher, family, and school characteristics and child outcomes. *Elementary School Journal, 102,* 225–238.

Reynolds, A. J., & Gill, S. (1994). The role of parental perspectives in the school adjustment of inner-city black children. *Journal of Youth and Adolescence, 23,* 671–694.

Rodkin, P. C., Farmer, T. W., Pearl, R., & Van Acker, R. (2000). Heterogeneity of popular boys: Antisocial and prosocial configurations. *Developmental Psychology, 36,* 14–24.

Romer, D., Black, M., Ricardo, I., Feigelman, S., Kaljee, L., Galbraith, J., Nesbit, R., Hornik, R. C., & Stanton, B. (1994). Social influences on the sexual behavior of youth at risk for HIV exposure. *American Journal of Public Health, 84,* 977–985.

Rubin, K. H., Bukowski, W., & Parker, J. G. (1998). Peer interactions, relationships, and groups. In W. Damon (Series Ed.) & N. Eisenberg (Vol. Ed.), *Handbook of child psychology* (5th ed., pp. 619–700). New York: John Wiley & Sons.

Sage, N. A., & Kindermann, T. A. (1999). Peer networks, behavior contingencies, and children's engagement in the classroom. *Merrill-Palmer Quarterly, 45,* 143–171.

Sampson, R., Raudenbush, S. W., & Earls, F. (1997). Neighborhoods and violent crime: A multilevel study of collective efficacy. *Science, 277,* 917–925.

Sandstrom, M. J., & Coie, J. D. (1999). A developmental perspective on peer rejection: Mechanisms of stability and change. *Child Development, 70,* 955–966.

Scales, P. C., & Leffert, N. (1999). *Developmental assets: A synthesis of the scientific research on adolescent development.* Minneapolis: Search Institute.

Shonkoff, J. P., & Phillips, D. A. (Eds.). (2000). *From neurons to neighborhoods: The science of early childhood development.* Washington, DC: National Academies Press.

Shumow, L., Vandell, D. L., & Posner, J. (1999). Risk and resilience in the urban neighborhood: Predictors of academic performance among low-income elementary school children. *Merrill-Palmer Quarterly, 45,* 309–331.

Simons, R. L., Lin, K.-H., Gordon, L. C., Brody, G. H., Murry, V., & Conger, R. D. (2002). Community differences in the association between parenting practices and child conduct problems. *Journal of Marriage and the Family, 64,* 331–345.

Simpkins, S. D., & Parke, R. D. (2001). The relations between parental friendships and children's friendships: Self-report and observational analysis. *Child Development, 72,* 569–582.

Smith, G. T., Miller, T. L., Kroll, L., Simmons, J. R., & Gallen, R. (1996). Children's perceptions of parental drinking: The eye of the beholder. *Journal of Studies on Alcohol, 60,* 817–824.

Sprague, J., Walker, H., Golly, A., White, K., Myers, D. R., & Shannon, T. (2001). Translating research into effective practice: The effects of a universal staff and student intervention on indicators of discipline and school safety. *Education and Treatment of Children, 24,* 495–511.

Stanton, W. R., & Silva, P. A. (1992). A longitudinal study of the influence of parents and friends on children's initiation of smoking. *Journal of Applied Developmental Psychology, 13,* 423–434.

Starkman, N., Scales, P. C., & Roberts, C. (1999). *Great places to learn: How asset-building schools help students succeed.* Minneapolis: Search Institute.

Stattin, H., & Kerr, M. (2000). Parental monitoring: A reinterpretation. *Child Development, 71*, 1072–1085.

Steinberg, L. (2001). We know some things: Parent-adolescent relationships in retrospect and prospect. *Journal of Research on Adolescence, 11*, 1–19.

Thompson, L. A., & Kelly-Vance, L. (2001). The impact of mentoring on academic achievement of at-risk youth. *Children and Youth Services Review, 23*, 227–242.

Tibbs, T., Haire-Joshu, D., Schechtman, K. B., Brownson, R. C., Nanney, M. S., Houston, C., & Auslander, W. (2001). The relationship between parental modeling, eating patterns, and dietary intake among African-American parents. *Journal of the American Dietetic Association, 101*, 535–541.

Vitaro, F., Brengden, M., & Tremblay, R. E. (2001). Preventive intervention: Assessing its effects on the trajectories of delinquency and testing for mediational processes. *Applied Developmental Science, 5*, 201–213.

Weinstein, R. S., Marshall, H. H., Sharp, L., & Botkin, M. (1987). Pygmalion and the student: Age and classroom differences in children's awareness of teacher expectations. *Child Development, 58*, 1079–1093.

Wentzel, K. R. (2002). Are effective teachers like good parents? Teaching styles and student adjustment in early adolescence. *Child Development, 73*, 287–301.

West, P., & Mitchell, L. (1999). Smoking and peer influence. In A. J. Goreczny & M. Hersen (Eds.), *Handbook of pediatric and adolescent health psychology* (pp. 179–202). Boston: Allyn & Bacon.

Whitbeck, L. B. (1987). Modeling efficacy: The effect of perceived parental efficacy on the self-efficacy of early adolescents. *Journal of Early Adolescence, 7*, 165–177.

A healthy community offers a rich array of constructive, engaging opportunities and activities to all young people.

4

The Constructive-Use-of-Time Assets

Why Is Constructive Use of Time Important?

The choices made by both parents and children concerning the activities in which children participate outside school hours can bestow on fortunate children a developmentally appropriate balance of scheduled and "free" time. These children benefit from plentiful interaction with responsible peers and caring adults, as well as from the private self-discovery enabled by sufficient amounts of free time. Child and parent choices regarding a child's use of time before and after school hours can also leave children either relatively unoccupied or overscheduled and overdirected, neither of which conditions supports developmental well-being.

Larson and Verma (1999) argue that time is a developmental variable allowing children, through accumulated exposure to particular contexts or experiences, to develop social and emotional competencies and life skills, such as initiative, self-regulation, and interpersonal success. During middle childhood, children's environments expand rapidly in scope and variety. Most children in this stage of development are increasingly able to function independently, without constant adult supervision (or constant structured programming), both inside and outside the home. Moreover, middle childhood has been thought of as a time of "industry," whereby a capacity for productive work helps define the child's view of her or his competence (Erikson, 1959). Together, these developments enable parents to (1) permit children to spend greater amounts of time caring for themselves without adult supervision (for more information on self-care, see pages 133–34); (2) encourage or even require children's participation in a variety of organized after-school activities; and (3) promote constructive use of time spent at home and outside of organized programs. In addition, children in middle childhood become increasingly aware of their own talents and interests (as well as their limitations and dislikes), leading them to seek friends and opportunities, inside and outside of school, that enhance their strengths and allow participation in activities they enjoy.

Halpern (2000) eloquently described why high-quality structured programs are so developmentally valuable for children, particularly in middle childhood:

> [A]ll children need times and places in their lives where the adult agenda is modest, if not held at bay; where the emotional temperature is low, and acceptance is generous; where learning is self-directed, experiential, and structured to be enjoyable; where talents can be identified and nurtured; and where possible identities can be explored without risk of failure or ridicule. (p. 186)

A variety of studies have shown the positive impact on children of regular participation in even relatively modest amounts of structured activities that occupy their time constructively. For example, students who participate in after-school programs sponsored by school or community agencies have been found to be less likely to commit delinquent or criminal offenses or to use alcohol or other drugs than are children who do not participate in such constructive activities (Eccles, 1999). Moreover, they have better grades and academic achievement, more cooperative behavior, and better conflict resolution and interpersonal communication skills (Fashola, 1998; U.S. Department of Education & U.S. Department of Justice, 2000).

Although the great majority of studies show numerous positive child outcomes associated with participation in structured after-school or extracurricular programs, studies do not invariably report positive effects. For example, Posner and Vandell (1999) studied nearly 200 White and African American students in Milwaukee elementary schools, following them from grades 3 through 5. They reported that the African American children were better adjusted emotionally in grade 5 if they had spent more cumulative time than their peers in nonsport extracurricular enrichment activities since grade 3. Interestingly, the same children earned better grades in grade 5 if they spent significantly *less* time in coached sports and *more* time socializing (with both friends and family) than did their peers. White children who spent significantly more cumulative time in extracurricular activities compared to their peers received poorer grades in grade 5 (perhaps an unintended result of those children being "overprogrammed").

Similarly, Moore and Glei (1995) reported in a longitudinal study of several thousand young people followed from age 7 to 22 that a simple measure of a child's participation in after-school clubs from ages 10 to 18 did not predict the child's likelihood of experiencing a "misstep," such as early sexual intercourse, pregnancy by age 17, or school dropout. This result was most likely due to lack of available data on the nature of those clubs' activities and the extent of children's involvement. Thus, although the bulk of evidence shows beneficial effects of organized child programs, some studies underscore the limitations of simply counting hours of participation.

Mathematica, Inc., conducted a federally funded study of a sample of after-school programs—21st Century Learning Centers—most in just their first or second years of implementation, and reported mixed results. Academic and behavioral impact overall for elementary students was reported as limited, but some significant impact was also observed on mathematics achievement among African American students, and parental involvement increased (Jacobson, 2003). Doubtless, some of the study's "no effect" findings can be attributed to the programs being quite early in their operation. The study does raise important questions about what the appropriate goals of after-school programs should be (e.g., emphasizing academic improvement, individual activity exploration, development of social skills), and how after-school programs can best achieve those goals.

But this study's "null" findings should be interpreted cautiously. The bulk of the research in this asset category shows positive associations between structured, constructive time use and developmental outcomes. For example, even though Moore and Glei (1995) found that participation in school clubs across middle childhood and adolescence did not predict *adolescent* risk behaviors well, youth program activities in adolescence did predict positive outcomes in *young adulthood.* Young people who participated significantly more than their peers in school clubs in childhood and adolescence were especially likely as 18- to 22-year-olds to be involved in community affairs or volunteer work and to report close relationships with their parents. This suggests, at the least, that the effects of after-school programs and other patterns of constructive time use may be most profound over time, as they accumulate, and may not be as notable in a study with a relatively brief time frame. Another example is a recent study of New York City 5th graders who participated in after-school programs for 3 years. In contrast to the Mathematica study, this study found improvements in attendance and math test scores for participants, compared to students not in the after-school program (Jacobson, 2003).

How such constructive activities are evaluated is important, because placing too much emphasis on the achievement of specific outcomes may not always be developmentally appropriate. For example, for many young people, middle childhood may be the last stage of development when they can participate in a variety of creative and athletic pursuits for the sheer joy that such activities offer, with less regard for personal performance and relative ability compared to their peers. In a study of 8- to 12-year-olds learning the martial arts, students in a mastery-oriented program that promoted the intrinsic benefits of skill development reported higher levels of enjoyment and perceived competence and motivation, and actually exhibited better motor skills, than did students in a traditional performance-oriented martial arts program that was aimed primarily at teaching students how to become better than their classmates at a particular set of skills (Theeboom, De Koop, & Weiss, 1995).

Of course, children do have differing levels of need for competition. On average, studies such as Theeboom et al., and a variety of studies on academic performance (see Chapter 5), suggest that a high level of emphasis on competition in middle childhood and early adolescence is not beneficial to children. On the other hand, some children, such as those who are athletically or musically gifted, may thrive and become more sharply focused and motivated by high-level competition.

Regardless of these individual differences, participation in high-quality structured out-of-school programs is favored by most children. Larson and Verma (1999) noted that during participation in structured sports, arts, and activities of volunteer organizations, young people report higher average levels of enjoyment, involvement, and motivation than for any other kind of activity, such as unstructured free time, television viewing, reading, or time at school. These positive experiences are likely to occur in part because the voluntary nature of these activities helps build a young person's sense of agency and efficacy in directing part of her or his life.

In a study of after-school programs attended by African American children in Chicago, Kahne and colleagues (2001) found, among 6th through 10th graders, that even though not all after-school programs provided comparable supports for positive youth development, almost all were considered by young people to be more attractive emotional contexts than those they experienced during the school day. Both genders, but especially males, were more likely to feel that they belonged and that they were respected, safe, comfortable, and trusted in the after-school programs than during the school day in the classroom.

In a study of 1st graders participating in after-school programs, Pierce, Hamm, and Vandell (1999) also found that the emotional climate of after-school programs, reflected in staff warmth and enthusiasm demonstrated with the children, was strongly related to adjustment in the school context, especially for boys. Boys displayed fewer externalizing (e.g., aggression) or internalizing (e.g., depression) problems in school when their after-school program staff were observed to be warm, affectionate, smiling, and reciprocal in their interactions with children. In contrast, boys who experienced negative staff interactions in their after-school programs earned poorer school grades in reading and math. None of these effects was observed for 1st-grade girls.

In addition to being fun and affectively positive, and thereby supporting emotional well-being, the relatively unconstrained exploration that can be experienced in high-quality, structured out-of-school programs may be an important element in a child's construction of a broad sense of competence and the gradual development of a strong, stable, positive identity. As children approach and enter early adolescence, they become increasingly aware of their strengths and weaknesses, in part because they increasingly understand how others see them, and in part because increased competition enters all phases of their lives. These developments can lead many young people to abandon pursuits in which they were otherwise interested, stunting their personal growth and prematurely foreclosing paths of identity development.

Out-of-school programs may also provide additional protective benefits to children who are at greater risk for problem behaviors (e.g., those who live in low-income families, who are academically behind or disinterested in school, or who exhibit behavior problems and difficulty with peers). For example, Morrison, Storino, Robertson, Weissglass, and Dondero (2000) evaluated the effects of one California after-school program, which combined academic enrichment activities, life skills development, and cultural activities, on 175 students in grades 5 and 6 who were judged to be at risk for substance abuse. The study group was compared to a control group of 175 ethnically and economically similar classmates from a largely poor community composed of White and Latino students. The researchers found that after-school program participants either increased or maintained their levels of key resilience factors, such as bonding to their school, whereas the control group reported decreased resilience factors in their lives.

Similarly, Cosden, Morrison, Albanese, and Macias (2001) reported that students who participated in an after-school homework help program had higher achievement test scores in language, reading, and math after 3 years of program participation. The program may have been especially effective for children with limited English proficiency (LEP). Those students, when enrolled in the program over its several-year span, were rated by teachers as exerting more effort and having better study skills, among other outcomes, than either LEP students in the control group or participant students who were fully proficient in English.

This introduction and the remainder of the research we discuss in this chapter clearly suggest the positive impact of constructive time use for children. But some caution is in order as well. As Larson (2001) observed, our knowledge of the relationships between how children spend their time and what they actually experience internally is fairly limited. Even more important, "individual and cultural differences in learning processes and developmental goals" make it inappropriate to prescribe hard-and-fast criteria about desirable levels of participation in one or another kind of activity. In the end, reminds Larson, "overemphasis on time allocation is certain to mislead" (2001, p. 163). Thus, it is important to remember that time use is just one of many variables that can influence development, and there is considerable individual variation in what constitutes "constructive" time use.

Through Search Institute's *Me and My World* survey, we measure several dimensions of constructive use of time: creative activities, sports and nonsports clubs and organizations, and time spent in religious community (see Appendix).

Using earlier and slightly different items than those listed in Table 8, the Appendix shows that the measure of *child programs* had a low alpha internal consistency reliability of .34–.40. But this may not be the most appropriate reliability measure for this construct, since we combine children's time spent in both sports and nonsports activities. Normal differences in children's interests may lead them to pursue one type of activity more than the other, and at a level of participation that satisfies the two or more times per week criterion for experiencing developmentally positive child program activities in general. Children may not have the additional time or interest to pursue much of the other kind of activity in a typical week. Research mentioned earlier in the chapter and studies we discuss later consistently reveal that boys are much more likely to participate in organized sports than are girls. Thus, the apparent low reliability

Table 8. The Constructive-Use-of-Time Assets	
Creative activities	Child participates in music, art, drama, or creative writing two or more times per week.
Child programs	Child participates two or more times per week in cocurricular school activities or structured community programs for children.
Religious community	Child attends religious programs or services one or more times per week.
Time at home	Child spends some time most days both in high-quality interaction with parent(s) and doing things at home other than watching TV or playing video games.

of the child programs measure is of less concern than the figure would normally suggest.

Summary of Research Findings:
The Constructive-Use-of-Time Assets in Middle Childhood

A substantial body of research addresses the importance of adults providing youth with constructive activities during the after-school hours. In a review of 22 studies published between 1980-2000 that examined children's time use, however, Ben-Arieh and Ofir (2002) concluded that children ages 6 to 12 are a group "still overwhelming neglected," and that most of the literature reflects the study of adolescents.

Nevertheless, there are still a reasonable number of studies on the time use of elementary-age children, and the findings about the impact of constructive use of time usually parallel those found with samples of adolescents. Newman, Fox, Flynn, and Christeson (2000) noted that while the period between 3 p.m. and 6 p.m. can be the "prime time" for delinquent and other high-risk behaviors, it can also be a time of positive child and youth enrichment through after-school programs. Numerous national reports and evaluation studies on after-school programs report that structured activities provide children with safe places to develop emotionally, socially, and academically (Fashola, 1998; Newman et al., 2000; U.S. Department of Education and U.S. Department of Justice, 2000).

A large proportion of the studies on after-school programs concern the impact of children's constructive use of time on their subsequent academic achievement and school-related outcomes. Relatively less research attention has been paid to the direct links between children's free-time activities and their socioemotional adjustment (Halpern, 2000; McHale, Crouter, & Tucker, 2001; Posner & Vandell, 1999). For example, Posner and Vandell (1999) found, for African American 5th graders, that participation in nonsports extracurricular activities in the 3rd grade had a significant positive association with teacher-reported emotional adjustment of the same children in the 5th grade. For White children, more time spent in unstructured outdoor activities was related to poorer grades, work habits, and emotional adjustment in grade 5 (as we shall discuss later in this chapter, these children probably were neither supervised nor monitored adequately). Additionally, in both African American and White samples, children's emotional adjustment in 3rd grade significantly predicted the type and extent to which children engaged in different after-school activities. It seems clear that free-time activities and emotional adjustment are linked, but in different ways for different children.

A recent compendium of studies focusing on the arts showed that youth participation in arts-centered activities is related to dozens of positive academic and social outcomes, ranging from higher reading skills and math proficiency to better self-efficacy, empathy, problem-solving strategies, and task persistence (Catterall, 2002b). However, while many studies demonstrate such positive outcomes for youth who participate in drama and music activities, only a handful of studies have been reported showing such effects for dance and the visual arts.

Unfortunately, it is often difficult to determine the effects of different kinds of after-school activities on positive outcomes. Some researchers combine all children's after-school program activities into one category, such as "extra-curricular" or "enrichment" activities. This single category may include activities as diverse as the arts, reading for pleasure, sports, music lessons, and more, thereby failing to make the necessary distinctions between arts activities and active or sport-oriented programs in order to investigate unique associations between different kinds of activities and various child outcomes. Nonetheless, these activities before and after school are threaded together by their structured, out-of-home nature. Similarly, studies have also reported the positive effects of unstructured, quality time at home (e.g., McHale et al., 2001), time in which the child is either engaged in something constructive of her or his own choosing, like reading, or being monitored by parents even if he or she is simply watching television. Children do not need a diet of time use that is wholly structured, but they do need most of it to be supervised or at least monitored by parents and other adults.

Less frequently investigated is the significance of children's involvement in religious community life in middle childhood. Our literature search identified few empirical studies involving samples of children who participated in religious activities in the middle childhood years. Of those studies, 6th graders were the only middle childhood age group represented, and of course, they also are considered a transitional grade that belongs in both the middle childhood and adolescent stages. However, research on adolescence shows that engagement in religious activities plays an influential role in the lives of young people, especially as activities contributing to young people's prosocial, caring attitudes and behaviors, and protecting them from engaging in high-risk behaviors (Donahue & Benson, 1995; Regnerus, 2000; Wright, Frost, & Wisecarver, 1993).

In much of our discussion in this chapter, emphasis is placed on the role of adult presence and supervision as a key element in the positive impact of high-quality child programs and constructive free-time activities at home. But "supervision" should not be construed narrowly to mean merely setting limits on children or keeping them out of harm's way. In much the same way authoritative parents foster positive development by doing more than setting boundaries, the caring adults children experience in high-quality child programs provide a developmentally appropriate mix of warmth, control, and promotion of children's psychological autonomy. Quite apart from how much those adults simply protect and monitor children, the quality of these adult-child relationships in fostering children's sense of support, empowerment, exploration of interests, and development of values and social skills is a critical reason there is a wealth of research showing the positive effects of child programs in particular.

For example, in a review of 48 "soundly evaluated" programs that showed positive outcomes among young people ages 10 to 18, Roth and Brooks-Gunn (2003) concluded that what sets genuine youth *development* programs apart from other youth programs is not so much different opportunities but a different atmosphere. Programs that do a better job of promoting what Lerner, Fisher, and Weinberg (2000) termed the "five C's" (competence, confidence, connections, character, and caring) are distinguished by providing young people with a supportive and empowering environment, "both at and away from the program" (Roth & Brooks-Gunn, 2003, p. 219). These programs try not only to "improve" young people but also more ambitiously to positively affect young people's lives in other contexts—family, school, peer, community—away from the program itself. The quality of the relationships adults foster with children and youth in such programs obviously must include but go far beyond simply keeping young people "occupied."

Creative Activities and Child Programs

Most studies that focus on positive development and youth involvement in structured creative arts activities (e.g., music, arts, drama, and creative writing) have examined children's experiences during the school day. Arts activities, as mentioned earlier, also are a common but undifferentiated part of out-of-school programs. A study of after-school programs in Boston, Chicago, and Seattle (Halpern, 1999) concluded that most "share a common activity structure." The programs mix periods of free time with organized sports, academic enrichment, cultural awareness activities, arts and crafts, board games, and field trips. Well-implemented out-of-school programs focusing on providing a mix of artistic, academic, cultural, and athletic activities for children have been associated, directly or indirectly, with:

Academic Outcomes

- **Reduced risk for school failure** (Cosden et al., 2001 [mediated by availability of homework assistance at home, quality of program, and the nature of the homework assigned]) and **early school dropout** (Mahoney, 2000); **greater academic achievement** (Hofferth &

Sandberg, 2001; Posner & Vandell, 1994 [for third graders]; U.S. Department of Education & U.S. Department of Justice, 2000); **better grades** (Nettles, 1991; U.S. Department of Education & U.S. Department of Justice, 2000); **improved reading ability** (Catterall, 2002a; Nettles, 1991; U.S. Department of Education & U.S. Department of Justice, 2000); **bonding to school** (Morrison et al., 2000; U.S. Department of Education & U.S. Department of Justice, 2000); and **better school attendance** (Nettles, 1991; U.S. Department of Education & U.S. Department of Justice, 2000).

Mental and Behavioral Health Outcomes

- **Fewer teacher-rated problem behaviors** (Hofferth & Sandberg, 2001 [for children who spend time playing sports]; Morrison et al., 2000; U.S. Department of Education & U.S. Department of Justice, 2000); **reduction in crime and risky behaviors** (Mahoney, 2000; Nettles, 1991 [if peers in children's social network also participated in extracurricular activities]; Newman et al., 2000; U.S. Department of Education & U.S. Department of Justice, 2000) and **increased sense of safety in children** (Halpern, 1992; Newman et al., 2000); **better socioemotional adjustment** (McHale et al., 2001; Posner & Vandell, 1999 [for African American children involved in nonsports extracurricular activities]; Scripp, 2002); and **increased self-esteem** (Reynolds, 1995 [for children participating in music education]).

Social Outcomes

- **Increased social skillfulness with peers** (Catterall, 2002a [for children participating in drama and theater programs]; Sandstrom & Coie, 1999 [for initially rejected children participating in extracurricular activities]; U.S. Department of Education & U.S. Department of Justice, 2000).

Factors influencing participation in creative activities and child programs
The way children spend their out-of-school time is affected by a variety of factors, such as age, gender, mother's employment status, educational background of parents, family income, parents' marital status, and cultural background. In a study of more than 2,000 children age 12 and under in the United States, Hofferth and Sandberg (2001) used diaries that children kept of their daily activities for an entire week to conclude that only 30% of the time in a child's week is truly discretionary (the remainder of the time is occupied with sleeping, eating,

personal care, school, and day care). Of the discretionary 51 hours per week, free play time accounts for 15 hours (29%), TV viewing takes 12 hours (24%), and structured activities such as sports, visiting others, and going to church occupy 9 hours (18%). Reading for pleasure and arts activities each are given an average of about 1 hour per week. The remaining time is occupied by activities such as out-of-school learning time, family time, movies, and sports viewing.

Compared to younger children in the study, children ages 9 to 12 devoted an increased amount of time to playing sports, studying, and watching television, while decreasing time was spent in other free play. As girls grow older, time spent reading and visiting others increased faster than it did for boys, and boys' involvement in sports increased faster than did girls' involvement. A U.S. Census Bureau study also reported that girls ages 6 to 11 were more likely to take lessons of various kinds than were boys, whereas boys ages 6 to 11 were more likely to participate in sports. Rates of participation in clubs were similar for both boys and girls (Fields, Smith, Bass, & Lugaila, 2001).

Hofferth and Sandberg (2001) reported that children from African American families spent greater amounts of time in church activities than White children. In contrast, White children and children from families with nonworking female heads of household spent more time in sports activities. Children from families with more highly educated family heads of household spent more time reading and studying, regardless of their racial/ethnic background. Spending more time reading for pleasure was strongly associated with better achievement test performance, and playing sports was associated with fewer behavior problems and greater problem-solving skills. Fields et al. (2001) also reported that children who participated in extracurricular sports, clubs, or after-school lessons were more likely to be educationally "on track"—in the modal grade for their age rather than being "held back"—than children who did not participate.

Evidence shows that both the kinds of activities children engage in, as well as the social context in which they occur, are associated with various developmental outcomes. In addition, children's levels of socioemotional, behavioral, and academic adjustment also seem to predict their subsequent patterns of free-time activity. For example, McHale and colleagues (2001) followed a U.S. sample population of 200 White 4th and 5th graders from rural and small towns in a northeastern state for 2 years. They reported that school grades, incidence of depression, and behavioral conduct at age 12 were all predicted by the way children spent their free time at age 10. Children who spent more time in the pursuit of hobbies and sports involvement at age 10 enjoyed better mental health and school adjustment at age 12, whereas those who spent more time playing outdoors and "hanging out" with no particular agenda had lower grades, more behavior problems, and less emotional adjustment. Time spent reading at age 10 was associated with both better grades *and* a higher incidence of depression at age 12. Of course, reading does not cause depression. However, it may be that the children who spend above-average amounts of time reading at age 10 have less well developed social skills than their peers who spend comparatively more time playing with age-peers. Regardless of the mechanism, this study's results are a reminder that fundamentally positive activities do not always contribute to positive outcomes.

McHale et al. also found gender differences in psychosocial adjustment, with girls' adjustment linked more to the social context in which their activities occurred, while boys' adjustment was related more strongly to the activities themselves. For example, by itself, outdoor play was not associated with subsequently poorer grades for girls. However, when time spent with mothers and time spent with peers in *unsupervised* settings were added to the prediction, the relationship between outdoor play and grades was mediated. Among girls who spent more time with their mothers, outdoor play did not negatively influence later grades, but for girls who spent more unsupervised time with peers, time spent in outdoor play did predict later poorer grades. These social contextual effects were not observed for boys.

Differential access to after-school programs   Not surprisingly, Halpern (1999) found that after-school programs for low-income children tend to have less adequate facilities, less well trained staff, and more limited financing than after-school programs for middle- and upper-income children. Low-income children also participate to a significantly lesser degree in structured after-school programs than more affluent children. For example, a U.S. Census Bureau report noted that 50% of children 6–17 years old participated in at least one extracurricular activity in 1994 (sports, clubs, and after-school or weekend lessons). However, the participation differences by monthly family income were startling. Only 12% of children ages 6 to 11 with family incomes of less than $1,500 per month participated in after-school lessons, while only 16% participated in sports and only 25% engaged in club activities. In contrast, twice as many children with family incomes of $4,500 or more per month participated in similar activities (28% in lessons, 51% in sports, and 51% in clubs; Fields et al., 2001). Halpern (2000) also reported that only 20%–30% of low-income children in Boston, Chicago, and Seattle participated even as much as twice per week in such programs.

Schools play an important role in providing children with access to structured activities. Several different program models are common across the United States, each with a somewhat different emphasis. For example, traditional extra- or cocurricular activities are primarily designed as enrichment programs, whereas extended-day programs (both before and after school and most common at the elementary school level) address families' needs for child care and safe sanctuaries for children. Community or full-service schools offer a broader array of services and activities, and are open and used both during and outside traditional school hours. They integrate a broad variety of educational, health, social, cultural, and recreational components that often blur traditional lines between school and community, and between time spent inside and outside school (Dryfoos, 1999). However, there is some evidence (Halpern, 1999; Kahne et al., 2001) that after-school programs sponsored by community organizations may attract young people who are less connected to school. Thus, despite the school's special capacity to provide youth with a variety of opportunities for constructive use of time during the nonschool hours, communities are advised to maintain programs provided by a range of alternative sponsors in order to meet the needs of the broadest possible cross section of young people.

Religious Community

The effect of young people's involvement in and commitment to religious activities has been examined almost entirely at the middle and high school levels. Few studies are available that examine the developmental benefits of a religious life for children (Benson, Masters, & Larson, 1997), and studies overwhelmingly concern Christian children, with little empirical research available on how other faith traditions may affect development in middle childhood (Bridges & Moore, 2002). Also more common is the line of research that examines direct and indirect associations between parents' religiosity or spirituality and children's well-being. The available research does suggest that children's participation in religious programs and services is associated, directly or indirectly, with:

Mental and Behavioral Health Outcomes

- **Reduced prevalence of alcohol dependence** in adolescents who attended church regularly while growing up (Clapper, Buka, Goldfield, Lipsitt, & Tsuang, 1995); **decreased risk-taking behaviors and attitudes** (Sutherland, Hale, Harris, Stalls, & Foulk, 1997); **increased self-esteem** (Thomas & Carver, 1990); **increased sense of well-being** (Moore & Glei, 1995); **fewer reported acts of delinquency** (Jagers & Mock, 1993; Thomas & Carver, 1990); **fewer externalizing behavior problems** if child's parents felt religion was important and frequently attended church (Brody, Stoneman, & Flor, 1996); and **reduced effects of neighborhood disorder on**

crime among African American youth (Johnson, Jang, De Li, & Larson, 2000).

Social Outcomes

- **Greater sense of connectedness to community** for African American children (Jagers, Smith, Mock, & Dill, 1997); **greater social responsibility** if parents' religious beliefs or attendance frequently affected their daily lives (Gunnoe, Hetherington, & Reiss, 1999); and **higher quality parent-child relationships** if mothers regarded religion with high importance (Pearce & Axinn, 1998).

Links between religiosity and well-being in childhood and adolescence

Measuring time spent in religious community captures only one dimension of a child's exposure to religious life inside and outside the family, and is perhaps not even the most important aspect of the religious experience. For example, through a unique interviewing and case study approach used with children involved in various Christian, Islamic, and Jewish faith traditions, Coles (1990) provides an illustrative examination of children's development, attitudes, and views concerning spiritual life. Going beyond reports of whether children attend their respective churches, mosques, or temples, Coles demonstrated children's interest and ability to grapple with fascinating questions such as: What does God look like? Who do you talk to when you pray and how do they respond? How does spirituality play out in everyday life? And, where and when do people call on spirituality?

Unfortunately, we could identify only a few empirical studies that examined the impact of religious life in middle childhood; most research on the effects of religiosity on young people is conducted with adolescents. That body of research generally finds that greater youth involvement with religion produces a variety of positive associations, such as better academic performance, lessened substance use, and more prosocial attitudes and behavior (see review in Scales & Leffert, 1999).

For example, Jeynes (1999) used the National Education Longitudinal Study to research how religious commitment might affect academic achievement among African American and Hispanic students. He found that students in grade 8 who described themselves as very religious, actively involved in a religious youth group, and attending church three or four times a month, consistently outperformed their less religiously committed peers by grade 12 on standardized achievement tests. They also were more likely to have taken a recommended basic core of courses and were less likely to have been "left back" a grade. Almost all these effects remained, when socioeconomic status and type of school the child attended (public, private, or religious) were controlled. Moore and Glei (1995) examined data from the National Study of Children, first undertaken in 1976 when the children were 7 to 11 years old, with follow-ups at adolescence and again at ages 18 to 22. The researchers reported that children who initially had low scores on the Peabody Picture Vocabulary Test, an indication of academic risk, had higher positive well-being scores as young adults, in comparison to other children, due to greater religiosity.

Benson, Scales, Sesma, and Roehlkepartain (2003) also reported that 6th–12th graders for whom religion or spirituality is important, and/or who participate often in religious activities, showed fewer risk-behavior patterns and more thriving than less religious or spiritual youth. They also reported that the importance of religion or spirituality is quite stable across grades 6–12, with 55% of students saying it is very important, even though young people's participation in religious activities drops over those years. We might hypothesize that participation in middle childhood would be even higher, since it is more likely to be dictated by parents, and that children's ascribed importance of being religious or spiritual would be at least as high as among adolescents, for whom importance is fairly stable. Benson and colleagues also pointed out, however, that reports of importance or attendance per se may be less significant an influence on risk and thriving than whether a young person's religiosity or spirituality promotes individualism or community. Those hypotheses need to be explored with adolescents as well as with those in middle childhood.

These examples demonstrate that children's time spent connected to religious institutions can provide direct, positive benefits; however, children may also enjoy indirect, positive benefits from their *parents'* religiosity. An interesting study reported by Pearce and Axinn (1998) helps tease out some of the mechanisms through which the positive effects of religious involvement may occur. They studied a sample of 867 White families, largely of Christian faiths, in the Detroit metropolitan area, following children involved in the study from infancy in 1961 through young adulthood to approximately 23 years old in 1985. Pearce and Axinn found that the more frequently the mothers attended religious services while their children were growing up, the more positively mothers described the parent-child relationships when their children were 23 years old. However, mothers' religious service attendance had no such effect on their 23-year-old adult children's descriptions of the parent-child relationship.

In contrast, the importance of religion to mothers while their children were growing up made a significant difference in how positively *both* mothers and adult children saw their relationship. The same patterns were seen when mothers and their 18-year-old children reported similarities in patterns of religious service attendance and degree of importance of religion. When mothers and children agreed on how often they attended services when the children were 18, and agreed on the importance of religion in their lives, the more frequently they described the parent-child relationship 5 years later as high in quality.

The Pearce and Axinn study does suggest that the importance attached to religion by both adults and children may be more critical to positive outcomes than attendance at religious services per se, a result also found in studies with adolescents (reviewed in Scales & Leffert, 1999). In fact, much of the strength of the effects associated with church attendance diminished when "importance of religion" was added to the prediction. This suggests that frequent parental attendance at religious services may reflect a high degree of importance that parents give to religious involvement. In middle childhood, parental attendance is likely to predict children's attendance, since few children of this age make independent decisions about participation in religious organizations.

Apart from the public evidence of commitment that religious service attendance represents and whether parents require their children's attendance, parents' level of internal commitment to the practice of religion may have important indirect effects on children's outcomes. Such religious commitment might also reflect and positively support parental values, such as tolerance, patience, forgiveness, and unconditional love, which are conducive to effective parenting practices and high-quality parent-child relationships. As noted in Chapter 1, those elements of child rearing are associated with a wide variety of positive developmental outcomes for children in the middle childhood years.

Time at Home

Children of all ages and in all stages of development need to use their leisure time well; we call this constructive use of time. Of course, aspects of constructive use of time that are relevant to one stage of development may not apply to another stage of development. Preschool children need a variety of stimulating objects to hold, look at, shake, and otherwise manipulate. School-age children need to spend solid chunks of their out-of-school time reading, singing, or playing musical instruments, being physically active, building, and discovering their talents and interests. The basic notion of the value of constructive use of time reflects a continuous developmental need of the growing child.

For instance, we name *time at home* as an adolescent developmental asset in the constructive-use-of-time category. Defined as spending no more than two nights a week out with friends with nothing special to do, the time-at-home asset suggests that adolescents who spend substantial amounts of time at home are more likely to be influenced by parents and peers with similar time use profiles than are adolescents who have a great deal of "free" time. For adolescents, who have considerably more decision-making power and influence over how they spend their free time in comparison to elementary-age children, the time-at-home asset is an appropriate measure that hints at adolescents' potential exposure to risky situations, their decision-making capabilities, and their values. Thus, asking about time spent at home in the evenings is a valid way to help assess how adolescents balance their growing independence with their continuing need to be occupied in what Clark calls "high-yield" leisure activities that protect them from risk and enhance their positive capacities (Clark, 1988).

Elementary-age children are increasingly decisive in how they spend after-school time. But typically, relative to adolescents, they have little freedom to decide whether to spend their time out of the home in the evening, and even fewer means to do so (e.g., being able to drive and having adequate amounts of their own money for entertainment). Thus, we suggest a more developmentally meaningful expression of this asset for preadolescents: What do they do during their at-home time? Do they spend time almost every day reading with parents, playing games with them, or working on a project together? In a study of 811 Caucasian families with children age 11 in the United States, drawn from the National Survey of Families and Households, Zick, Bryant, and Österbacka (2001) reported that this kind of high-quality time yielded important "human capital enrichment" for the children, as reflected in fewer behavioral problems and better school grades.

Time at home also includes "free" time, albeit with parents around monitoring children's whereabouts. Larson (2001) concluded that, although there is little evidence children are in danger of being "overprogrammed" (despite some popular press accounts to the contrary), it is also undoubtedly true that some level of unstructured free time can contribute to children's well-being. Thus, it is important to know whether children have some time almost every day also to do things they want to, such as just read for fun, listen to music, work on a hobby, or reflect on the events of their day. Time at home thus includes both a dimension of parents interacting with the child in developmentally stimulating ways and a dimension of the child having some amount of unstructured time that provides a developmental balance to the time they spend in structured programs and activities. Time spent at home is associated, directly or indirectly, with:

Academic Outcomes

- **Greater academic achievement** (Hofferth & Sandberg, 2001 [for children who spend time reading for pleasure]); **better grades** (McHale et al., 2001 [for children who spend time reading for pleasure and for children who spend time in activities with their father]; Zick et al., 2001); and **increased overall cognitive and**

linguistic development (Fisher, 1992 [for children who frequently participate in imaginary play]).

Mental and Behavioral Health Outcomes

- **Better socioemotional adjustment** (Fisher, 1992 [for children who frequently participate in imaginary play]; McHale et al., 2001 [for children who spend time participating in hobbies]; **fewer externalizing behaviors** (Pettit, Laird, Bates, & Dodge, 1997); **fewer behavior problems at home** (Zick et al., 2001); and **less depression** (McHale et al., 2001 [for children who spend time in activities with parents].

Social Outcomes

- **Increased social skillfulness with peers** (Pettit et al., 1997).

Contextual impact on children's constructive use of time at home McHale and colleagues (2001) reported a reciprocal dynamic at work between play and adjustment. Children's activities at age 10 did predict adjustment at age 12, but somewhat more evidence showed that adjustment at age 10 also predicted activity trends at age 12. For example, children with better grades at age 10 spent less time hanging out and in unsupervised peer settings at age 12, and spent more time with unrelated adults. Similarly, children who were depressed at age 10 spent less time in sports activities and with unrelated adults at age 12, and more time hanging out. These findings do not suggest that all "hanging out" with nothing special to do is negative for children. But they do suggest that the more children spend "free" time in such unstructured settings, relatively unmonitored by adults, the more likely they are to be affected negatively.

Although time spent alone was associated with later negative outcomes in the McHale et al. study, alone time is not invariably a negative developmental experience, just as McHale and colleagues reported that time spent reading was not always a positive experience. Among young adolescents, for example, Larson (1997) reported that a moderate amount of time alone, up to 25 % of discretionary time for some children, was associated with better emotional well-being. He also reported that younger children in middle childhood did not seem to benefit from such levels of time alone.

However, a *small* amount of time spent alone (perhaps 10% of discretionary time) may not be harmful to younger children, and may even have a net positive impact in terms of increasing feelings of competence and contributing to identity development. For children in middle childhood, the ability to successfully spend some time alone may be an important developmental task that contributes to a growing ability to coregulate and eventually self-regulate behavior. And it may be a normal part of development that this alone time increases in the upper elementary years. In a sample of nearly 500 students in grades 5 through 9, for example, Larson and Richards (1991) found that nearly half of 5th graders' discretionary time was spent with family, a proportion that dropped to only about 25% by grade 9. Between 5th and 7th grades especially, both boys and girls increased the proportion of their time spent alone (and girls the proportion of time with friends). Larson and Richards suggested that children may increasingly be able to use alone time in a developmentally advantageous way for relaxation, self-renewal, and self-discovery.

Consider the issue of child "self-care," in which children may spend an extended period without adult supervision. A significant number of early elementary-grade children spend *some* time in self-care. A report from the National Center for Education Statistics (1999) indicates that about 39%, or 6.1 million, of 1st through 3rd graders receive some kind of nonparental care before or after school. Not all of this nonparental care is self-care, of course. But some portion of "self-care" involves managing physical needs, such as making snacks or going to the bathroom. And an important part of self-care is children's decision making and time management in ways that both keep them out of trouble and build developmental strengths.

Distinctions can be made within the broader category of self-care: Vandell, Posner, Shumow, and Kang (1995) distinguished self-care types whereby children are alone, with a sibling, with peers, or with older adolescents who serve as providers. They found that time alone predicted later behavior problems for 3rd graders (but not for 5th graders), and time alone with peers predicted later behavior problems for both 3rd and 5th grade children. McHale and colleagues (2001) reported that the time children spent in activities with parents and unrelated adults also was related to positive adjustment, but that the more time they spent alone, the poorer their emotional adjustment. Similarly, Larson (1997) reported that solitude was not nearly as positive an experience during middle childhood as it could be, in moderation, for young adolescents. This may be because being alone in middle childhood may signify children's lack of social competencies more than it reflects a choice.

Not all studies report those negative effects. For example, in a study of 166 White, rural and suburban 4th through 6th graders from middle-class families in Colorado, Pettine and Rosen (1998) reported that spending even several hours a day alone in self-care was not necessarily associated with deviant behaviors or tolerance for deviance. In that study, nearly 25% of 4th and 5th graders and 40% of 6th graders reported three or more hours of self-care on most days, but 90% reported no deviant behavior or tolerance for deviance. The researchers concluded that self-care can reasonably be considered a "normal developmental process" (p. 641).

However, depending on children's environmental contexts, the developmental value that some self-care might have is largely outweighed by its association with more negative outcomes. For example, Posner and Vandell (1994) studied a sample of more than 200 children in grade 3 from Milwaukee, half African American and half White, with about half of each racial/ethnic group also considered poor on the basis of family income. Among the low-income urban children, regardless of race/ethnicity, those who spent more time in self-care spent less time under adult supervision, a finding that was correlated with more antisocial behaviors. In contrast, children who spent more time in formal after-school programs had better grades, school conduct, peer relations, and emotional adjustment. Children in the formal after-school programs were involved in more academic and enrichment activities, such as music and dance, than children in other types of care, and spent less time watching television and engaging in unsupervised activities in their neighborhoods than did children in self-care.

Similarly, in a study of an urban sample of 1st through 4th graders, diverse in race/ethnicity and family income, Marshall and colleagues (1997) also reported that time spent unsupervised after school was associated with more behavior problems. In contrast, formal after-school program participation was associated with fewer internalizing problems (e.g., depression, low self-esteem) among low-income children. No such effects were observed among middle-income children.

The Constructive-Use-of-Time Assets across the Early Childhood-Adolescence Life Span

As is often the case for older youth, the out-of-school hours have the potential to be either beneficial or detrimental to younger children's growth. As a result of demographic and secular changes in American society, including more single parents and greater numbers of working mothers, young children face more free, unstructured time than in years past (National Center for Education Statistics, 1999).

Creative Activities and Child Programs

A tremendous opportunity exists for adults to maximize children's before- and after-school time by engaging them in meaningful, constructive activities. A review of the literature on what happens to children during the after-school hours suggests three conclusions. First, self-care (e.g., time spent alone without supervision) emerges as a consistent predictor of problem behaviors, both concurrently and longitudinally; this effect appears to be stronger for younger children than older children. As mentioned earlier in this chapter, Vandell and colleagues (1995; cited in Vandell & Posner, 1999) reported that for 3rd graders, unsupervised time during the after-school hours predicted behavior problems 2 years later; however, this relation was not found for 5th graders. Likewise, Pettit and colleagues (1997) found that self-care among 1st graders predicted negative results for social competence and achievement test scores in grade 6. There also seemed to be an amplification process whereby children who exhibited external-izing behaviors in 1st grade *and* participated in self-care subsequently showed significant increases in behavior problems in grade 6 (Pettit et al., 1997).

Second, when children are involved in some sort of structured, adult-supervised activity outside school hours, there seems to be a relationship be-tween the activity and positive developmental outcomes, both concurrently and longitudinally, for children in the kindergarten through grade 3 years, similar to positive outcomes for those in middle childhood and adolescence. Posner and Vandell (1994) examined a sample of grade 3 children from low-income set-tings and found that children who participated in formal after-school programs had better academic achievement and social adjustment than nonparticipants. Formal programs included a variety of types, such as programs with academic, recreational (sports, games, dance, crafts), and remedial orientations (reading and math).

Similarly, Pettit and colleagues (1997) reported that children who attended adult-supervised activity-oriented programs in grade 1 were rated by teachers as more socially competent in grade 6 than children who engaged in other kinds of after-school arrangements. However, they also reported a curvilinear relation between children's time spent in adult-supervised, activity-oriented programs and their later externalizing problems. Children who spent either no time or in excess of 4 hours per day in these types of programs evinced greater levels of externalizing problems than did grade 1 children who spent only 1 to 3 hours a day in programs. (Similar findings have been reported with adolescents and paid work: some may be beneficial, but too much can be a negative influence; see Mortimer & Finch, 1996.) While such a curvilinear pattern should be replicated before this finding is accepted, it does serve as a reminder that overtaxing young children can be as problematic as not giving them enough to do.

Finally, the relative benefits of one kind of activity vis-à-vis others—sports, dance, music, academic programs—may not be as salient for young children as they seem to be for older youth (Vandell & Posner, 1999). For younger chil-dren, especially for those in kindergarten or 1st grade, having adult supervision and opportunities to interact safely and constructively with adults and peers is probably more important than the type of activities per se. For our purposes, ensuring that children are supervised by adults in meaningful activities during out-of-school hours suffices as a putative asset.

Religious Community

As previously noted, a paucity of data exists regarding the developmental importance of religious involvement for younger children. There is more information regarding the links between religious involvement and subsequent outcomes in adolescence, but few studies address the potential developmental significance of this relationship in middle childhood, or among even younger children. It is likely that religious institutions play an important role in the moral education of children (Becker & Hofmeister, 2001), but systematic research in this area has not yet been conducted.

Of course, religious involvement may affect development via indirect pathways. Pearce and Axinn (1998) delineate three such possibilities, all describing how religious institutions can set in motion mechanisms that strengthen family relationships and promote positive child development. First, a common theme among Judeo-Christian religions is the idea that positive family relationships are important and should be achieved. By promulgating norms such as love among family members, respect for parents and elders, and strong marital bonds, religious institutions may help shape or reinforce parents' attitudes regarding healthy families and the steps toward strengthening family ties.

The second mechanism Pearce and Axinn (1998) discuss is that religious institutions often have formal support groups and/or programs for families, including picnics, volunteer opportunities, and religious counseling services, all of which provide occasions for families to spend "quality time" together. Finally, attending religious functions and services puts families into physical contact with others who may share similar values regarding families and parenting, and who are also ostensibly similarly influenced by the first two mechanisms described above. By enlarging the social network of parents with other families who also putatively want to have strong families, religious institutions facilitate social bonds that can promote healthy parent-child relationships. However, mechanisms such as these, as well as the claim that religious involvement plays a direct role in the moral education of children, need to be addressed more often in research in order to better understand the role of religious involvement in child development.

Time at Home

What is the nature of young children's unstructured free time at home, and are there qualities to this time that are known to promote positive development? As discussed above, time at home can include positive parent-child and sibling interactions as well as engagement in positive solitary activities. Relevant to this discussion is the dimensional approach described in the Introduction. This approach posits that adult-child relationships that are characterized by (1) warmth and affection, (2) boundaries and limit setting, and (3) activities of discovery, exploration, or learning are most likely to facilitate positive development. Although much of the research in this area looks at factors that increase or decrease the *amount* of time parents spend with children (e.g., maternal employment), recent research underscores the significance of the *quality* of parent-child activities and developmental outcomes (Zick et al., 2001).

For example, in a sample of preschool children and their mothers, Wood (2002) reported that children whose mothers frequently engaged in a number of developmentally rich activities with them (e.g., singing, reading, playing games) had higher reading level scores one year later than did children who did not have these experiences. Notably, these activities were based on descriptions of what parents and children normally do, and were thus construed to be relatively common activities between parents and their children. Zick et al. (2001) found that the frequency of parents' positive interactional activities (e.g., playing, reading, helping) with children had a positive effect on both grades and behavior problems.

Much has been written about the significance of literacy and other cognitively stimulating activities (see Chapter 5), but the significance of play in fostering development deserves special mention. Play constitutes a special interactional context in which children learn and elaborate new skills, as well as being an arena for emotional expression and regulation (Dehart, Sroufe, & Cooper, 2000; Fisher, 1992). Russ (1998) argues that play—and in particular, pretend play—is integrally linked to both creativity and everyday coping and adjustment via cognitive and affective mechanisms; that is, play positively affects children's intellectual and emotional development. For example, a longitudinal study by Russ (cited in Russ, 1998) found predictive relations between play in early childhood and self-reports of coping 4 years later.

Measuring the Constructive-Use-of-Time Assets in Middle Childhood

About 50%–70% of 4th–6th graders in our three field tests of the *Me and My World* survey in Nevada, California, and New York (and in our two earlier pilot tests in Oklahoma) report experiencing three of the constructive-use-of-time assets (items to measure the time-at-home asset were added after the field tests). There were meaningful variations across samples in all three of the assets measured (see Table 9). Regarding religious community, two explanations may be at work. The California sample included a higher proportion of students of color. Adults and adolescents of color, especially African Americans, generally have been found to report that religion is more important to them and that they are more active in religious activities than White adults or adolescents (Moore & Glei, 1995; Taylor, 1988). Because of this greater involvement in religious activities by the adolescents and the adults who surround them, preadolescent African American and Hispanic children may be exposed to greater immersion in religious community as an outgrowth of their cultural backgrounds. Both the California and New York samples also included significantly higher proportions of 4th graders than the Nevada sample, and parents would be expected to have greater influence on those younger children's exposure to religious community.

The difference in reported child program experience and time in creative activities, with the California children reporting less than children in both the New York and the Nevada communities, is a little less clearly explained. On the one hand, children from more affluent, suburban samples typically report more involvement in structured child and youth programs (Carnegie Council on Adolescent Development, 1992; Damore, 2002). The California sample reported lower parental education levels, our proxy for socioeconomic status, so this result may reflect differences across the field test samples in parents being able to afford such programs for their children. On the other hand, the Nevada site, although including suburban children, also was the most rural of our three field test sites, and thus the large proportion of students in child programs was somewhat surprising. The experience of this state over the past 2 years in an intentional asset-building initiative, Raising Nevada, may have positively influenced young people's access to structured programs.

Table 9. Proportion of Field Test 4th–6th Graders Who Report Experiencing the Constructive-Use-of-Time Assets

Asset	% Who Report Experiencing Asset		
	Nevada	California	New York
Creative activities	64	58	69
Child programs	62	47	64
Time at home[a]	--	--	--
Religious community	53	61	65

From field tests in 2003; N = 1,294. Items to measure the time-at-home asset were added after the field tests, so no percentages for that asset are included.
[a] *No data available; added after field tests.*

Although the majority of children participating in both our two pilot studies in Oklahoma and these three field tests said they experienced the constructive-use-of-time assets, it is clear that about 30%–50% do not. To the extent that other samples of children report similar patterns, there is much room for improvement in how well children in the middle childhood years use their time and in how well adults in their lives supervise them to those ends.

References

Becker, P. E., & Hofmeister, H. (2001). Work, family, and religious involvement for men and women. *Journal for the Scientific Study of Religion, 40, 707–722.*

Ben-Arieh, A., & Ofir, A. (2002). Time for (more) time-use studies: Studying the daily activities of children. *Children: A Global Journal of Child Research, 9,* 225–248.

Benson, P. L., Masters, K. S., & Larson, D. B. (1997). Religious influence on child and adolescent development. In J. D. Noshpitz & N. E. Alessi (Eds.), *Handbook of child and adolescent psychiatry: Vol. 4. Varieties of development* (pp. 206–219). New York: John Wiley & Sons.

Benson, P. L., Scales, P. C., Sesma, A., & Roehlkepartain, E. C. (2003, March). *Indicators of positive development: Adolescent spirituality.* Paper presented at the Indicators of Positive Youth Development Conference, convened by Child Trends, Washington, DC.

Bridges, L. J., & Moore, K. A. (2002). *Religion and spirituality in childhood and adolescence.* Washington, DC: Child Trends.

Brody, G. H., Stoneman, Z., & Flor, D. (1996). Parental religiosity, family processes, and youth competence in rural, two-parent, African American families. *Developmental Psychology, 32,* 696–706.

Carnegie Council on Adolescent Development. (1992). *A matter of time: Risk and opportunity in the non-school hours.* Washington, DC: Author.

Catterall, J. S. (2002a). Research on drama and theater in education. In R. J. Deasy (Ed.), *Critical links: Learning in the arts and student academic and social development* (pp. 58–62). Washington, DC: Arts Education Partnership.

Catterall, J. S. (2002b). The arts and transfer of learning. In R. J. Deasy (Ed.), *Critical links: Learning in the arts and student academic and social development* (pp. 151–157). Washington, DC: Arts Education Partnership.

Clapper, R. L, Buka, S. L., Goldfield, E. C., Lipsitt, L. P., & Tsuang, M. T. (1995). Adolescent problem behavior as predictors of adult alcohol diagnoses. *International Journal of the Addictions, 30,* 507–523.

Clark, R. M. (1988). *Critical factors in why disadvantaged children succeed or fail in school.* New York: Academy for Educational Development.

Coles, R. (1990). *The spiritual life of children.* Boston: Houghton Mifflin.

Cosden, M., Morrison, G., Albanese, A. L., & Macias, S. (2001). When homework is not home work: After-school programs for homework assistance. *Educational Psychologist, 36,* 211–221.

Damore, D. T. (2002). Preschool and school age activities: Comparison of urban and suburban populations. *Journal of Community Health, 27,* 203–211.

Dehart, G. B., Sroufe, L. A., & Cooper, R. G. (2000). *Child development: Its nature and course* (4th ed.). Boston: McGraw-Hill.

Dryfoos, J. G. (1999). The role of the school in children's out-of-school time. *The Future of Children: When School Is Out, 9,* 117–133.

Donahue, M. J., & Benson, P. L. (1995). Religion and the well-being of adolescents. *Journal of Social Issues, 51,* 145–160.

Eccles, J. S. (1999). The development of children ages 6 to 14. *The Future of Children: When School Is Out, 9,* 30–44.

Erikson, E. (1959). *Childhood and society.* New York: Norton.

Fashola, O. S. (1998). *Review of extended-day and after-school programs and their effectiveness* (Report No. 24). Baltimore, MD: Center for Research on the Education of Students Placed at Risk, Johns Hopkins University.

Fields, J. M., Smith, K., Bass, L. E., & Lugaila, T. (2001). *A child's day: Home, school, and play (selected indicators of child well-being)* (Current Population reports, P70-68). Washington, DC: U.S. Census Bureau.

Fisher, E. P. (1992). The impact of play on development: A meta-analysis. *Play and Culture, 5,* 159–181.

Gunnoe, M. L., Hetherington, E. M., & Reiss, D. (1999). Parental religiosity, parenting style, and adolescent social responsibility. *Journal of Early Adolescence, 19,* 199–225.

Halpern, R. (1992). The role of after-school programs in the lives of inner-city children: A study of the "urban youth network." *Child Welfare, 21,* 215–230.

Halpern, R. (1999). After-school programs for low-income children: Promises and challenges. *The Future of Children: When School Is Out, 9,* 81–95.

Halpern, R. (2000). The promise of after-school programs for low-income children. *Early Childhood Research Quarterly, 15,* 185–214.

Hofferth, S. L., & Sandberg, J. F. (2001). How American children spend their time. *Journal of Marriage and the Family, 63,* 295–308.

Jacobson, L. (2003, February 12). Study critiques federal after-school program. *Education Week, 22,* 10.

Jagers, R. J., & Mock, L. O. (1993). Culture and social outcomes among inner-city African American children: An Afrographic exploration. *Journal of Black Psychology, 19,* 391–405.

Jagers, R. J., Smith, P., Mock, L. O., & Dill, E. (1997). An Afrocultural social ethos: Component orientations and some social implications. *Journal of Black Psychology, 23,* 328–343.

Jeynes, W. H. (1999). The effects of religious commitment on the academic achievement of Black and Hispanic children. *Urban Education, 34,* 458–479.

Johnson, B. R., Jang, S. J., De Li, S., & Larson, D. (2000). The "invisible institution" and black youth crime: The church as an agency of local social control. *Journal of Youth and Adolescence, 29,* 479–498.

Kahne, J., Nagaoka, J., Brown, A., O'Brien, J., Quinn, T., & Thiede, K. (2001). Assessing after-school programs as contexts for youth development. *Youth and Society, 32,* 421–446.

Larson, R. W. (1997). The emergence of solitude as a constructive domain of experience in early adolescence. *Child Development, 68,* 80–93.

Larson, R. W. (2001). How U.S. children and adolescents spend time: What it does (and doesn't) tell us about their development. *Current Directions in Psychological Science, 10,* 160–165.

Larson, R., & Richards, M. H. (1991). Daily companionship in late childhood and early adolescence: Changing developmental contexts. *Child Development, 62,* 284–300.

Larson, R. W., & Verma, S. (1999). How children and adolescents spend time across the world: work, play, and developmental opportunities. *Psychological Bulletin, 125,* 701–736.

Lerner, R. M., Fisher, C. B., & Weinberg, R. A. (2000). Toward a science for and of the people: Promoting the civil society through the application of developmental science. *Child Development, 71,* 11–20.

Mahoney, J. L. (2000). School extracurricular activity participation as a moderator in the development of antisocial patterns. *Child Development, 71,* 502–516.

Marshall, N. L., Coll, C. G., Marx, F., McCartney, K., Keefe, N., & Ruh, J. (1997). After-school time and children's behavioral adjustment. *Merrill-Palmer Quarterly, 43,* 497–514.

McHale, S. M., Crouter, A. C., & Tucker, C. J. (2001). Free-time activities in middle childhood: Links with adjustment in early adolescence. *Child Development, 72,* 1764–1778.

Moore, K. A., & Glei, D. (1995). Taking the plunge: An examination of positive youth development. *Journal of Adolescent Research, 10,* 15–40.

Morrison, G. M., Storino, M. H., Robertson, L. M., Weissglass, T., & Dondero, A. (2000). The protective function of after-school programming and parent education and support for students at risk for substance abuse. *Evaluation and Program Planning, 23,* 365–371.

Mortimer, J. T., & Finch, M. D. (1996). Work, family, and adolescent development. In J. T. Mortimer & M. D. Finch (Eds.), *Adolescents, work, and family* (pp. 1–125). Thousand Oaks, CA: Sage.

National Center for Education Statistics. (1999). *Participation of kindergartners through third graders in before- and after-school care.* Washington, DC: U.S. Department of Education, Office of Educational Research and Improvement. (NCES 1999:013).

Nettles, S. (1991). Community involvement and disadvantaged students: A review. *Review of Educational Research, 61,* 379–406.

Newman, S. A., Fox, J. A., Flynn, E. A., & Christeson, W. (2000). America's after-school choice: The prime time for juvenile crime, or youth enrichment and achievement. In *Fight crime: Invest in kids* [On-line]. Retrieved June 10, 2002. Available: http://www.fightcrime.org/reports/as2000.pdf.

Pearce, L. D., & Axinn, W. G. (1998). The impact of family religious life on the quality of mother-child relations. *American Sociological Review, 63,* 810–828.

Pettine, A., & Rosen, L. A. (1998). Self-care and deviance in elementary school-age children. *Journal of Clinical Psychology, 54,* 629–643.

Pettit, G. S., Laird, R. D., Bates, J. E., & Dodge, K. A. (1997). Patterns of after-school care in middle childhood: Risk factors and developmental outcomes. *Merrill-Palmer Quarterly, 43,* 515–538.

Pierce, K. M., Hamm, J. V., & Vandell, D. L. (1999). Experiences in after-school programs and children's adjustment in first-grade classrooms. *Child Development, 70,* 756–767.

Posner, D. K., & Vandell, D. L. (1994). Low-income children's after-school care: Are there beneficial effects of after-school programs? *Child Development, 65,* 440–456.

Posner, J. K., & Vandell, D. L. (1999). After-school activities and the development of low-income urban children: A longitudinal study. *Developmental Psychology, 35,* 868–879.

Regnerus, M. D. (2000). Shaping schooling success: Religious socialization and educational outcomes in metropolitan public schools. *Journal for the Scientific Study of Religion, 39,* 363–370.

Reynolds, J. W. (1995). Music education and student self-concept: A review of literature. In *Research perspectives in music education* [On-line]. Tallahassee: Florida, Music Educators Association. Available: music.arts.usf.edu/rpme/rpmereyn.htm

Roth, J. L., & Brooks-Gunn, J. (2003). What is a youth development program? Identification of defining principles. In F. Jacobs, D. Wertlieb, & R. M. Lerner (Eds.), *Handbook of applied developmental science: Vol. 2. Enhancing the life chances of youth and families: Contributions of programs, policies, and service systems* (pp. 197–224). Thousand Oaks, CA: Sage.

Russ, S. W. (1998). Play, creativity, and adaptive functioning: Implications for play interventions. *Journal of Clinical Child Psychology, 27,* 469–480.

Sandstrom, M. J., & Coie, J. D. (1999). A developmental perspective on peer rejection: Mechanisms of stability and change. *Child Development, 70,* 955–966.

Scales, P. C., & Leffert, N. (1999). *Developmental assets: A synthesis of the scientific research on adolescent development.* Minneapolis: Search Institute.

Scripp, L. (2002). An overview of research on music and learning. In R. J. Deasy (Ed.), *Critical links: Learning in the arts and student academic and social development* (pp. 132–136). Washington, DC: Arts Education Partnership.

Sutherland, M. S., Hale, C. D., Harris, G. J., Stalls, P., & Foulk, D. (1997). Strengthening rural youth resiliency through the church. *Journal of Health Education, 28,* 205–218.

Taylor, R. J. (1988). Structural determinants of religious participation among Black Americans. *Review of Religious Research, 30,* 114–125.

Theeboom, M., De Koop, P., & Weiss, M. R. (1995). Motivational climate, psychological responses, and motor skill development in children's sport: A field-based intervention study. *Journal of Sport and Exercise Psychology, 17,* 294–311.

Thomas, D. L., & Carver, C. (1990). Religion and adolescent social competence. In T. P. Gullotta, G. R. Adams, & R. Montenmayor (Eds.), *Advances in adolescent development: Vol. 3. Developing social competency in adolescence* (pp. 195–219). Newbury Park, CA: Sage.

U.S. Department of Education & U.S. Department of Justice. (2000). *Working for children and families: Safe and smart after-school programs.* Washington, DC: Authors.

Vandell, D. L., & Posner, J. K. (1999). Conceptualization and measurement of children's after-school environments. In S. L. Friedman & T. D. Wachs (Eds.), *Measuring environment across the life span: Emerging methods and concepts* (pp. 167–196). Washington, DC: American Psychological Association.

Vandell, D. L., Posner, J., Shumow, L., & Kang, K. (1995, March). *Concurrent, short-term and long-term effects of self-care.* Poster session presented at the biennial meeting for the Society for Research in Child Development, Indianapolis, IN.

Vandell, D. L., & Shumow, L. (1999). After-school child care programs. *Future of Children, 9,* 64–80.

Wood, C. (2002). Parent-child pre-school activities can affect the development of literacy skills. *Journal of Research in Reading, 25,* 241–258.

Wright, L. S., Frost, C. J., & Wisecarver, S. J. (1993). Church attendance, meaningfulness of religion, and depressive symptomology among adolescents. *Journal of Youth and Adolescence, 22,* 559–568.

Zick, C. D., Bryant, W. K., & Österbacka, E. (2001). Mothers' employment, parental involvement, and the implications for intermediate child outcomes. *Social Science Research, 30,* 25–49.

The Internal Assets

A young person's commitment to learning is strongly influenced by relationships with family, peers, and others, as well as by the school environment.

5

The Commitment-to-Learning Assets

Why Is Commitment to Learning Important?

Middle childhood is the period during which children develop the capacity for meaningful productivity that they will need later in adulthood. It is also the time when a variety of critical self-perceptions, values, and skills evolve. A child's continued academic engagement and achievement depend upon these developments. As Kowaleski-Jones and Duncan (1999) describe it, in middle childhood children "begin to learn what constitutes success in the larger society. . . . [Their] sense of personal adequacy is developing and therefore vulnerable" (p. 931). Children's academic and personal interests, sense of competence and efficacy, perceptions about the usefulness of particular subject matter, motivation, classroom goals, and belief that school is an enjoyable and accepting place become differentiated and unique. During middle childhood, these and other variables, including children's peer relationships and general social competencies, combine to either strengthen or weaken developmental trajectories favorable to strong school bonding and school performance.

The widely varying effects of these developmental influences can be dramatic and occur at early ages. For example, in a study of mostly White, middle- to lower-middle-class, suburban students in grades 3 and 4, Miserandino (1996) reported that children's perceptions of their academic abilities and the degree to which they feel teachers overcontrol them are related to emotional expression, connection to school, and internal motivation, even in above-average achievers.

Children who felt uncertain about their academic abilities and excessively controlled by teachers were anxious and bored with school and did the minimum to "get by" on their schoolwork. In contrast, students who expressed confidence in their abilities, and who felt they were granted relative autonomy by their teachers, enjoyed school more and were more curious, involved, and persistent in their schoolwork.

Notable in this study is that teacher "overcontrol" was measured by children's perceptions, not by observers using validated criteria. Some of those teachers may have been simply practicing good classroom management that *felt* overcontrolling to students. Others may have been sufficiently overcontrolling that trained observers also would have rated them as such. Some likely guided their students in ways that exerted control but that did not feel overcontrolling to their students. Nevertheless, the key message of this study was that how students *felt* about teachers' classroom management styles had profound effects on their engagement with schoolwork.

Eccles, Roeser, Wigfield, and Freedman-Doan (1999) concluded that unfortunately, children's expectations for success and positive beliefs in their own competence generally decline as they move through middle childhood and early adolescence, a decline often beginning around grade 3, when schools increase the emphasis on competition among students. Wigfield and colleagues (1997) also reported a decline over the same period in children's sense of the usefulness of, and their interest in, subjects such as math, reading, sports, and instrumental music, although interest declined less in math and sports.

With declines in both the perceived usefulness of academic subjects and their competence in them, children are less likely to choose to engage with those content areas. A study of 233 British students in grades 4 through 6 found that when students could choose between working on easier or harder math, spelling, and vocabulary problems, students at all grade levels chose much easier problems than the 50% difficulty level (i.e., problems that on average 50% of students will get right and 50% will get wrong) that theory posits as optimal for motivation (Clifford, 1988). Moreover, as grade level increased, students were even less likely to choose problems of higher difficulty; that is, they took less academic risk, perhaps because they felt increasingly less capable of success.

Underlying these changes in children's competency beliefs may be developmental changes in children's understanding of perceived control, as reported in two studies by Skinner (1990) totaling more than 500 children in grades 1 through 6. Perceived control may be viewed as the extent to which children believe that their academic and other outcomes can be affected by their own efforts or are, instead, more a product of luck, unchanging innate ability, or the influence of powerful agents such as teachers. Skinner reported that, as children age from approximately 7 to 12 years old, their notions of control become much more differentiated. For children around age 7, causes of outcomes are essentially known or unknown; by age 8 or 9, causes are internal, external, or unknown, but are not specific. It is only around age 11 or 12 that children's attributions of causes for various outcomes differentiate into several factors, including ability, effort, external factors such as luck and the role of others, and unknown causes. This development suggests that middle childhood is a critical time for promoting in children the belief that their abilities are, in fact, malleable, and that individual effort can play a great role in successfully meeting their needs, academically and otherwise.

Adding depth to these findings are the results of Vartuli's (1999) study of Head Start through 3rd-grade teachers. She reported that as grade level *increased*, teachers' self-reported, developmentally appropriate beliefs and practices *declined*. For example, when asked how important it was for early childhood classroom activities to be responsive both to individual differences in development and to individual differences in interest, Head Start teachers scored significantly higher than 1st- and 2nd-grade teachers. It appears that the decreases in students' competency beliefs and in teachers' levels of developmentally appropriate teaching beliefs and practices occur around the same time. From a developmental point of view, these declines are almost surely a result of the reciprocal influence of teachers and students on each other. Because these events occur just as students are firming up personal theories of how much control they have over the academic and nonacademic outcomes in their lives, this combination of developmental phenomena can act as a potentially powerful disengagement influence on children's commitment to learning in middle childhood.

Considerable evidence suggests that children's inability to adapt well to school in the upper elementary years, especially in their sense of their own competence and ability, can have significant negative consequences in middle childhood and beyond. Consequences include school problems such as poor attendance, lower grades, and higher dropout rates, as well as problems such as depression, social rejection by peers, and inappropriate acts of anger and aggression (Eccles et al., 1999).

Children's achievement expectations and motivation, engagement in learning in and outside school, bonding to adults at school, participation in homework, and reading for pleasure all represent important strengths that, when present, contribute to their positive connections to school and schoolwork and greater intrinsic motivation to learn. The Appendix shows that two of the commitment-to-learning assets (achievement motivation and learning engagement) were measured at the acceptable .70 level of internal consistency reliability in field tests of the *Me and My World* survey. Bonding to adults at school was measured at a promising level (in the .60s), but the reliability for reading for pleasure was somewhat low. (The item for homework was added after the field test.)

Factors That Influence a Commitment to Learning

By the time children enter middle childhood, they have amassed and been affected by countless experiences that shape their commitment to learning, including the socioeconomic status (SES) into which they were born, the parenting styles they experience, and the achievement-related norms of their peers. For example, in a study of 174 children followed from grade 1 through age 16, Jimerson, Egeland, and Teo (1999) found, even in this sample in which all the families lived below the poverty line, that *relatively* higher levels of SES made a significant positive difference in math and reading achievement test scores. Higher SES, even at poverty levels, predicted higher test scores at the end of grade 1, and just as or even more important, also predicted improvement in test scores by grade 6 and later at age 16. Higher SES, whether measured by parents' education, income, or occupation, has generally been found to be a significant predictor of children's intellectual attainment and cognitive skills, particularly verbal abilities, across a variety of cultures, with the effects often indirect and attributed to the relationship between higher SES and better parenting (Bradley & Corwyn, 2002).

Jimerson and colleagues (1999) also reported, as have numerous other studies (see review in Eccles et al., 1999) that parent involvement in schooling and a high-quality home environment (measured by cognitive stimulation, parent support, and organization) were related both to children's early achievement and to their subsequent improvement in achievement across the elementary years and into adolescence. Mattanah's study (2001) of a small sample of middle- and upper-middle-class White 4th graders and their parents showed that other parenting variables may contribute considerable additional influence to academic functioning in middle childhood. The degree to which fathers did *not* try to psychologically control their 4th-grade children and prevent them from expressing their own ideas or making autonomous decisions was significantly related to more academic motivation, less depression, and less aggression in the children. These results were found even after controlling for parent warmth and boundary setting, which are also associated with positive academic adjustment, as noted earlier. However, the degree to which *mothers* granted psychological autonomy to their children did not mirror the positive results found for fathers' granting of autonomy.

Kindermann (1993) illuminated the role of peers in children's commitment to learning. In a small, brief (school-year) longitudinal study of 109 students in 4th and 5th grades, he demonstrated that children's peer groups are selected partly on the basis of academic motivation levels, and that these groups also play a role in socializing children further according to the peer group's prevailing level of motivation. Even though the membership of a given peer group in the study changed dramatically over the school year, its prevailing commitment to a certain level of achievement motivation did not. Overall, children affiliated at the start of the school year with peers who displayed similar motivation levels. Old and new group members alike continued throughout the school year to experience social expectations and reinforcement for the level of academic motivation (relatively higher or lower) characteristic of their particular peer group.

Kurdek and Sinclair (2000) conducted a study of several hundred 1st through 5th graders and examined how several kinds of academic outcomes were determined by psychological, family, and peer group variables. The average academic performance of one's peer group was significantly correlated with all but one of seven academic outcome variables. In multiple regression analyses, peer group achievement did not play a unique role in individual aptitude scores or passing scores on proficiency tests, but did contribute uniquely to end-of-the-year teacher ratings of children's verbal and math skills. These results collectively suggest that peer groups are selected on the basis of fit with individual children's current orientations toward school and academic motivations. They can also provide social norms that may support and promote desirable academic outcomes.

However, each child has a unique developmental trajectory. For example, even though most research shows that socioemotional adjustment and school engagement have important relationships to academic achievement (see, for example, Malecki & Elliott, 2002), Roeser, Eccles, and Sameroff's study (2000) is a reminder that individual paths and relations among these variables can be quite varied. Some children succeed academically in spite of being neither emotionally happy nor excited by their schoolwork. The common denominator among successful students, despite socioemotional differences, seems to be their belief in their general academic competence and efficacy. In this sense, apart from socioemotional issues, children can arrive at academic-engagement-reinforcing answers to several fundamental motivational questions posed by Eccles and Wigfield (2000): Can I succeed at this task? Do I want to do this task? Why am I doing this task? What do I have to do to succeed at this task?

Socioemotional status, measured in terms of levels of depression, anxiety, anger, or aggression, should not be confused with students' levels of social skills, which have consistently been found to be important correlates of and contributors to academic performance among both adolescents (see review in

Scales & Leffert, 1999) and elementary-age children (see chapter 7). For example, Malecki and Elliott (2002) studied 139 low-income 3rd- and 4th-grade children who were Hispanic, African American, or White. They reported that the students' self- and teacher-rated social skills—including cooperation, assertiveness, responsibility, empathy, and self-control—were significantly related both to standardized test scores in math, reading, and language and to self- and teacher-rated academic competence assessments. Children who evidenced more prosocial skills had stronger beliefs in their own abilities, as did their teachers, and the children actually performed better academically than did their classmates with lower levels of prosocial skills.

Bandura, Barbaranelli, Caprara, and Pastorelli (1996) reported on a study of 6th and 7th graders, in which children's belief in their ability to regulate their own learning and influence their academic achievement contributed both directly and indirectly to actual academic achievement. The indirect path reflected academic self-efficacy's influence on enhancing children's academic goals or aspirations, increasing prosocial behavior, and lessening vulnerability to depression. Wentzel (1993), too, found among 6th and 7th graders that children's valuing social goals in the classroom (e.g., cooperating, sharing, helping others, keeping promises, and thinking about how their behavior affects others) more strongly predicted good grades than did either intrinsic mastery motivation or striving for good grades. These studies suggest that although individual paths to academic success are varied and complex, children's social skills and sensitivities play important roles in attaining desirable academic outcomes.

Motivation and Achievement Trajectories

Researchers have investigated whether children's basic competencies and behavior during middle childhood become "crystallized" into patterns that are relatively stable throughout adolescence. For example, Kowaleski-Jones and Duncan (1999) studied two samples totaling about 1,500 children from the National Longitudinal Survey of Youth. They demonstrated that, although children's *average* math and reading achievement scores increased across four data collection points from ages 6 and 7 to ages 12 and 13, the *individual* achievement trajectories of most children varied widely in adjacent time periods. Typically, a period of positive change in achievement in one developmental period was followed by a more negative change in the next period, and vice versa. In other words, one should not expect *continuous* improvement in a child's achievement across middle childhood and adolescence.

Although achievement paths from early childhood through middle childhood to adolescence may rise slightly on the average, despite wide individual variations over time, researchers have also found that *intrinsic academic motivation* tends to be relatively stable for each individual and tends to decline in terms of group average over the same period. The concept of intrinsic academic motivation includes curiosity, enjoyment of learning, persistence in the face of subject matter difficulty, and an orientation toward exploration and mastery of content more than toward grades. Intrinsic motivation and mastery motivation have been associated with better academic performance generally (Shiner, 2000; Wentzel, 1993) and with the amount and breadth of children's reading (Wigfield & Guthrie, 1997).

In Gottfried, Fleming, and Gottfried's study (2001) of nearly 100 children followed from infancy through age 17, mean levels of intrinsic motivation declined steadily with the exception of a slight increase between the ages of 16 and 17, as students neared the end of high school. Specifically, students whose intrinsic motivation was low in middle childhood were more likely to remain at low levels and did not enjoy an increase in motivation through middle and high school. Even though motivation for "school in general" declined slightly in the study population, it declined less than intrinsic motivation to achieve in math, science, and reading. However, intrinsic motivation for social studies achievement did not decline. Gottfried and colleagues (2001) also found that by age 9, children have developed a "substantial degree" of motivation. Motivational levels at age 9 are not only predicted by motivation levels from earlier years, but also considerably predict subsequent motivation in later years.

Intrinsic Motivation and Learning Outside School

The discussion of intrinsic motivation, up to this point framed by aspects of schooling and the school curriculum, is not complete without considering another aspect of the commitment-to-learning category: measures of learning that takes place outside school. Processes that affect young people's orientation toward school and schoolwork are emphasized because of the importance of successful academic adjustment to students' current and future well-being. "Commitment to learning," however, does not mean merely a commitment to schooling. The term also is intended to convey the developmental importance of showing intellectual curiosity beyond school walls, exploring new interests and talents, and being exposed to numerous informal opportunities outside the realm of formal schoolwork. Such outside-of-school learning can broaden self-knowledge and forge connections to an increasingly expanding personal ecology. Thus, we include enjoyment of learning outside of school and reading for pleasure within the commitment-to-learning category, as each is important in its own right and because the experience of these assets may also strengthen students' more formal school orientation and performance.

For example, Marks (2000) studied more than 3,600 elementary, middle, and high school students in schools identified as having made considerable progress toward restructuring to promote greater student engagement and achievement (through such practices as team teaching, integrated and interdisciplinary curriculum, and expanded cocurricular/after-school programs). About one-third of the sample was composed of elementary students. Although Marks found that students' engagement with academics decreased as their grade level increased, she also found that whether students experienced a supportive school climate and "authentic instructional work" made a significant difference in those engagement patterns. Authentic instructional work includes opportunities for higher-order thinking rather than emphasis on memorization; deep intellectual exploration of topics rather than merely "covering" the curriculum; and, most important for the present discussion, opportunities for connecting schoolwork to the "real" world beyond the classroom, such as through community service or service-learning. The desired result is that students can understand the purpose, value, and meaning of both one's knowledge and one's contributions to the world, allowing for a deeper, longer-lasting engagement with a variety of intellectual work.

Marks found that students who reported higher levels of "authentic instructional work" were more engaged with subject matter at every grade level. This positive effect was strong enough to eliminate the negative effect of elementary students' prior levels of achievement on their current engagement. That is, not taking authentic instruction into account, students who had poor achievement records at school in earlier years reported lower current levels of engagement with subject material, but if they also experienced higher levels of authentic work that connected them to the world outside school, their academic engagement levels rose significantly higher, despite having had earlier experiences of poor school achievement. The compensatory effects of authentic instructional work were especially strong for boys, whose general levels of academic engagement were lower than the levels of girls.

Gender and Commitment to Learning

Among the most commonly studied topics related to the commitment-to-learning category are differences between boys and girls in their levels of academic achievement, motivation, engagement, bonding to school, and related variables. Girls generally are found to achieve academically at higher levels but to doubt themselves more, especially in particular subject matter domains. For example, in a 3-year longitudinal study of 1st, 2nd, and 4th graders who were followed through the 3rd, 4th, and 6th grades, respectively, Wigfield and colleagues (1997) reported that children's gender-linked competency beliefs existed in the earliest grades and did not change over time: Boys held greater competency beliefs than girls in math and sports, and girls held greater competency beliefs than boys in reading and instrumental music.

Moreover, Pomerantz, Altermatt, and Saxon (2002) studied nearly 1,000 White, lower- to middle-class 4th through 6th graders, and reported that although girls outperformed boys in science, language arts, math, and social studies, they evaluated their competence in these areas, except in language arts, more poorly than boys did their own. In addition, the girls worried significantly more than boys about their school performance. Even high-performing girls reported significantly less global self-worth and significantly more anxiety and depression than did boys. Complex gender differences in academic motivation were found in Thorkildsen and Nicholls's (1998) study of more than 550 students in grade 5. But the study results generally supported the view that girls are both more aware of teachers' differing expectations for different students and more sensitive to negative feedback.

Jacobs, Lanza, Osgood, Eccles, and Wigfield (2002) followed 761 children from the 1st through 12th grades. They reported that gender differences in competence beliefs were specific to the subjects or domains studied—language arts, math, and sports—and were not simply general effects. For example, in grade 1, boys had significantly higher competence beliefs in math, but their beliefs declined faster than did girls' over the elementary school years. By high school, boys' and girls' competence beliefs in their math abilities were equal. In contrast, both boys and girls began grade 1 having the same levels of competence beliefs in language arts, but boys' beliefs declined rapidly through elementary school, while girls' beliefs declined much more slowly, with the result that girls' beliefs in their language arts abilities were higher than boys in middle school and beyond. Boys' sports competence beliefs started at higher levels than girls'; however, both genders experienced a decline over elementary school at the same rate, leaving boys' sports competency beliefs consistently higher than girls' throughout school.

Stetsenko, Little, Gordeeva, Grasshof, and Oettingen (2000) conducted a study of more than 3,000 students in grades 2 through 6 in East and West Berlin, Moscow, Tokyo, Bern, Los Angeles, and Prague between 1990 and 1993. They reported that in 90% of the cases in which girls outperformed boys in language or math grades, girls' self-assessments of how able and smart they were equaled, but did not exceed, boys' self-assessments. In general, better-achieving boys and girls held higher perceptions of their potential for achievement than did the lower-achieving students. When girls earned higher grades than did boys, they also held higher beliefs regarding their ability to obtain teachers' help, be lucky in school, and exert the effort needed to do well. Thus, there were more similarities between boys' and girls' beliefs about their own agency or ability to take actions to get good grades than there were differences. The one observed exception was the consistent difference in boys' and girls' self-perceptions of their intellectual talent, such that higher-performing girls consistently underassessed their own "smartness" across varied cultural settings. The researchers attributed these results to differential feedback received by girls and boys from parents and teachers, who are more likely to tell girls that their academic problems are due to lack of ability and boys that their problems arise from a lack of effort.

Finally, girls may generally enjoy greater exposure to the commitment-to-learning assets and experience higher achievement, but they may also be more vulnerable to disturbances of that orientation to school and to learning. For example, in a national longitudinal study, Kowaleski-Jones and Duncan (1999) found that boys had a higher degree of variability in their achievement trajectories from ages 6 to 13. In contrast, girls had generally more consistent achievement paths, but if knocked offstride academically, tended to take longer to recover to better achievement. Girls may take longer than boys to recover from an interruption of their achievement arc because they value both high achievement and meeting others' expectations of them more than do boys, as well as because their academic self-confidence appears more vulnerable.

The commitment-to-learning assets measured in the *Me and My World* survey reflect many, although not all, of the themes discussed here. The powerful influence that children's competence beliefs can exert on their motivation and ultimate performance is an important aspect of the broader concept of commitment to learning, as evidenced in the preceding discussion, but is not included within this asset category. These beliefs appear to have both a general component, perhaps best called *academic competence,* and an even more important, specific component *(perceived competence)* related to particular subject areas that are beyond the scope of measurement in the MMW survey.

In a more general sense, it is highly unlikely that *any* set of five or six measures could comprehensively reflect as vast and complex a concept as a commitment to learning. For example, in presenting a model of achievement for cultural minority children, Okagaki (2001) noted that characteristics of *home* (family cultural norms and values surrounding schooling and education), *school* (how the school is organized and what the purpose of going to school is seen to be), and *individual students* (their efficacy beliefs) must be considered together.

Further, Wang, Haertel, and Walberg (1990) observed in a metareview and synthesis of research on learning that schooling processes alone, not to mention the broader learning constructs included in the commitment-to-learning category, "respond to a multitude of influences interacting in kaleidoscopic patterns" (p. 37). The result is that although countless variables are moderately related to various learning outcomes, few if any variables alone are strongly related. It is the *connections* among all these variables, and what they signify about the child's person-environment interactions, that are more important than any single variable. Thus, although the five assets in the commitment-to-learning category adequately capture sufficient aspects of this concept for many research and applied purposes, the assets also present an incomplete picture that may need to be supplemented by additional measures.

Table 10. The Commitment-to-Learning Assets	
Achievement motivation	Child is motivated and strives to do well in school.
Learning engagement	Child is responsive, attentive, and actively engaged in learning at school and enjoys participating in learning activities outside of school.
Homework	Child usually hands in homework on time.
Bonding to adults at school	Child cares about teachers and other adults at school.
Reading for pleasure	Child enjoys and engages in reading for fun most days of the week.

Summary of Research Findings: The Commitment-to-Learning Assets in Middle Childhood

The literature on child development is rich with topics relevant to our understanding of a child's commitment to learning, both in and out of school. The research we reviewed examines issues surrounding motivation, goals, homework, and self-efficacy and competency beliefs in middle childhood. A significant number of studies demonstrate that a commitment to learning, by which we mean that children are motivated to learn, are engaged in school and non-school-related learning activities, and are connected to teachers and staff at school, is a positive contributor to academic competence and well-being. Less evident in the research, however, is how children's commitment to learning may influence their relationships with others (e.g., peer social skills), emotional competency (e.g., internal states and externalized behaviors), and overall mental health. Nevertheless, an array of positive developmental outcomes, such as higher standardized test scores, increased engagement in learning activities, school attendance, and lessened antisocial behavior, have been associated with a commitment to learning among children and youth.

Achievement Motivation and Learning Engagement

We group these two assets together because of their close relationship, as evidenced in our discussion of influences on commitment to learning. Associations between children's motivation to do well in school, their engagement in learning (especially at school), and academic achievement are particularly abundant in the literature. Achievement motivation (especially intrinsic or mastery motivation) has been found to predict higher grades and test scores, more positive perceptions of academic competence, and increased willingness to tackle difficult tasks. Achievement motivation has also been associated with better behavioral competence in the classroom (e.g., Shiner, 2000). Achievement motivation has been associated, directly or indirectly, with:

Academic Outcomes

- **Higher grades and standardized test scores** (Gottfried, 1990; Gutman & Midgley, 2000 [for low-income African American children across the middle school transition]; Leondari & Gialamas, 2002 [moderated relationship between achievement goals and achievement]; Shiner, 2000; Skinner, Wellborn, & Connell, 1990; Stetsenko et al., 2000; Wentzel, 1993 [especially for students high in mastery motivation]); **perceptions of academic competence** (Guay, Boggiano, & Vallerand, 2001 [intrinsic motivation mediates relationship between teacher autonomy support and perceived academic competence]); **elevated willingness to perform challenging academic tasks** (Leondari & Gialamas, 2002 [when children believe intelligence can be increased through one's own efforts]); **increased likelihood to seek teachers' help with difficult academic tasks** (Ryan, Hicks, & Midgley, 1997); **increased engagement in learning** (Kindermann, 1993 [through self-selected peer groups of similar motivational orientation]; Miserandino, 1996; Patrick, Skinner, & Connell, 1993; Skinner et al., 1990 [when authoritative teaching style present in students' lives]; **increased time spent on reading** (Wigfield & Guthrie, 1997 [especially for intrinsically motivated students]); and **better academic competence** (Shiner, 2000).

Mental and Behavioral Health Outcomes

- **Lessened antisocial behavior and better academic competence** (Shiner, 2000).

Research also consistently shows that children who are responsive, attentive, and actively engaged in learning are more connected to school, attend school more regularly, behave better, and have higher grades than children less engaged in learning at school. More specifically, learning engagement, especially at school, has been associated, directly or indirectly, with:

Academic Outcomes

- **Higher standardized grade point averages** (Connell, Spencer, & Aber, 1994 [among African American sample]; Peet, Powell, & O'Donnel, 1997 [when mother and teachers had similar perceptions about children's school engagement]; Shiner, 2000) and **standardized test scores** (Connell et al., 1994 [among African American sample]; Shiner, 2000); **better social competence at school** (Shiner, 2000); **higher school attendance** (Connell et al., 1994 [among African American sample]); and **increased interest in science-related courses** (Joyce & Ferenga, 1999 [especially for girls]).

Mental and Behavioral Health Outcomes

- **Increased positive expectations for the future** (Dubow, Arnett, Smith, & Ippolito, 2001 [6th–8th grade sample]); **reduction of alienation and withdrawal** (Finn, 1989); and **lessened antisocial behavior** (Shiner, 2000).

Collectively, the research on children's achievement motivation and engagement in learning at school suggests that students' intrinsic motivation can be discouraged by both school environment issues and specific motivation and engagement issues associated with particular curriculum and the manner in which the subject matter is taught. The effects of school climate and curriculum on students' motivations combine with the broader influences of socioeconomic status, personality characteristics, family support variables, and peer relationships. The overall impact of these variables can be discerned quite early in children's school careers and appears to have considerable influence, for better or worse, on their future academic pathways.

Young people's engagement in learning outside school is represented in the literature by studies examining the potential benefits of activities such as museum education, community education opportunities, and informal science education. Engagement in learning outside of school has been associated, directly or indirectly, with:

- **Increased academic achievement and literacy skills** (Christenson, Rounds, & Gorney, 1992 [structure for learning in the home]; Hull & Schultz, 2001; Nettles, 1991 [learning through community activities]); and
- **Greater sense of intrinsic motivation to do well in school** (Gottfried, Fleming, & Gottfried, 1998); **increased motivation and enthusiasm for science learning** (Joyce & Ferenga, 1999 [for girls only]; Ramey-Gassert, 1997).

Differentiating between Learning in and out of School   We include the enjoyment of learning outside the classroom walls along with engagement in learning at school to emphasize the closeness of the two aspects of engagement in learning. Hull and Schultz (2001) observe that distinguishing between the two contexts for learning often presents a "false dichotomy . . . [that ignores] the presence of school-like practice at home . . . , or nonschool-like activities in the formal classroom" (p. 577), and that school and out-of-school learning activities can either support or compensate for each other. In fact, in a pair of studies, Ferenga and Joyce (1998) and Joyce and Ferenga (1999) showed that a significant relationship existed between formal (e.g., school science lessons) and informal (e.g., museums and zoos) science learning experiences and, subsequently, the number of science courses taken by 9- to 13-year-old boys and girls with high science ability. In addition, girls' leisure interest in science (as evidenced by their desire for science books as presents) significantly predicted the number of science courses they took.

Moreover, a majority of schools in the United States (including 46% of elementary schools) now provide Internet access to their students outside regular school hours (Cattagni & Farris, 2001). Given that much of school-related Internet use is dedicated to supporting schoolwork, albeit with blocking and filtering software, this opportunity provides millions of children with the chance to do exploratory, interest-based learning outside school hours through the use of a school resource. Availability and use of this technological development further blur the lines between in-school and out-of-school influences on commitment to learning.

Homework

Researchers' efforts to examine the effects of youth's time spent on homework have produced mixed results, contributing not only to great debate in the research arena, but also among practitioners, policy makers, and parents (Cooper & Valentine, 2001; Warton, 2001). For elementary school students in particular, findings of small and sometimes even negative associations between homework time and academic achievement are widespread (Cooper, 1989; Cooper & Valentine, 2001). Contrary findings have also been noted among adolescents (Scales & Leffert, 1999).

Perhaps more important during middle childhood than the hours young people spend on homework (the way the "homework" asset is defined for adolescents) may be simply whether they do homework when it is assigned (Benson, Roehlkepartain, & Leffert, 1997) and hand it in on time. For example, in his large meta-analysis of 120 empirical studies on the effects of homework on achievement in students elementary school through high school, Cooper (1989) found that *amount assigned* and *time spent* had relatively little impact on achievement gains in elementary students compared to junior high and high school students. However, when researchers (Cooper, Lindsay, Nye, & Greathouse, 1998; Cooper & Valentine, 2001) included a measure of the amount of homework *completed* in more recent studies on children and adolescents, they found a positive relation to school grades in elementary school students similar to that of correlations found in the meta-analysis for adolescents. Unfortunately, most correlational research that relates homework to academic outcomes relies on either students' or parents' reports of children's time spent doing homework and fails to make the distinction between the proportion of homework assigned and homework completed (Cooper et al., 1998). As described above, measuring this distinction may have important implications on the assessment of homework's influence on children's development.

Not surprisingly, most empirical studies investigate homework's influence on standard achievement outcomes (e.g., GPA and standardized test scores). Far fewer emphasize the links between homework and non-achievement-related outcomes such as levels of personal responsibility, self-discipline, and interest in learning. In addition to promoting commitment to learning more generally and academic achievement more specifically, homework may also support the growing ability of the child to regulate herself or himself with the guidance of adults. Homework has been associated, directly or indirectly, with:

Academic Outcomes

- **Higher achievement test scores, grades, or both** (Cooper, Jackson, Nye, & Lindsay, 2001; Cooper et al., 1998; Leone & Richards, 1989; Posner & Vandell, 1994); and **greater completion and accuracy of homework** (Miller & Kelley, 1991 [if accuracy in homework was required]).

Social Outcomes

- **More positive conduct in school** (Posner & Vandell, 1994).

Bonding to Adults at School

Although much of the literature on bonding to school pertains to the relationship between children's connectedness to teachers and peers and positive developmental outcomes (see Chapter 1), studies that examine students' relationships to a broader network of adults at school (i.e., principals, nurses, and school staff) also show significant associations between school bonding and healthy development. Together, these studies indicate that when children care for teachers *and* other staff at school, they are more likely to report positive developmental outcomes, such as a sense of satisfaction in and enjoyment of learning, better academic performance, better emotional health, and fewer risky behaviors. Bonding or "connectedness" to adults at school has been associated, directly or indirectly, with:

Academic Outcomes

- **Greater school satisfaction** (Baker, 1998, 1999 [for at-risk African American students]; Griffith, 2000; Samdal, Nutbeam, Wold, and Kannas, 1998 [in children from Finland, Latvia, Norway, and Slovakia]) and **enjoyment in school activities** (Griffith, 1997); **increased commitment, engagement, and motivation toward learning in school** (Osterman, 2000; Tucker et al., 2002 [among African American 1st- through 12th-grade children]); **greater school competence and fewer emotional problems at school** (Murray & Greenberg, 2000); and **higher grades for behaviorally and/or mentally disturbed students** if they perceive socioemotional and instructional support from teachers (Griffith, 2002 [for schools having more socioeconomically disadvantaged students]).

Mental and Behavioral Health Outcomes

- **Protection against later alcohol dependence and abuse** (Guo, Hawkins, Hill, & Abbott, 2001); **less aggression in school** (Hughes, Cavell, & Jackson, 1999); and **fewer emotional problems at school** (Murray & Greenberg, 2000).

Bonding to school, in the sense that children care for teachers and staff, is a critical component of children's engagement in and commitment to learning. Although the bonding-to-adults-at-school asset may appear similar to the teachers component of the caring-school-climate asset, it is important to note two distinctions. First, the bonding-to-adults-at-school asset encompasses children's attitudes and perceptions about a wide range of adults encountered in the academic setting, including not only teachers but other staff as well. Second, these two assets reflect different perspectives on emotional connection to school. That is, in measuring the teachers component of the caring-school-climate asset, we measure the degree to which children perceive teachers to be caring, encouraging, and supportive in the school environment. In this relationship, children are merely passive participants who either do or do not perceive their teachers to be caring presences in their lives. On the other hand, measuring the degree to which children feel bonded to adults at school looks at the level to which children feel connected to adults in the school environment; we assume children are active participants in that relationship of connection.

Unfortunately, few studies that address students' relationships with adults at school make the distinction between the passive "being cared for" and the active "caring for" in their methodological and conceptual underpinnings. Of the studies we did find, a large portion either considers the two constructs as one and the same or entirely omits our definition of bonding to adults at school. Consequently, it is difficult to assess the potential influence this asset may have on positive child development outcomes.

Nonetheless, the literature does show it is particularly important to child well-being that children care for adults at their school. In a relatively diverse sample of 289 children in late middle childhood (the mean age was about 11.5 years), Murray and Greenberg (2000) examined the connections between children's school and teacher bonding and the children's socioemotional adjustment. Our notion of bonding to adults at school (i.e., children care about the adults at their school) was used as part of a more global measure of student-teacher affiliations. The researchers found that children who reported stronger bonds with teachers and schools, less dissatisfaction with teachers, and fewer school danger factors also reported significantly better social and school competence and significantly fewer symptoms of depression.

Bonding to adults at school may also have significant long-term affects. Lonczak, Abbott, Hawkins, Kosterman, and Catalano (2002) analyzed comprehensive longitudinal data from a sample of children followed from grade 5 to 21 years of age. Children who were provided with a social developmental intervention (i.e., a program promoting academic achievement, social competence, and bonding to school through teacher, parent, and child training) experienced significantly more responsible sexual behavior, fewer sexual partners, and a reduced likelihood of contracting a sexually transmitted disease by age 21 than did the control group (who experienced no intervention). Another paper on the same sample revealed that avoidance of alcohol abuse and dependence at age 21 was more reliably predicted by young people's strong school bonding at ages 10, 14, and 16 than by other meaningful predictors, including parents' monitoring behaviors and students' refusal skills (Guo et al., 2001).

Students' sense of a high degree of belonging to their school community is affected by a complex mix of parent and teacher practices, peer relationships, and student competence beliefs. In a small study of African American families with 5th graders who were making the transition to middle school, Gutman and Midgley (2000) found that the students who experienced both parent involvement in schooling (a support asset) and school belonging (similar in meaning to the bonding-to-adults-at-school asset within the commitment-to-learning category) had higher grade point averages (GPAs) throughout the often problematic middle school transition years than did students who reported neither or only one of those assets.

In another small study of urban African American students in grades 3 through 5, Baker (1999) also reported that the differential social relationships students have with teachers and peers at school creates two groups of students as early as grade 3: those who already like school and find it a satisfying place to be, and those who do not.

Research has also shown that teachers prefer and provide more support and caring to students who are already engaged, well behaved, and prosocial; that peer acceptance patterns mirror those teacher preferences; and that student engagement and academic performance are affected by these variables from kindergarten through high school (Osterman, 2000). For example, Hamre and Pianta (2001) reported that kindergartners whose teachers reported them to be highly negative in their relationships with the teacher and dependent on the teacher displayed poor academic and behavioral outcomes through grade 8, particularly if the children already had shown behavior problems in kindergarten.

The extent to which children can "access the instructional and socialization resources of the classroom environment" (Hamre & Pianta, 2001, p. 636) may be significantly lower for children with early histories of classroom behavior disorders. Those children may begin to withdraw physically from participation in curricular and extracurricular activities, thus further depressing teacher support, peer acceptance, and their own sense of competence, and leading ultimately to emotional withdrawal and school dropout (Finn, 1989). Because this cycle feeds on itself, children who fail in their early school years to show the kind of motivation and social behavior valued by teachers and peers especially need a school environment in middle childhood that promotes a strong sense of bonding to teachers or other adults at school.

Although not directly measuring student bonding to adults at school, Griffith's study (2002) of more than 25,000 suburban, racially and ethnically diverse students in grades 3 through 6 (i.e., half were students of color) offered further evidence of the importance of what he called "expressive" support, particularly for socioeconomically disadvantaged children. Students who reported that they felt able to express their ideas and work in class without being bothered by other students also reported higher GPAs. Moreover, gaps in GPAs between White students and students of color were smaller in schools in which students reported both school-level "expressive support" and classroom-level "instrumental support" (e.g., teachers held high expectations for them). Expressive support at the school level includes students identifying an adult at school to whom they could go for help with problems or who would help them if they were hurt, as well as feeling that the principal was fair and the office staff was nice and helpful. Finally, in schools composed of greater proportions of disadvantaged students, somewhat higher GPAs were found among students who said they had both expressive and instrumental support from the adults at their school.

Reading for Pleasure

Unfortunately, although the developmental significance of reading for pleasure is apparent, it is not numerically well represented in the child development literature. Among the few studies we identified, reading for pleasure has been associated, directly or indirectly, with:

- **Higher basic achievement test scores** (Hofferth & Sandberg, 2001) and **higher reading achievement scores** (Donahue, Voelkl, Campbell, & Mazzeo, 1999 [when children are given time to read books of their own choosing during school]; Taylor, Frye, & Maruyama, 1990 [when children either read assigned texts or read for pleasure in school, but not at home]); **increased gains in reading fluency** (Clarke-Stewart, 1998 [when the child reads with a parent]); and
- **Increased enjoyment of reading fluency** (Clarke-Stewart, 1998 [when the child reads with a parent]).

Parental practices leading to a cognitively stimulating home environment have important short- and long-term positive impacts on children's school commitment and their broader learning outside school (Gottfried et al., 1998), as well as on children's specific reading habits (Korpan, Bisanz, Bisanz, Boehme, & Lynch, 1998). For example, Clarke-Stewart (1998) studied a small sample of children 8 to 10 years old, and reported that when parents *and* children took turns reading children's books aloud, children enjoyed reading more, paid greater attention, and achieved better reading fluency than when parents alone read the books. A finding from the 1998 National Assessment of Educational Progress report on reading reinforces the notion that child participation, as a form of self-regulation or agency, may be especially beneficial to children in middle childhood. More than half of 4th graders (56%) reported that their teachers gave them opportunities almost daily to decide what they could read, compared with only 21% of 8th graders and just 6% of 12th graders, results that suggest that elementary school teachers consider free-choice reading an important instructional practice (Donahue et al., 1999).

The Commitment-to-Learning Assets across the Early Childhood-Adolescence Life Span

Clearly, the assets comprising the commitment-to-learning category are important—though not exhaustive—contributors to children's connections with, and success in, school and learning in general. What do these dimensions of a commitment to learning look like in the early elementary grades? The following discussion places the significance of these qualities into a broader developmental context.

Young children tend to begin formal schooling (i.e., kindergarten and grade 1) with positive, even lofty, beliefs, attitudes, and perceptions regarding their involvement and performance in various school and academic competencies, as noted earlier. In one of the more comprehensive studies addressing the developmental trend in children's academic competence beliefs and values, Wigfield et al. (1997) followed two cohorts of children for 3 years, starting in the early elementary grades (kindergarten and grade 1). Consistent with previously cited research, a decline occurred in children's perceptions of their competence in, and their beliefs regarding the usefulness and importance of, reading and math, indicating that young children start school with generally optimistic beliefs about their competencies and positive attitudes toward reading and math.

Children's beliefs and values regarding their academic competence in reading and math were more unstable from grade 1 to grade 2 than in higher grades. That is, as children grow older, an enduring self-portrait of abilities and attitudes solidifies as they become more adept at social comparisons and are more able to incorporate parental and teacher feedback on their behavior and performance. Wigfield and colleagues (1997) note that the early instability is not necessarily a negative phenomenon, as young children's beliefs about their academic competence are still amenable to change. Finally, the relationship between a child's belief in her or his competence in an academic domain and *actual* competence (as rated by teachers or parents) is relatively weak—there is a disconnection between children's subjective beliefs and adults' objective reports. Wigfield and colleagues comment that this unsupported optimism of children represents an important "window of time" before children's beliefs about their academic efficacy become more stable.

Of course, not all young children hold rosy beliefs about their academic abilities and motivation. Wigfield and colleagues's study, and others like it, showing initially high levels of achievement motivation and perceived academic competence beliefs among young children (e.g., Eccles, Wigfield, Harold, & Blumenfeld, 1993; Marsh, 1989) all use group-level measurement as their unit of analysis, and therefore may mask important individual variations in children's achievement motivation and competence belief trajectories.

Another approach to evaluating the evolution of children's motivation and beliefs over time is to model the trajectories of individual children's beliefs and perceptions. This approach, also called the *person-centered approach*, was referenced earlier in the chapter; it highlights the significant intraindividual variability that often is masked by an approach that compares statistical means (Kowaleski-Jones & Duncan, 1999). Unfortunately, Kowaleski-Jones and Duncan (1999) only addressed actual achievement levels and behavior problems— they did not address the kinds of beliefs and attitudes representative of the commitment-to-learning category, such as academic goals, motivation, competence beliefs, and academic valuing. Kowaleski-Jones and Duncan's (1999) findings are important, though, in that they point to the role of stability and change in beliefs and perceptions at the individual level; research addressing individual growth trajectories of children's motivation and academic attitudes is needed to elucidate the way these attitudes develop and "crystallize" over time.

One study that approximates motivation trajectories comes from Eccles and her colleagues (Eccles et al., 1999). Describing a series of studies from their research group, Eccles and colleagues (1999) categorized children as "at-risk" or "not-at-risk" at two points in time: early elementary (grade 1) using teacher ratings of academic competence, and early adolescence (grades 7 and 8) using self-reports of academic competence. This categorization yielded four student groups: those at risk during both time periods, at risk only in the early elementary period, at risk only in the early adolescent period, and not at risk during either time period. A data plot of the individual trajectories of these four groups of children revealed no differences in the teacher perceptions of academic competence of the 1st-grade groups or of the value children ascribed to doing well at school at that time. Distinct differences emerged along these dimensions by early adolescence, however, including self-ratings of academic competence, GPA scores, and measures of self-esteem (Eccles et al., 1999). Thus, the available evidence suggests that although individual differences exist, young children generally have optimistic beliefs in their abilities and motivation to learn and achieve. If these optimistic beliefs are still relatively malleable until later in development (Wigfield, 1994), then efforts should focus on creating contexts and relationships likely to support the development of adaptive academic competence pathways.

Relationships

The effect that all adults, but especially parents, can have on children's engagement in and enjoyment of learning and achievement motivation is predicated first on the presence of a warm, supportive relationship between children and adults (Brazelton & Greenspan, 2000). Within this responsive interpersonal climate, adults can promote comfort and a desire for learning in children through intentional interactions that include encouraging exploration, identifying and building upon children's individual interests and talents, and providing opportunities for discovery (Ramey & Ramey, 1992; Shonkoff & Phillips, 2000). The essence of the research is that simply being engaged *with* the child in all manner of learning activities fosters positive growth (Ramey & Ramey, 1998; 2000; Shonkoff & Phillips, 2000).

Sènèchal and LeFevre (2002), for example, distinguished between formal literacy interactions, in which the adult and child focus on reading and writing skills, and informal literacy activities, in which the focus is not on reading skills per se but rather on a shared activity in which the child is exposed to storybooks in the presence of parents. In noting that these two activities are unrelated, Sènèchal and LeFevre (2002) reported that among kindergarten and 1st-grade children, shared book reading between parent and child was uniquely related to development of receptive language skills (vocabulary and listening comprehension). In contrast, formal teaching interactions were uniquely related to emergent literacy skills (e.g., alphabet knowledge and invented spelling). Each of these types of literacy activities in early childhood was then indirectly related to the child's reading proficiency at the end of grade 3 (see also Aram & Levin, 2002, for a similar example using joint writing as the child-parent interaction).

The significance of offering children adult-structured learning opportunities echoes the work of Vygotsky (1978), who spoke of the "zone of proximal development." The zone represents the distance between a task too complicated for a child to perform alone and the same task performed by the child with the assistance of an adult. Adult support for activities within the zone of proximal development is a powerful factor in promoting a child's cognitive development (Rogoff, 1998).

This learning by "collaborative process" (Rogoff, 1998) does not necessarily require an adult to be present. Children as young as 5 years old who were experts at a planning task (a game that involved planning and reversing sequence in a series of steps) have been found to be effective learning partners for 5-year-olds who were novices at the same planning task (Duran & Gauvain, 1993). Indeed, also related to children's motivation and achievement is the degree to which they have opportunities to engage in collaborative tasks and cooperative learning with their peers. Osterman (2000), in a comprehensive review of children's reported sense of belonging to their school, suggests that opportunities to collaborate with age-mates significantly affect children's sense of belonging, as well as providing them opportunities to engage in prosocial positive interactions with peers.

Peer friendships can also indirectly influence children's feelings and attitudes about schools. In a now classic study, Ladd examined the effects of peer interactions and friendships among kindergartners (Ladd, 1990). Ladd was interested in understanding whether the kinds of peer relations children constructed as they made the transition to kindergarten affected their school adjustment or, conversely, whether the degree to which children adjusted and adapted positively to the school environment affected the kinds of peer relationships they subsequently established. Evidence for supporting both hypotheses was found. As Ladd (1990) notes, however, the preponderance of the results was consistent with the first hypothesis: Children's peer relationships across the kindergarten year predicted overall school adjustment two months into the school year (i.e., positive perceptions of school, school academic performance, and anxiety and avoidance at school) and again at the end of the school year, after controlling for prior preschool experience and initial levels of school adjustment variables.

One of the most studied nonparental, adult-child relationships is that of the child and teacher. Pianta has shown that if children engage in positive relationships with teachers, their academic and social outcomes are likely to be better in the short term as well as 8 years later (Hamre & Pianta, 2001). Skinner and Belmont (1993) found that students' reported emotional engagement in learning was most strongly predicted by the quality of student-teacher relationships. Wigfield, Eccles, and Rodriguez (1998) noted, "The implication of this finding is that positive relationships with teachers are crucial to motivation" (p. 95).

Interestingly, although a wealth of research documents the significance of *teacher* reports of the quality of the student-teacher relationship, the significance of *child* reports of this relationship during the primary grades remains unclear. For example, Valeski and Stipek (2001) found that kindergartners' perceptions of relationships with their teachers were unrelated to teachers' perceptions of the relationships. However, 1st-grade children's and teachers' perceptions were modestly correlated to each other ($r = .28$), an indication that—at least for 1st graders—at a very young age, children's perceptions begin to coincide with teachers' perceptions. Although neither kindergarten nor 1st-grade student ratings of the student-teacher relationship were related to teacher ratings of students' school engagement, students' positive relationships with teachers were related to generally positive attitudes toward school (Valeski & Stipek, 2001). Clearly more work is necessary to better understand the bidirectional nature of young students' and teachers' perceptions of their relationships.

Contexts That Influence a Commitment to Learning

The two most influential contexts in which a commitment to learning takes root for children during the primary grades are the home and the school. Here we review the role of each setting in instilling a devotion to learning in children.

Home environment   A cognitively stimulating home, characterized by books, other learning materials, a good deal of verbal stimulation, and parents who read and learn with children, is reliably linked to IQ measures, as well as to measures of academic achievement skills (Hart & Risley, 1995; Smith, Brooks-Gunn, & Klebanov, 1997). As mentioned earlier, Jimerson and colleagues (1999) were interested in examining whether specific variables—the home environment among them—were related to achievement scores (obtained by means of a regression equation) that were both higher and lower than predicted (termed "upward" and "downward deflections") in a low-income sample of children and mothers. Jimerson and colleagues found that stimulating aspects of the home environment in 1st grade, including facets such as organization, play materials, and quality of the language environment, were related to upward deflections in math and reading scores in grade 6 and in reading scores at age 16. Likewise, in a sample of older children, Gottfried et al. (1998) reported that a cognitively stimulating home environment at age 8 directly predicted achievement motivation at ages 9 and 13, and indirectly predicted it at ages 10 and 13, after controlling for socioeconomic status at age 8. Studies such as these serve as reminders that important variations exist within socioeconomic classes, and that the home environment has the potential to be an important facilitator of achievement outcomes (Ramey & Ramey, 2000).

School environment   One of the most consistent findings to emerge from the "effective schools" research is the relationship between student achievement levels and classroom management style (Eccles, Wigfield, & Schiefele, 1998; Pianta, La Paro, Payne, Cox, & Bradley, 2002). Not surprisingly, classrooms characterized by orderliness, predictability, and efficiency enhance student achievement, motivation, and behavior. Furthermore, this is a curvilinear relation, in which both too little and too much classroom control are related to poorer academic outcomes (Eccles & Wigfield, 2000).

Specifically, *child-centered* classrooms have been found to be related to teacher reports of social competence in kindergarten children, when researchers control for family income and maternal education (Pianta et al., 2002). Child-centered classrooms are characterized by a positive, supportive emotional tone, an absence of negativity, and opportunities for students to exercise some choice in pursuit of their interests. The National Association for the Education of Young Children's position statement on effective schools for children in the early elementary grades also enumerates these same classroom characteristics (Bredekamp & Copple, 1997).

Each of these factors—children's relationships with parents, teachers, and peers, and the contexts of home and school in which these relationships occur—is believed to be important in children's acquisition and maintenance of the commitment-to-learning assets. However, these kinds of influences are almost certainly bidirectional: Teachers tend to have close relationships with children who are warm and pleasant; stimulating home environments will be more motivating for a child who already gravitates toward enriching stimuli and is curious; and so on. As we consider commitment to learning in the early elementary years, it remains important to think not only about the kinds of relationships and experiences likely to foster a love of learning, but also the ways in which home and school contexts and the child interact together to produce positive outcomes.

Measuring the Commitment-to-Learning Assets in Middle Childhood

Across all three MMW field test sites, the majority of 4th through 6th graders reported experiencing all of the commitment-to-learning assets.

Asset	% Who Report Experiencing Asset		
	Nevada	California	New York
Achievement motivation	74	79	79
Learning engagement	53	54	54
In school	54	56	51
Outside of school	64	65	71
Bonding to adults at school	76	82	81
Homework[a]			
Reading for pleasure	56	54	59

Table 11. Proportion of Field Test 4th–6th Graders Who Report Experiencing the Commitment-to-Learning Assets

From field tests in 2003; N = 1,294.
[a] *Added after field tests.*

Learning engagement was the least commonly reported commitment-to-learning asset, with only about 50% of students saying they were engaged in learning, and reading for pleasure was the next least common, with about 55% reporting it; but about 60%-70% of the students reported each of the remaining assets. Thus, in regard to commitment to learning, most of these young people appear to be motivated to achieve, are engaged in learning *outside* of school, and feel positive emotional connections to adults at school. Engagement in learning *in* school appears to be a weak area, however, with only about 50% reporting that component of the learning-engagement asset.

References

Aram, D., & Levin, I. (2002). Mother-child joint writing and storybook reading: Relations with literacy among low SES kindergartners. *Merrill-Palmer Quarterly, 48*, 202–224.

Baker, J. A. (1998). The social context of school satisfaction among urban, low-income, African-American students. *School Psychology Quarterly, 13*, 25–44.

Baker, J. A. (1999). Teacher-student interaction in urban at-risk classrooms: Differential behavior, relationship quality, and student satisfaction with school. *Elementary School Journal, 100*, 57–70.

Bandura, A., Barbaranelli, C., Caprara, G. V., & Pastorelli, C. (1996). Multifaceted impact of self-efficacy beliefs on academic functioning. *Child Development, 67*, 1206–1222.

Benson, P. L., Roehlkepartain, J. L., & Leffert, N. (1997). *Starting out right: Developmental assets for children.* Minneapolis: Search Institute.

Bradley, R. H., & Corwyn, R. F. (2002). Socioeconomic status and child development. *Annual Review of Psychology, 53*, 371–399.

Brazelton, T. B., & Greenspan, S. I. (2000). *The irreducible needs of children: What every child must have to grow, learn, and flourish.* Cambridge, MA: Perseus.

Bredekamp, S., & Copple, C. (1997). *Developmentally appropriate practice in early childhood programs.* Washington, DC: National Association for the Education of Young Children.

Cattagni, A., & Farris, E. (2001). *Internet access in U.S. public schools and classrooms: 1994–2000* (Statistics in Brief, NCES 2001-071). Washington, DC: National Center for Education Statistics.

Christenson, S. L., Rounds, T., & Gorney, D. (1992). Family factors and student achievement: An avenue to increase student's success. *School Psychology Quarterly, 7*, 178–206.

Clarke-Stewart, K. A. (1998). Reading with children. *Journal of Applied Developmental Psychology, 19*, 1–14.

Clifford, M. M. (1988). Failure tolerance and academic risk-taking in ten- to-twelve-year-old students. *British Journal of Educational Psychology, 58*, 15–27.

Connell, J. P., Spencer, M. B., & Aber, J. L. (1994). Educational risk and resilience in African-American youth: Context, self, action, and outcomes in school. *Child Development, 65*, 493–506.

Cooper, H. (1989). *Homework.* White Plains, NY: Longman.

Cooper, H., Jackson, K., Nye, B., & Lindsay, J. J. (2001). A model of homework's influence on the performance evaluations of elementary school students. *Journal of Experimental Education, 69*, 181–193.

Cooper, H., Lindsay, J. J., Nye, B., & Greathouse, S. (1998). Relationships among attitudes about homework, amount of homework assigned and completed, and student achievement. *Journal of Educational Psychology, 90,* 70–83.

Cooper, H., & Valentine, J. C. (2001). Using research to answer practical questions about homework. *Educational Psychologist, 36,* 143–153.

Donahue, P. L., Voelkl, K. E., Campbell, J. R., & Mazzeo, J. (1999). *Reading: Report card for the nation and the states* (NCES 1999: 500). Washington, DC: U.S. Department of Education, Office of Educational Research and Improvement..

Dubow, E. F., Arnett, M., Smith, K., & Ippolito, M. F. (2001). Predictors of future expectations of inner-city children: A 9-month prospective study. *Journal of Early Adolescence, 21,* 5–28.

Duran, R. T., & Gauvain, M. (1993). The role of age versus expertise in peer collaboration during joint planning. *Journal of Experimental Child Psychology, 55,* 227–242.

Eccles, J. S., Roeser, R., Wigfield, A., & Freedman-Doan, C. (1999). Academic and motivational pathways through middle childhood. In L. Balter & C. S. Tamis-LeMonda (Eds.), *Child psychology: A handbook of contemporary issues* (pp. 287–317). Philadelphia: Psychology Press.

Eccles, J. S., & Wigfield, A. (2000). Schooling's influences on motivation and achievement. In S. Danziger & J. Waldfogel (Eds.), *Securing the future: Investing in children from birth to college—The Ford Foundation series in asset building* (pp. 153–181). New York: Russell Sage Foundation.

Eccles, J., Wigfield, A., Harold, R. D., & Blumenfeld, P. (1993). Age and gender differences in children's self- and task perceptions during elementary school. *Child Development, 64,* 830–847.

Eccles, J. S., Wigfield, A., & Schiefele, U. (1998). Motivation to succeed. In W. Damon (Series Ed.) & N. Eisenberg (Vol. Ed.), *Handbook of Child Psychology: Vol. 3. Social, emotional, and personality development* (5th ed., pp. 1017–1095). New York: John Wiley & Sons.

Ferenga, S. J., & Joyce, B. A. (1998). Science-related attitudes and science course selection: A study of high-ability boys and girls. *Roeper Review, 20,* 247–251.

Finn, J. D. (1989). Withdrawing from school. *Review of Educational Research, 59,* 117–142.

Gottfried, A. E. (1990). Academic intrinsic motivation in young elementary school children. *Journal of Educational Psychology, 82,* 525–538.

Gottfried, A. E., Fleming, J. S., & Gottfried, A. W. (1998). Role of cognitively stimulating home environment in children's academic intrinsic motivation: A longitudinal study. *Child Development, 69,* 1448–1460.

Gottfried, A. E., Fleming, J. S., & Gottfried, A. W. (2001). Continuity of academic intrinsic motivation from childhood through late adolescence: A longitudinal study. *Journal of Educational Psychology, 93,* 3–13.

Griffith, J. (1997). Student and parent perceptions of school social environment: Are they group based? *Elementary School Journal, 98,* 135–150.

Griffith, J. (2000). School climate as group evaluation and group consensus: Student and parent perceptions of the elementary school environment. *Elementary School Journal, 101,* 35–61.

Griffith, J. (2002). A multilevel analysis of the relation of school learning and social environments to minority achievement in public elementary schools. *Elementary School Journal, 102,* 349–442.

Guay, G., Boggiano, A. K., & Vallerand, R. J. (2001). Autonomy support, intrinsic motivation, and perceived competence: Conceptual and empirical linkages. *Personality and Social Psychology Bulletin, 27,* 643–650.

Guo, J., Hawkins, J. D., Hill, K. D., & Abbott, R. D. (2001). Childhood and adolescent predictors of alcohol abuse and dependence in young adulthood. *Journal of Studies on Alcohol, 62,* 754–802.

Gutman, L. M., & Midgley, C. (2000). The role of protective factors in supporting the academic achievement of poor African American students during the transition to middle school. *Journal of Youth and Adolescence, 29,* 223–248.

Hamre, B. K., & Pianta, R. C. (2001). Early teacher-child relationships and the trajectory of children's school outcomes through eighth grade. *Child Development, 72,* 625–638.

Hart, B. M., & Risley, T. R. (1995). *Meaningful differences in the everyday experience of young American children.* Baltimore, MD: Paul H. Brookes.

Hofferth, S. L., & Sandberg, J. F. (2001). How American children spend their time. *Journal of Marriage and Family, 63,* 295–308.

Hughes, J. N., Cavell, T. A., & Jackson, T. (1999). Influence of teacher-student relationship on child conduct problems: A prospective study. *Journal of Clinical Child Psychology, 28,* 173–184.

Hull, G., & Schultz, K. (2001). Literacy and learning out of school: A review of theory and research. *Review of Educational Research, 71,* 575–611.

Jacobs, J. E., Lanza, S., Osgood, D. W., Eccles, J. S., & Wigfield, A. (2002). Changes in children's self-competence and values: Gender and domain differences across grades one through twelve. *Child Development, 73,* 509–527.

Jimerson, S., Egeland, B., & Teo, A. (1999). A longitudinal study of achievement trajectories: Factors associated with change. *Journal of Educational Psychology, 91,* 116–126.

Joyce, B. A., & Ferenga, S. J. (1999). Informal science experience, attitudes, future interest in science, and gender of high-ability students: An exploratory study. *School Science and Mathematics, 99,* 431–437.

Kindermann, T. A. (1993). Natural peer groups as contexts for individual development: The case of children's motivation in school. *Developmental Psychology, 29,* 970–977.

Korpan, C. A., Bisanz, G. L., Bisanz, J., Boehme, C., & Lynch, M. A. (1998). What did you learn outside school today? Using structured interviews to document home and community activities related to science and technology. *Science Education, 81,* 651–662.

Kowaleski-Jones, L., & Duncan, G. J. (1999). The structure of achievement and behavior across middle childhood. *Child Development, 70,* 930–943.

Kurdek, L. A., & Sinclair, R. J. (2000). Psychological, family, and peer predictors of academic outcomes in first- through fifth-grade children. *Journal of Educational Psychology, 92,* 449–457.

Ladd, G. W. (1990). Having friends, keeping friends, making friends, and being liked by peers in the classroom: Predictors of children's early school adjustment? *Child Development, 61,* 1081–1100.

Leondari, A., & Gialamas, V. (2002). Implicit theories, goal orientations, and perceived competence: Impact on students' achievement behavior. *Psychology in the Schools, 39,* 279–291.

Leone, C. M., & Richards, M. H. (1989). Classwork and homework in early adolescence: The ecology of achievement. *Journal of Youth and Adolescence, 18,* 531–548.

Lonczak, H. S., Abbott, R. D., Hawkins, J. D., Kosterman, R., & Catalano, R. F. (2002). Effects of the Seattle Social Development Project on sexual behavior, pregnancy, birth, and sexually transmitted disease outcomes by age 21 years. *Archives of Pediatric and Adolescent Medicine, 156,* 438–447.

Malecki, C. K., & Elliott, S. N. (2002). Children's social behaviors as predictors of academic achievement: A longitudinal analysis. *School Psychology Quarterly, 17*, 1–23.

Marks, H. M. (2000). Student engagement in instructional activity: Patterns in the elementary, middle, and high school years. *American Educational Research Journal, 37*, 153–184.

Marsh, H. W. (1989). Age and sex effects in multiple dimensions of self-concept: Preadolescence to early adulthood. *Journal of Educational Psychology, 81*, 417–430.

Mattanah, J. F. (2001). Parental psychological autonomy and children's academic competence and behavioral adjustment in late childhood: More than just limit-setting and warmth. *Merrill-Palmer Quarterly, 47*, 355–376.

Miller, D. L., & Kelley, M. L. (1991). Interventions for improving homework performance: A critical review. *School Psychology Quarterly, 6*, 174–185.

Miserandino, M. (1996). Children who do well in school: Individual differences in perceived competence and autonomy in above-average children. *Journal of Educational Psychology, 88*, 203–214.

Murray, C., & Greenberg, M. T. (2000). Children's relationship with teachers and bonds with school: An investigation of patterns and correlates in middle childhood. *Journal of School Psychology, 38*, 423–445.

Nettles, S. M. (1991). Community involvement and disadvantaged students: A review. *Review of Educational Psychology, 61*, 379–406.

Okagaki, L. (2001). Triarchic model of minority children's school achievement. *Educational Psychologist, 36*, 9–20.

Osterman, K. F. (2000). Students' need for belonging in the school community. *Review of Educational Research, 70*, 323–368.

Patrick, B. C., Skinner, E. A., & Connell, J. P. (1993). What motivates children's behavior and emotion? Joint effects of perceived control and autonomy in the academic domain. *Journal of Personality and Social Psychology, 65*, 781–791.

Peet, S. H., Powell, D. R., & O'Donnel, B. (1997). Mother-teacher congruence in perceptions of the child's competence and school engagement: Links to academic achievement. *Journal of Applied Developmental Psychology, 18*, 373–393.

Pianta, R. C., La Paro, K. M., Payne, C., Cox, M. J., & Bradley, R. (2002). The relation of kindergarten classroom environment to teacher, family, and school characteristics and child outcomes. *Elementary School Journal, 102*, 225–238.

Pomerantz, E. M., Altermatt, E. R., & Saxon, J. L. (2002). Making the grade but feeling distressed: Gender differences in academic performance and internal distress. *Journal of Educational Psychology, 94*, 396–404.

Posner, D. K., & Vandell, D. L. (1994). Low-income children's after school care: Are there beneficial effects of after-school programs. *Child Development, 65*, 440.

Ramey, C. T., & Ramey, S. L. (1998). Early intervention and early experience. *American Psychologist, 53*, 109–120.

Ramey, S. L., & Ramey, C. T. (1992). Early educational intervention with disadvantaged children: To what effect? *Applied and Preventive Psychology, 1*, 131–140.

Ramey, S. L., & Ramey, C. T. (2000). Early childhood experiences and developmental competence. In S. Danziger & J. Waldfogel (Eds.), *Securing the future: Investing in children from birth to college* (pp. 122–150). New York: Sage Foundation.

Ramey-Gassert, L. (1997). Learning science beyond the classroom. *Elementary School Journal, 97*, 433–450.

Roeser, R. W., Eccles, J. S., & Sameroff, A. J. (2000). School as a context of early adolescents' academic and social-emotional development: A summary of research findings. *Elementary School Journal, 100,* 443–471.

Rogoff, B. (1998). Cognition as a collaborative process. In W. Damon (Series Ed.) & D. Kuhn & R. S. Siegler (Vol. Eds.), *Handbook of Child Psychology: Vol. 2. Cognition, perception, and language* (5th ed., pp. 679–744). New York: John Wiley & Sons.

Ryan, A. M., Hicks, L., & Midgley, C. (1997). Social goals, academic goals, and avoiding seeking help in the classroom. *Journal of Early Adolescence, 17,* 152–171.

Samdal, O., Nutbeam, D., Wold, B., & Kannas, L. (1998). Achieving health and educational goals through schools: A study of school climate and students' satisfaction with school. *Health Education Research, 13,* 383–397.

Scales, P. C., & Leffert, N. (1999). *Developmental assets: A synthesis of the scientific research on adolescent development.* Minneapolis: Search Institute.

Sènèchal, M., & LeFevre, J. (2002). Parental involvement in the development of children's reading skill: A five-year longitudinal study. *Child Development, 73,* 445–460.

Shiner, R. L. (2000). Linking childhood personality with adaptation: Evidence for continuity and change across time into late adolescence. *Journal of Personality and Social Psychology, 78,* 310–325.

Shonkoff, J. P., & Phillips, D. A. (Eds.). (2000). *From neurons to neighborhoods: The science of early childhood development.* Washington, DC: National Academies Press.

Skinner, E. A. (1990). Age differences in the dimensions of perceived control during middle childhood: Implications for developmental conceptualizations and research. *Child Development, 61,* 1882–1890.

Skinner, E. A., & Belmont, M. J. (1993). Motivation in the classroom: Reciprocal effects of teacher behavior and student engagement across the school year. *Journal of Educational Psychology, 85,* 571–581.

Skinner, E. A., Wellborn, J. G., & Connell, J. P. (1990). What it takes to do well in school and whether I've got it: The role of perceived control in children's engagement and school achievement. *Journal of Educational Psychology, 82,* 22–32.

Smith, J. R., Brooks-Gunn, J., & Klebanov, P. K. (1997). Consequences of living in poverty for young children's cognitive and verbal ability and early school achievement. In G. J. Duncan & J. Brooks-Gunn (Eds.), *Consequences of growing up poor* (pp. 132–189). New York: Sage Foundation.

Stetsenko, A., Little, T. D., Gordeeva, T., Grasshof, M., & Oettingen, G. (2000). Gender effects in children's beliefs about school performance: A cross-cultural study. *Child Development, 71,* 517–527.

Taylor, B. M., Frye, B. J., & Maruyama, G. M. (1990). Time spent reading and reading growth. *American Educational Research Journal, 27,* 351–362.

Thorkildsen, T. A., & Nicholls, J. G. (1998). Fifth graders' achievement orientations and beliefs: Individual and classroom differences. *Journal of Educational Psychology, 90,* 179–201.

Tucker, C. M., Zayco, R. A., Herman, K. C., Reinke, W. M., Trujillo, M., Carraway, K., Wallack, C., & Ivery, P. D. (2002). Teacher and child variables as predictors of academic engagement among African American children. *Psychology in the Schools, 39,* 477–488.

Valeski, T. N., & Stipek, D. J. (2001). Young children's feelings about school. *Child Development, 72,* 1198–1213.

Vartuli, S. (1999). How early childhood teacher beliefs vary across grade level. *Early Childhood Research Quarterly, 14,* 489–514.

Vygotsky, L. S. (1978). *Mind in society: The development of higher psychological processes.* Cambridge, MA: Harvard University Press.

Wang, M. C., Haertel, G. D., & Walberg, H. J. (1990). What influences learning? A content analysis of review literature. *Journal of Educational Research, 84,* 30–43.

Warton, P. M. (2001). The forgotten voices in homework: Views of students. *Educational Psychologist, 36,* 155–165.

Wentzel, K. R. (1993). Motivation and achievement in early adolescence: The role of multiple classroom goals. *Journal of Early Adolescence, 13,* 4–20.

Wigfield, A. (1994). Expectancy-value theory of achievement motivation: A developmental perspective. *Educational Psychology Review, 6,* 49–78.

Wigfield, A., Eccles, J. S., & Rodriguez, D. (1998). The development of children's motivation in school contexts. *Review of Research in Education, 23,* 73–118.

Wigfield, A., Eccles, J. S., Yoon, K. S., Harold, R. D., Arbreton, A. J. A., Freedman-Doan, C., & Blumenfeld, P. C. (1997). Change in children's competence beliefs and subjective task values across the elementary school years: A 3-year study. *Journal of Educational Psychology, 89,* 451–469.

Wigfield, A., & Guthrie, J. T. (1997). Relations of children's motivation for reading and the amount and breadth of their reading. *Journal of Educational Psychology, 89,* 420–432.

Positive values learned in the family and elsewhere eventually become deep commitments that guide how young people think and act.

6

The Positive-Values Assets

Why Are Positive Values Important?

The values children learn as they grow up form the center of their moral being. If one of the fundamental processes of human development is the gradual expansion of the child's ability to regulate her- or himself, it is essential that the child assimilate *positive values* in order to ensure that self-regulation is not merely selfish. That is, a truly "thriving" person makes choices and acts in ways that not only meet her or his needs but also promote the well-being of others and contribute to the numerous ecologies to which the person belongs (e.g., family, neighborhood, social groups, and wider community) (Lerner, Brentano, Dowling, & Anderson, 2002). The positive-values asset category reflects a number of principles that guide individuals as they balance the dual goals of enhancing their personal growth and contributing to the positive development of their environment.

Our focus in regard to the positive-values assets in middle childhood is on whether children perceive that their parents teach them the importance of various values, not on whether children "have" these values. Of course, children in these years clearly demonstrate their evolving values. Children share their snacks or toys or do not. They join in teasing someone or do not, or even ask other children to stop. They admit responsibility for a misdeed or they blame someone or something else. There is no question that these behaviors are evidence of value *development*.

But these value-demonstrating behaviors are not necessarily consistent in the middle childhood years. The altruistic child one day or in one situation might not be so giving the next day or in even slightly different circumstances, and hence in our way of thinking does not yet "have" that value. We can think of this gradual development in much the same way as other talents develop for most people. For example, in singing, one might "hit" a beautiful high or low note out of one's vocal range now and then. But a singer does not "have" that note unless he or she can sing the note reliably, nearly all the time that he or she is faced with singing it.

Similarly, the cognitive-moral development of upper-elementary-age children is not yet stabilized or internalized sufficiently in order for them to report reliably that a value is "theirs," in the sense that the value provides a steady beacon consistently guiding their decision making across a variety of situations. Walker, Henning, and Krettenauer (2000), for example, reported evidence that considerable changes occur in children's levels of moral reasoning from grade 5 through grade 10. Wainryb (2000) also concluded that the more complex aspects of moral reasoning, such as understanding that people can draw differing moral interpretations from the same experience, are not fully developed until late adolescence.

The Positive-Values Assets

The asset category of positive values is another example of the themes of developmental continuity and stage uniqueness, and of assets for which we have suggested a slight change in emphasis on the basis of developmental stage. The formation and subsequent reshaping of a personal value system constitute a process one can argue continues throughout life. This process is not limited to a particular stage of development, nor is it likely to be widely debated whether children in the elementary school years ought to acquire values such as honesty, responsibility, and integrity. Families, schools, religious congregations, youth programs, peers, and media certainly are among the formative influences, intentionally or unintentionally, on children's growing sense of such values.

To what degree are children in middle childhood equipped developmentally to "have" core values in the same sense we mean when we say adolescents or adults have personal values that act as internal, self-regulating sets of principles to guide their behavior? Some 4th and 5th graders may indeed internalize some of those values, at least in certain circumstances. However, the research on cognitive moral development suggests that stage uniqueness enters the picture here as well. For many young people, it may not be until they have passed through the middle school years, or early adolescence, that they can be said to truly "have" a core set of personal values that begin to act reliably and regularly as internal compasses (see review in Scales & Leffert, 1999).

Some young people in the middle childhood years may indeed "have" these positive values. But for most, perhaps a better way to think of these assets is to ask whether the child's *family* is laying the groundwork for the eventual personal ownership of a value system by actively teaching them the importance of personal values. This was the frame of reference articulated for early childhood in *Starting Out Right* (Leffert, Benson, & Roehlkepartain, 1997), and although the issue is certainly debatable, we believe there is merit in extending that view to middle childhood. Thus, we do define the positive values in middle childhood by whether children say their parents tell them how important these values are, not by whether children say they "have" them.

Schools, congregations, peers, media, neighborhood adults, and other influences certainly also shape children's developing value system. All those sources have a role and some responsibility to help promote the positive values we enumerate. But the literature we review throughout this book suggests the primary importance of parents and primary caregivers for children's acquisition of core values.

Progression in stages of moral thinking, a process fundamental to value development, also is related strongly and positively to age in studies of children. For example, Helwig and Jasiobedzka (2001) reported that 10-year-olds were more likely than 6-year-olds to think positively about socially beneficial laws (such as those requiring vaccinations) and about the government's role in making sure those things happen. In several situations, 10-year-olds were also more likely than 6-year-olds to invoke fairness or equality when describing their reasoning for holding a particular viewpoint (as were 8-year-olds in one situation).

In a study of 113 young people ages 9–20, Lamborn, Fischer, and Pipp (1994) found that 9- to 12-year-olds, those closest to the age level we define as middle childhood, could explain only under conditions of high support (probing, guiding) how the values of honesty and kindness can both be present and interact when one offers constructive criticism. Even among the 16- to 20-year-olds surveyed, only a minority of young people understood how simultaneously praising a friend's strengths and criticizing her weaknesses could be done for kind reasons, such as to help the friend improve herself. Yet under conditions of high support, and with practice, children studied at all age levels could reason more abstractly about these values. In addition, understandings about honesty and kindness affected children's prosocial problem solving (e.g., scenarios involving friends), but not problem solving in nonsocial scenarios. Together, these findings suggest that children's understanding and use of values as their behavioral guides vary, independently of age, as a function of the type of situation, how much support they have in clarifying the role of values in that situation, and how much practice they have had with similar situations.

Damon (1994) also reported a study of "positive justice" among 4- to 8-year-olds. Positive justice concerns the distribution of material and emotional rewards in society. Children's positive justice choices range from a primitive focus on the choice itself, without giving a reason ("I want it, so I should get it") to notions of who deserves justice more because of merit or reciprocity ("payback"). At higher levels of moral reasoning, egalitarian views are common ("All should have the same chances"). Children may also evidence what Damon calls a more "benevolent" view, when they assert that some have extra needs or reasons for getting more than their "fair share." This view may reflect children's understanding that certain situations call for attempts to make up for previous inequalities in access to resources. Along this progression of positive justice perspectives, Damon (1994) reported that the correlation coefficient between age and level of "positive justice" was, for social science research, a remarkable .85 (by comparison, the correlation between SAT scores and subsequent college grades is .20 [Meyer et al., 2001]).

A study of 132 children between the ages of 5 and 17 showed that five stages of the conceptualization of conscience were strongly correlated (.78) with age (Stilwell, Galvin, Kopta, & Padgett, 1998). Children ages 7 to 11 were found to be motivated most often by a "morality of mastery." They defined moral self-worth in terms of satisfying external and internal rules or standards, such as "beds made, dogs fed, homework done, music lessons practiced, and bases run" (p. 206).

Of course, developing a high level of positive values or a more advanced stage of moral development is not a simple, linear process. Research suggests there is no single age progression that applies equally well to the mature development of all moral principles or acquisition of all the values in the positive-values category (Warton & Goodnow, 1991). Even in considering one value, such as responsibility, Warton and Goodnow found that, among 3rd, 6th, and 9th graders, several components of that particular value (one is responsible if one causes a situation, one should not have to be reminded of one's responsibility, and one's responsibility is ongoing) emerged at different levels among each age group. Nevertheless, a clearly observable developmental progression took place: Students in grade 3 used simpler moral assertions, those in grade 6 showed evidence of applying moral principles to their reasoning, and those in grade 9 modified the principles of personal responsibility in relationship to other principles (e.g., trust, reciprocity in relationships).

Damon (1994) reported that most children applied not just one stage of moral reasoning to their decision making but instead used a mixture, with more advanced levels of reasoning predominating as they grew older. A longitudinal study of several hundred children in grades 1, 4, 7, and 10 also suggested that moral reasoning for most young people progresses in a cyclical pattern, in which *stages of consolidation* of existing belief systems and moral capabilities alternate with *stages of disequilibrium* and transition to different levels (Walker & Taylor, 1991a). Even in Walker and Taylor's study, however, about one in four young people showed more linear developmental paths in their moral reasoning.

Moreover, Walker, Henning, and Krettenauer (2000) found that both parents and peers contribute, in different ways, to the rate of change in children's moral development. Parents certainly contribute to values acquisition through direct role modeling. For example, Houghton, Carroll, and Odgers (1998) studied exposure to alcohol among a mixed socioeconomic sample of Australian young people that included about 250 elementary students. The authors reported that 75% of the elementary students (and 95% of the older ones) had tried alcohol. Parents, not peers, and usually fathers at that, were primarily responsible for giving children the alcohol.

Parental and peer influence on children's development of values differs also in subtler ways. For example, parents are more likely than peers to use a gentle style of "drawing reasoning out through the use of appropriate probes" (Walker et al., 2000, p. 1045). This approach to moral dialogue consistently predicted higher rates of moral development in children than did approaches featuring more lectures or cognitive challenges. Parents were found to use "representational" styles of discussing moral dilemmas more often with 5th graders than with 10th graders. This style is perhaps a reflection of parents' understanding that younger children derive more benefit from a conflict-free approach in the family setting, where there are considerable differences in power distribution between adults and children.

In an earlier report, Walker and Taylor (1991b) also found that parents generally simplify their reasoning with their children, trying to reason at moral levels only slightly higher than their children's present levels, especially when children are at lower levels of moral development. Such a disparity is conducive to children's moral growth, because it enables parents to help children make the intellectual leap to higher levels of moral understanding. This is yet another example of what Vygotsky (1978) called the "zone of proximal development" (see p. 166), wherein adults help children "stretch" a little further than their current capabilities in a task or skill in order to help them continue growing in their competence at that skill.

Of course, as Grusec, Goodnow, and Kuczynski (2000) noted, most parents do not apply one rigid approach to child rearing. Rather, they employ a variety of strategies that differ depending on numerous factors, including the specific situation, the parents' and child's moods, the child's developmental level, the parent's perspective-taking ability (a component of empathy), and the parent's goal at that particular moment. All these factors contribute to children's acquisition of values, but in differing ways. For example, parents may be appropriately rigid with regard to compliance on certain issues, such as child safety. For other situations, such as those involving manners or social customs, compliance is conditional: Parents may expect it only when the child is in their presence and be less demanding of compliance when they, the parents, are absent. Finally, parents may deem some issues negotiable and may allow or even encourage the child's emergent sense of agency. All these situations affect the mix of values children come to hold, as well as the intensity and comprehensiveness with which those values serve as behavior guides. This is the inevitable outcome of parents' attempts to steer a course between keeping children close and fostering their autonomy.

The positive-values category includes assets that reflect prosocial orientations, such as caring, equality and social justice, honesty, and responsibility, as well as values that more directly promote an individual child's well-being, such as integrity and valuing a healthy lifestyle. Promoting values in middle childhood is important because the evidence, although spotty, does suggest that prosocial tendencies shown by children even as young as 2 years of age may decline in the ensuing years (Hay, 1994). However, not all such declines in prosocial proclivities may be due to a lessening in the *values* thought to contribute to prosocial behavior. Children's personalities, as well as the values to which they have been exposed, may also play important roles in the decline. For example, children whose parents have modeled and exposed them to the value of caring for and helping others may not themselves display such prosocial behaviors if they also happen to be fearful and anxious (Hay, 1994).

Moreover, parents might also model a value such as caring for other people, but may not sufficiently nurture children's appropriate regulation of their emotions. In Eisenberg, Fabes, Schaller, Carlo, and Miller's (1991) study of 3rd and 6th graders, the researchers found that empathy in children—often a key trigger for prosocial behaviors—developed best when mothers restricted hurtful emotional expressions in their daughters and fathers likewise in their sons. In addition, empathy development in boys was related to parental acceptance of moderate levels of emotional expression of feelings not typically hurtful to others, such as sadness or anxiety.

In the literature, considerable attention has been paid to whether parents value a healthy lifestyle and model it for their children. Research has consistently shown that children's valuing a healthy lifestyle is influenced by a multitude of factors, such as a cognitive understanding of healthy behavior, socioeconomic variables, family dynamics, peers, schools, and the media (Tinsley, 1992). Yet, of those factors, parental and familial socialization of preventive health behaviors, in particular, commands the focus of a majority of the studies. Tinsley (1992) conducted a comprehensive overview of research on factors that influence the socialization processes of positive health behaviors and attitudes in children. She concluded that "life-style . . . substantially has its origin in early family life, where health-related behaviors take form in childhood and are nurtured through adulthood" (p. 1,048).

For example, Jackson and Henriksen (1997) conducted a study examining the effects of parental smoking and antismoking practices on the onset of child-hood smoking in a sample of 1,213 children in grades 3 and 5. Regardless of whether parents smoked, the authors found that children who perceived their parents as engaged in antismoking socialization techniques with them (e.g., parents communicated the dangers of smoking, knew if children smoked, set clear rules against and consequences for smoking) were significantly less likely to start smoking than were children who felt their parents did not clearly use antismoking strategies. Although this study also reported that children are sig-nificantly more likely to start smoking at an early age if they have parents who smoke, it suggests that parents can have a profound effect, by their speech as well as by their modeling, on children's internalization of attitudes and values about high-risk behaviors.

Each of the positive-values assets is measured by only one item, except for healthy lifestyle, which is measured with multiple items at a generally accept-able level of internal consistency reliability (see Appendix; in one site the reli-ability was low, at .57, but the other two sites showed reliabilities of .64 and .71).

Further development of each of these values in middle childhood strength-ens the foundation for the flourishing in adolescence of a more dependable and integrated value system that can guide young people through myriad difficult decisions. The one positive-values asset that is phrased somewhat differently for middle childhood than for adolescence is healthy lifestyle. In adolescence, this positive-values asset is called restraint and focuses on adolescents' belief that it is important to avoid sexual intercourse or use alcohol or other drugs while they are still teenagers.

It is even more important for preadolescents to avoid such behaviors, and the healthy-lifestyle asset reflects that concern. But in middle childhood, the meaning of "healthy lifestyle" is broader than setting the stage for avoid-ing sex- or alcohol-related problems. Lessening the chances of unintentional injuries and developing healthy eating habits are also critical parts of physical health in the upper elementary years. In addition, an important contributor to young people dealing effectively and responsibly with sexual issues and choices in adolescence is gaining from parents, schools, religious organizations, and other positive sources in middle childhood an understanding of healthy sexuality. For example, among 4th–6th graders, puberty is in the air: For most, it is just around the corner; for many it has already begun. Upper elementary children are intensely curious, sharply observant of physical and social changes in their peers, and often worried about whether their body development is too fast or too slow. If adolescents are to deal with sexual choices in "caring, respectful, and responsible ways," they need in middle childhood to know that sexual feelings are normal and that it is "important to talk with parents and other trusted adults about sexuality" (Wilson, 1994). Thus, we include parents' valuing an understanding of healthy sexuality as an important component of the healthy-lifestyle asset in middle childhood.

Table 12. The Positive-Values Assets	
Caring	Parent(s) tell the child it is important to help other people.
Equality and social justice	Parent(s) tell the child it is important to speak up for equal rights for all people.
Integrity	Parent(s) tell the child it is important to stand up for one's beliefs.
Honesty	Parent(s) tell the child it is important to tell the truth.
Responsibility	Parent(s) tell the child it is important to accept personal responsibility for behavior.
Healthy lifestyle	Parent(s) tell the child it is important to have good health habits and an understanding of healthy sexuality.

Summary of Research Findings: The Positive-Values Assets in Middle Childhood

Although a wealth of popular books discuss the importance of positive values, and numerous research studies have investigated how values and a moral orientation may develop, few studies actually examine the positive *impact* that such values can have on children's development. For example, Grusec and colleagues (2000) highlight the widely accepted notion that parental contributions (i.e., socialization techniques such as parenting styles and disciplinary practices) are of primary importance to our understanding of the transmission, acquisition, and subsequent internalization of values among children. The authors extended the discussion by proposing conceptual and theoretical refinements of the existing, well-established theory of parental influence. However, they did not suggest an exploration of the beneficial effects that the internalization of values may have on developmental outcomes for children.

A more illustrative example of this gap in the research can be found in Eisenberg and Fabes's (1998) exhaustive review of prosocial development (a concept related to various aspects of the positive-values assets) in the *Handbook of Child Psychology*. Their review is devoted almost entirely to research and methodology involving correlates or factors that influence the development of prosocial values and behavior in children. In these studies, as in many others, positive values are viewed as ends in themselves (i.e., outcomes), rather than as means to an end (i.e., contributing factors to other outcomes).

Moreover, most of the studies available also involve small samples, often far fewer than 100 children, in which an increased likelihood exists that results are excessively affected by design, measurement, and/or sampling error. This scant empirical research into the contribution of various values to developmental outcomes in middle childhood is reminiscent of the similarly limited, research-based knowledge regarding the effects of positive values on adolescent development (see Scales & Leffert, 1999).

Still, some studies do show that children's internalized positive values, as well as their perceptions of their parents as models of the importance of caring, equality, justice, integrity, honesty, responsibility, and a healthy lifestyle, are associated with positive developmental outcomes. Those positive outcomes related to values acquisition include better school behavior, increased social skills, a more positive view of self, and higher academic achievement. Positive values have been associated, directly or indirectly, with:

Academic Outcomes

- **Increased academic achievement** (Bandura, Barbaranelli, Caprara, & Pastorelli, 1996b; Caprara, Barbaranelli, Pastorelli, Bandura, & Zimbardo, 2000); **higher perceived scholastic competence and less worry about school** (Johnson, 1993); and **higher grades** (Wentzel, 1991a [for children in grades 6–8; for review of literature, see Wentzel, 1991b]).

Mental and Behavioral Health Outcomes

- **More positive problem-solving ability** (Lamborn et al., 1994); **fewer problem behaviors in school** (Bandura et al., 1996b); **increased empathic and sympathetic responsiveness** (Eisenberg et al., 1987); **decreased delinquent and aggressive behaviors** (Bandura, Barbaranelli, Caprara, & Pastorelli, 1996a); **more positive**

sense of well-being for African-American children (Moore & Glei, 1995); **higher self-esteem** and **more hopefulness** (Bandura et al., 1996b; Johnson, 1993); **greater engagement with moral issues** (Bandura et al., 1996a); **lower fat-eating patterns and higher consumption of fruits and vegetables** in African American children whose parents model healthful dietary behavior (Tibbs et al., 2001); **decreased early onset rates for childhood smoking** when parents promote an antismoking message (Jackson & Henriksen, 1997 [even if parents smoke]; Jackson, Henriksen, Dickinson, & Levine, 1997); and **reduced risk for early alcohol use and abuse** (Jackson et al., 1997).

Social Outcomes

- **Being socially preferred among peers** in a sample of Italian youth (Bandura et al., 1996b; Caprara et al., 2000); and **better conflict resolution skills for children** in kindergarten through grade 4 participating in a program promoting prosocial development (Battistich, Solomon, Watson, Solomon, & Schaps, 1989).

Among the studies that report on the impact that positive values may have was Miller, Eisenberg, Fabes, and Shell's (1996) small study of 74 4- and 5-year-olds. They found that children who felt sympathy for other children in distress and whose moral reasoning showed high levels of concern for others' needs were more likely than other children to help their peers in a crayon-sorting task. Moral reasoning levels were not related, however, to helping adults in need (offering comfort after a simulated injury), but a number of research method issues may have prevented that association.

In another very small study of 20 children, Eisenberg, Wolchik, Goldberg, and Engel (1992) studied 1- and 2-year-olds, following them until they were 3 and 4 years old. They found that fathers' valuing of prosocial behavior (but not mothers') was related to children's later compliance with peer requests for help. However, overall, a parental focus on child obedience and compliance with requests for helping behaviors was associated with less compliance and more defensiveness later with peers. Despite the small sample size, this study offered an intriguing hint that parents' support and reinforcement of particular values may not necessarily lead to the later emergence of those values, which also depend on the constellation of other parent values and child-rearing practices the child experiences.

If prosocial values do take root, the effects can be significant. Caprara and colleagues (2000) reported in a study of several hundred Italian children that children's prosocial behavior in grade 3 predicted their peer status and school grades in grade 8. To the degree children had been cooperative, helping, sharing, and consoling, they were found later to have better grades and higher social status among peers than were their classmates who had not been as prosocial. In fact, the commonsense relationship often found in research between earlier and later academic performance (in Caprara et al.'s study, between children's 3rd grade and 8th grade academic performances) "disappears" after taking into account the level of children's 3rd-grade prosocial behavior. This finding suggests that prosocial values can contribute to a variety of positive developmental outcomes. The mechanisms may include not only fostering supportive relationships among adults and peers, but also lessening children's depression and aggressive behavior and increasing their sense of self-efficacy.

Of course, beginning to develop, or even "having," prosocial values such as caring or supporting equality and social justice does not ensure the emergence of prosocial *behavior*. Roberts and Strayer (1996) illustrated how social competencies enter this picture in a small study of 73 5-, 9-, and 13-year-olds. The authors found that emotional expressiveness, emotional insight, and the ability to understand the perspective of others were all strongly related to children's levels of empathy. In turn, empathy levels were strongly related to boys' prosocial behaviors, and to girls' prosocial behaviors with their friends (but not with their other peers). These gender differences may have been observed because empathy tends to be more common among girls; thus, its presence among boys may be more important in differentiating some boys from others (Eisenberg & Fabes, 1998).

Gender differences in moral or prosocial orientations have long been reported, perhaps most notably in the work of Gilligan (1984). However, Hay (1994) cautioned that methodological problems have plagued research on gender differences in prosocial orientations. Girls do report more empathy than boys do and are seen as more prosocial by others, but Hay concluded that direct observation studies often fail to find gender differences in prosocial behavior. Smetana, Killen, and Turiel (1991) reported in two small studies of 48 and 76 children respectively, that among 3rd-, 6th-, and 9th-grade boys and girls, notions of "justice" and interpersonal (caring) frameworks for resolving moral conflict situations coexisted, with use of them depending more upon a specific situation than on a child's gender. Regardless of gender, they found that "at least by middle childhood children have formed concepts of justice and rights that they apply to a range of situations" (p. 643).

In another small sample of 72 6-, 8- and 10-year-olds, Helwig and Jasiobedzka (2001) found that even the youngest children applied a mixture of moral concepts such as fairness, rights, prevention of harm, and justice to their determination of whether it was acceptable to break a particular law. No significant gender differences were found. Lourenco (1991) also reported that children did not distinguish "caring" situations from "justice" situations. In a study of 32 Portuguese 10- and 11-year-olds, Lourenco found that even in situations where a caring response is considered morally appropriate, children's hypothetical responses were shaped by their ideas about duties and rights more than by their compassion per se.

The Positive-Values Assets
across the Early Childhood-Adolescence Life Span

Much like the research base for positive values in middle childhood, the empirical scrutiny paid to the effects of positive values in the early primary grades is scant. Certainly, the evanescent qualities of these values in the kindergarten through grade 3 period require less comment on the enduring effects of these values on children's later development, and more discussion on contextual and relational conditions that set the stage for these kinds of values in later childhood and adolescence.

Chase-Lansdale, Wakshlag, and Brooks-Gunn (1995) posit that the following qualities must be present for children to fully develop as caring individuals, and we hypothesize that these are foundational qualities for positive-values assets discussed elsewhere in this chapter: "a secure, autonomous self, trust in others, and confidence in his/her ability to effect change" (p. 518). Voluminous research indicates that family interactions characterized by warm, supportive relationships that are firm but not overcontrolling and that are responsive to children's needs are most consistently related to a host of positive outcomes, including the qualities described in this chapter (Eisenberg & Fabes, 1998; Sroufe, Egeland, & Carlson, 1999).

Although this general description of effective parenting is often cited and discussed, blind adoption of these parenting parameters masks important variations in parent-child relationships. Grusec and colleagues (2000) caution against assuming such a unidirectional model of parenting effects (i.e., authoritative parenting automatically leads to positive outcomes). Important factors such as class, culture, and child characteristics also play an important role in the ways in which parents interact with their children. Grusec and colleagues (2000) propose the need for more complex models of parenting effects on children's values. Included in these models would be a differentiation among kinds of parental warmth (e.g., mutual reciprocity, warmth, sensitivity) and acknowledgment that different kinds of parental warmth may be related to different child outcomes.

Empirical support for the assertion that the development of prosocial behaviors and positive values may come from a variety of sources is seen in Kochanska's research (1995) on conscience development among toddlers, which illustrates the active role that parents as well as children play in the child's acquisition of positive values. Based on observations made when the children were toddlers (approximately 2–3 years of age), Kochanska assessed both the quality of the attachment relationship between the child and the primary caregiver (either secure or insecure attachment) and the level of fearfulness in the child (either fearful or not fearful). Kochanska also assessed parental discipline strategies, defining them along various dimensions of gentle control and guidance, negative control, and power assertion. Kochanska wanted to test the traditional model of parenting, which states that gentle and warm discipline, emphasizing discussion and reasoning, predicts conscience development and internalization of values (Eisenberg & Fabes, 1998), against an alternate parenting model positing conscience development as a function of both parenting style and child factors. Kochanska defined "conscience," or internalization, as toddlers' compliance with mothers' directives during a cleanup task as well as ability to follow orders not to touch a number of attractive items in the testing room.

Kochanska found that for children who were relatively fearful as toddlers, the use of warm and gentle discipline predicted a stronger conscience, at toddler ages as well as a year later. On the other hand, gentle discipline and induction were not related to internalization for toddlers who were relatively fearless, but a secure attachment relationship to the parent was. Her interpretation of these findings was that for fearful children, any mild rebuke by the parent that elicited slight discomfort in the child was sufficient to instill internalization of values. In essence, for fearful children, effective parenting consisted of capitalizing on mild discomfort (all in the context of warm and positive interactions) to foster internalization. For fearless children, though, this kind of interaction was less effective, as these children possessed a certain comfort level with anxiety-provoking situations. Rather, for these children, "a mother-child mutually cooperative, positive, responsive orientation was associated with strong conscience development at toddler and preschool age" (Kochanska & Thompson, 1997, p. 71).

Thus, as we begin thinking about the various experiences and relationships that undergird the development of the positive-values assets, it is also important to understand the role of both child and adult—whether parent, teacher, or neighbor—in fostering these qualities.

Measuring the Positive-Values Assets in Middle Childhood

Results from both our three field tests of MMW in Nevada, California, and New York (see Table 13), as well as from the earlier two pilot studies in Oklahoma, suggest that the great majority of children say their parents tell them of the importance of all these values. The *least* common positive-values asset is equality and social justice, but still, about 70% of the 4th–6th graders in our field test samples say their parents teach them that this value is important.

Two cautions are in order, however, in reflecting on these field test results. First, we did not ask whether they think their parents *have* these values; instead, we asked whether their parents *"tell* me it is important to help other people," *"tell* me it is important to tell the truth, even when it is hard," and so on. Thus, these data do not reflect whether parents actually hold these values, but describe how readily their children can affirm that their parents *speak to or teach them about* the importance of these values. As noted earlier, these items are about the environment parents create in which children are taught these values, but not about whether children "have" the values themselves.

Second, the very high level of affirmation children give that their parents do tell them the importance of these values may reflect a tendency for these children to respond with answers they think are "right" or socially desirable. It is entirely possible that these values are among those as relatively "universal" as values get in American society. Therefore, overwhelming majorities of parents might actually tell their children these values are important. But it is also possible that children understand they are "supposed" to believe these values are

Asset	% Who Report Experiencing Asset		
	Nevada	California	New York
Caring	89	88	88
Equality and social justice	73	67	68
Integrity	90	87	87
Honesty[a]	90	89	86
Responsibility[a]	80	88	85
Healthy lifestyle	82	84	92

Table 13. Proportion of Field Test 4th–6th Graders Who Report Experiencing the Positive-Values Assets

From field tests in 2003; N = 1,294.

[a] *Note.* Honesty and responsibility were divided after field tests. When combined in a single measure, the proportion of 4th–6th graders reporting honesty-responsibility was 81, 89, and 83 in Nevada, California, and New York, respectively, with reliabilities ranging from .74 to .76.

important, and that "good" parents teach their kids these values. We cannot disentangle these possible explanations for the high levels of reported experience of these assets, and so, despite the positive implications, these field test data should be interpreted cautiously.

References

Bandura, A., Barbaranelli, C., Caprara, G. V., & Pastorelli, C. (1996a). Mechanisms of moral disengagement in the exercise of moral agency. *Journal of Personality and Social Psychology, 71,* 364–374.

Bandura, A., Barbaranelli, C., Caprara, G. V., & Pastorelli, C. (1996b). Multifaceted impact of self-efficacy beliefs on academic functioning. *Child Development, 67,* 1206–1222.

Battistich, V., Solomon, D., Watson, M., Solomon, J., & Schaps, E. (1989). Effects of an elementary school program to enhance prosocial behavior on children's cognitive-social problem-solving skills and strategies. *Journal of Applied Developmental Psychology, 10,* 147–169.

Caprara, G. V., Barbaranelli, C., Pastorelli, C., Bandura, A., & Zimbardo, P. (2000). Prosocial foundations of children's academic achievement. *Psychological Science, 11,* 302–306.

Chase-Lansdale, P. L., Wakshlag, L. S., & Brooks-Gunn, J. (1995). A psychological perspective on the development of caring in children and youth: The role of the family. *Journal of Adolescence, 18,* 515–556.

Damon, W. (1994). Fair distribution and sharing: The development of positive justice. In B. Puka (Ed.), *Fundamental research in moral development* (pp. 189–254). New York: Garland.

Eisenberg, N., & Fabes, R. A. (1998). Prosocial development. In W. Damon (Series Ed.) & N. Eisenberg (Vol. Ed.), *Handbook of child psychology: Vol. 3. Social, emotional, and personality development* (5th ed., pp. 701–778). New York: Wiley.

Eisenberg, N., Fabes, R. A., Schaller, M., Carlo, G., & Miller, P. A. (1991). The relations of parental characteristics and practices to children's vicarious emotional responding. *Child Development, 62,* 1393–1408.

Eisenberg, N., Shell, R., Pasternack, J., Lennon, R., Beller, R., & Mathy, R. M. (1987). Prosocial development in middle childhood: A longitudinal study. *Developmental Psychology, 23,* 712–718.

Eisenberg, N., Wolchik, S. A., Goldberg, L., & Engel, I. (1992). Parental values, reinforcement, and young children's prosocial behavior: A longitudinal study. *Journal of Genetic Psychology, 153,* 19–36.

Gilligan, C. (1984). *In a different voice: Psychological theory and women's development.* Cambridge, MA: Harvard University Press.

Grusec, J. E., Goodnow, J. J., & Kuczynski, L. (2000). New directions in analyses of parenting contributions to children's acquisition of values. *Child Development, 71,* 205–211.

Hay, D. F. (1994). Prosocial development. *Journal of Child Psychology and Psychiatry, 35,* 29–71.

Helwig, C. C., & Jasiobedzka, U. (2001). The relation between law and morality: Children's reasoning about socially beneficial and unjust laws. *Child Development, 72,* 1382–1393.

Houghton, S., Carroll, A., & Odgers, P. (1998). Young children, adolescents, and alcohol—Part I: Exploring knowledge and awareness of alcohol and related issues. *Journal of Child and Adolescent Substance Abuse, 7,* 1–29.

Jackson, C., & Henriksen, L. (1997). Do as I say: Parent smoking, antismoking socialization, and smoking onset among children. *Addictive Behaviors, 22,* 107–114.

Jackson, C., Henriksen, L., Dickinson, D., & Levine, D. W. (1997). The early use of alcohol and tobacco: Its relation to children's competence and parents' behavior. *American Journal of Public Health, 87,* 359–364.

Johnson, E. A. (1993, March). *The relationship of self-blame and responsibility attributions and motivations, for schoolwork and conduct, to self-worth and self-perceptions.* Paper presented at the biennial meeting of the Society for Research in Child Development, New Orleans, LA.

Kochanska, G. R. (1995). Children's temperament, mothers' discipline, and security of attachment: Multiple pathways to emerging internalization. *Child Development, 66,* 597–615.

Kochanska, G. R., & Thompson, R. A. (1997). The emergence and development of conscience in toddlerhood and early childhood. In J. E. Grusec & L. Kuczynski (Eds.), *Parenting and children's internalization of values* (pp. 53–77). New York: John Wiley & Sons.

Lamborn, S. D., Fischer, K. W., & Pipp, S. (1994). Constructive criticism and social lies: A developmental sequence for understanding honesty and kindness in social interactions. *Developmental Psychology, 30,* 495–508.

Leffert, N., Benson, P. L., & Roehlkepartain, J. L. (1997). *Starting out right: Developmental assets for children.* Minneapolis: Search Institute.

Lerner, R. M., Brentano, C., Dowling, E. M., & Anderson, P. M. (2002). Positive youth development: Thriving as the basis of personhood and civil society. In R. M. Lerner, C. S. Taylor, & A. von Eye (Eds.), *New directions for youth development: No. 95. Pathways to positive development among diverse youth* (pp. 11–13). San Francisco: Jossey-Bass.

Lourenco, O. M. (1991). Is the care orientation distinct from the justice orientation? Some empirical data in ten- to eleven-year-old children. *Archives de Psychologie, 59,* 17–30.

Meyer, G. J., Finn, S. E., Eyde, L. D., Kay, G. G., Moreland, K. L., Dies, R. R., Eisman, E. J., Kubiszyn, T. W., & Reed, G. M. (2001). Psychological testing and psychological assessment: A review of evidence and issues. *American Psychologist, 56,* 128–165.

Miller, P. A., Eisenberg, N., Fabes, R. A., & Shell, R. (1996). Relations of moral reasoning and vicarious emotion to young children's prosocial behavior toward peers and adults. *Developmental Psychology, 32,* 210–219.

Moore, K. A., & Glei, D. (1995). Taking the plunge: An examination of positive youth development. *Journal of Adolescent Research, 10,* 15–40.

Roberts, W., & Strayer, J. (1996). Empathy, emotional expressiveness, and prosocial behavior. *Child Development, 67,* 449–470.

Scales, P. C., & Leffert, N. (1999). *Developmental assets: A synthesis of the scientific research on adolescent development.* Minneapolis: Search Institute.

Smetana, J. G., Killen, M., & Turiel, E. (1991). Children's reasoning about interpersonal and moral conflicts. *Child Development, 62,* 629–644.

Sroufe, L. A., Egeland, B., & Carlson, E. A. (1999). One social world: The integrated development of parent-child and peer relationships. In W. A. Collins & B. Laursen (Eds.), *The Minnesota symposium on child psychology: Vol. 30. Relationships as developmental context* (pp. 241–262). Hillsdale, NJ: Lawrence Erlbaum.

Stilwell, B. M., Galvin, M. R., Kopta, S. M., & Padgett, R. J. (1998). Moral volition: The fifth and final domain leading to an integrated theory of conscience understanding. *Journal of the American Academy of Child and Adolescent Psychiatry, 37,* 202–210.

Tibbs, T., Haire-Joshu, D., Schechtman, K. B., Brownson, R. C., Nanney, M. S., Houston, C.,

& Auslander, W. (2001). The relationship between parental modeling, eating patterns, and dietary intake among African-American parents. *Journal of the American Dietetic Association, 101*, 535–541.

Tinsley, B. J. (1992). Multiple influences on the acquisition and socialization of children's health attitudes and behavior: An integrative review. *Child Development, 63*, 1043–1069.

Vygotsky, L. S. (1978). *Mind in society: The development of higher psychological processes.* Cambridge, MA: Harvard University Press.

Wainryb, C. (2000). Values and truths: The making and judging of moral decisions. *New Directions in Child and Adolescent Development, 89*, 33–46.

Walker, L. J., Henning, K. H., & Krettenauer, T. (2000). Parent and peer contexts for children's moral reasoning development. *Child Development, 71*, 1033–1048.

Walker, L. J., & Taylor, J. H. (1991a). Stage transitions in moral reasoning: A longitudinal study of developmental processes. *Developmental Psychology, 27*, 330–337.

Walker, L. J., & Taylor, J. H. (1991b). Family interactions and the development of moral reasoning. *Child Development, 62*, 264–283.

Warton, P. M., & Goodnow, J. J. (1991). The nature of responsibility: Children's understanding of "your job." *Child Development, 62*, 156–165.

Wentzel, K. R. (1991a). Relations between social competence and academic achievement in early adolescence. *Child Development, 62*, 1066–1078.

Wentzel, K. R. (1991b). Social competence at school: Relations between social responsibility and academic achievement. *Review of Educational Research, 61*, 1–24.

Wilson, P. M. (1994). Sexuality education in the upper elementary classroom. In J.C. Drolet & K. Clark (Eds.), *The sexuality education challenge: Promoting healthy sexuality in young people* (pp. 123–136). Santa Cruz, CA: ETR Associates.

Social competencies are the skills young people need to develop satisfying relationships with others, deal with new and challenging situations, and sharpen their decision-making capacities.

7

The Social-Competencies Assets

Why Are Social Competencies Important?

One of the hallmarks of middle childhood is the expansion of children's opportunities for developing effective relationships with adults and peers. Children's competence in forging these relationships emerges as a central aspect of positive development in middle childhood. John (2001) defines social competence as "the ability to function appropriately in interpersonal interactions" (p. 182).

Among the developments that heighten the importance of social competencies in the middle childhood years are children's greater independence from direct parental supervision and their exposure to larger numbers of adults and peers, especially those who may differ from the child in race, ethnicity, religious background, ability, socioeconomic status, and other characteristics. In addition, more chances arise for children to contribute to decisions about how they spend their time, and the need increases for children to manage interpersonal situations involving frustration, disappointment, moral dilemmas, and conflict.

Social competence—particularly operationalized as social success with peers—is seen as one of the three primary, distinct dimensions of competence in middle childhood, along with academic competence and conduct (Masten et al., 1995). Although distinct, the three dimensions are also moderately interconnected, as this chapter illustrates.

A variety of factors affect children's levels of social competence, including temperament and personality, the given social situation, cognitive and emotional developmental stage, and developmental history of social interactions, beginning with parents and primary caregivers. A number of studies report that children's social adjustment is predicted by effective parenting; parenting practices are themselves affected by other factors that indirectly affect social functioning.

For example, the neighborhood a family lives in, the quality of the parents' marital/partner relationship, poor parental mental health, stress, the number of siblings a child has, and the family's economic well-being all have been associated with effects on parenting practices (O'Connor, 2002). In one study, Mistry, Vandewater, Huston, and McLoyd (2002) examined social adjustment among a sample of more than 400 African American and Hispanic children, ages 5 through 12, whose mothers were, for the most part, single parents. Due to the association of single parenting with lower economic status, this sample was characterized by high overall levels of economic distress. But even in such samples, some families are relatively better off than others. Those mothers who reported *relatively lower* levels of economic well-being had children whose teachers rated the children as less well adjusted socially and more engaged in behavior problems. The research demonstrated that the path of influence of lower economic status on child social adjustment was likely a result of those parents' less capable disciplinary behavior and fewer displays of affection with their children.

Of course, lower income does not always contribute to parental ineffectiveness any more than higher income assures high-quality parenting. In another study of urban, predominantly African American children 8 to 12 years old, Plybon and Kliewer (2001) found that children who were from the most impoverished neighborhoods but whose families were cohesive and supportive had fewer behavior problems than peers in the same neighborhoods but who experienced less cohesive and supportive parenting. In fact, the level of behavior problems shown by low-income children with positive parenting was similar to the levels of problem behavior shown by children in high-income neighborhoods who also experienced positive parenting.

Just as effective parenting predicts social competence, abusive parenting predicts the opposite. Following a sample population from childhood through adolescence, Bolger and Patterson (2001) found that young people who experienced early and chronic parental maltreatment showed more aggressive behavior toward their peers, resulting in repeated rejection by their peers throughout those years. These behavior patterns were established as early as grades 2 to 4 and remained stable through early adolescence (grades 6 through 8). Similarly, the impact of mother's depression on early childhood development has been widely studied and found repeatedly to be related to children's poorer behavioral and cognitive competence, patterns that become very stable over time (Krishnakumar & Black, 2002).

Children in the upper elementary years who demonstrate competence in a variety of social skills ranging from planning and decision making to empathy and positive self-control enjoy numerous positive outcomes. Among those positive outcomes are more satisfying, supportive peer and adult relationships, greater connection to institutions such as schools, better academic achievement, and less loneliness or depression than is experienced by peers who are less socially skilled.

Many of these relationships are doubtless reciprocal, conferring on fortunate children the circular benefits of the social-competencies assets leading to positive outcomes, which in turn lead to further strengthening of the assets, and so on. For example, in a study of even younger children in grades 1 and 2, Meisel (1989) found that school achievement was strongly related to teacher and peer ratings of social competence. It may be that children who already excel at achievement (i.e., school's central expectation) benefit from their academic performances in terms of peer acceptance, which in turn reinforces their socially competent behaviors.

A study of 163 children followed from grade 1 through grade 3 supports this reasoning about the reciprocal effects of achievement, peer acceptance, and social competence. Walsh, Parke, Widaman, and O'Neil (2001) reported that academic achievement in grade 1 directly contributed to teacher- and peer-rated social competence in grade 2. The same findings were reported for children in the period from grade 2 through grade 3. In addition, social competence in grade 2 predicted academic achievement in grade 3.

These relations appear to operate at least through elementary school, but may reverse in a negative manner by adolescence. For example, in a longitudinal study (Prinstein & LaGreca, 2002), adolescents who described their peer crowd as "brains," rather than as "populars," "jocks," or another label, were less likely in middle childhood to be lonely or depressed; they also had less social anxiety and higher self-esteem. The "brains," however, were the only adolescent group whose self-esteem decreased significantly across the transition to adolescence.

Conversely, social isolation, shyness, and withdrawal seem to have less significant effects on children at younger ages, but, during middle childhood, these same conditions have been found to be associated with both greater anxiety and lesser feelings of global self-worth (Fordham & Stevenson-Hinde, 1999).

This probably occurs because group relations among peers become much more developmentally important in middle childhood, and a relative lack of positive interactions in such peer groups may reduce children's ability to develop a variety of emotional and cognitive skills.

Children's social competence involves a combination of cognitive and affective skills, such as their ability to send messages effectively, to accurately understand and decode signals or cues from others' messages and expressions of emotions, and to effectively regulate their own emotional responses in social relationships. A considerable proportion of overall social competence may be related to this type of "emotional intelligence" (Goleman, 1995). For example, a number of studies have reported that aggressive children tend mistakenly to attribute hostile intent to their peers in ambiguous situations (Ladd, 1999). Unless the verbal and nonverbal signals sent to them are exceptionally clear, less socially competent children misread them and assume that their peers are being mean-spirited. They then respond with aggressive behavior and set in motion a cycle that can lead to repeated and consistent rejection by peers.

Of course, aggression is not per se a sign of incompetent social behavior, nor does it guarantee rejection, at least among boys. In a study of 450 White and African American boys in grades 4 through 6, Rodkin, Farmer, Pearl, and Van Acker (2000) showed that highly aggressive boys had the ability to be among the most popular and socially connected children in school, rivaling the well-behaved "model" boys in popularity. However, this phenomenon occurred only if the "tough" or aggressive boys were also perceived as "cool," athletic, not shy, reasonably friendly, and academically competent. In other words, his other personal attributes defined the context in which an aggressive boy was either popular or rejected.

Social competence is not a static ability that children either do or do not "have." Halberstadt, Denham, and Dunsmore (2001) use the metaphor of a pinwheel in motion to describe a child's developing social competence. "There is no one source of wind, nor is there one force tilting or turning the pinwheel; the child and his or her social partners, and the contexts in which they interact, give the pinwheel its unique impetus at any given time" (p. 87). Nevertheless, a child's temperament and early experiences do contribute to patterns of social competence that show some stability over time.

With the exception of a greater importance given to athletic and academic competence by older children, popular and unpopular children alike are distinguished in *both* early and middle childhood by the presence or absence of qualities such as friendliness, helpfulness, aggressiveness, and disruptiveness (Hartup, 1999). Similarly, preschool temperament has been shown to significantly predict aspects of personality in middle childhood. Hagekull and Bohlin (1998) reported a longitudinal study of Swedish children in which they found that extroversion and agreeableness (the latter including such descriptors of prosocial orientation as cooperativeness, sensitivity, trust, and unselfishness) in middle childhood were predicted by preschool levels of activity, shyness, and impulsivity. Active children who were low in shyness in the preschool years were more extroverted in middle childhood, and children low in both activity and impulsivity, but higher in shyness, were more agreeable in middle childhood. How these constellations of early temperament and later personality affect children's social competencies varies with the individual child and her or his middle childhood context, but that they impact social competencies is clear.

Positive self-control is an important element of social competence. Eisenberg and colleagues (1997) reported in a study of children in kindergarten through 3rd grade that children who were better able to regulate their emotions were more resilient and viewed by teachers and peers as more socially appropriate and likeable. Behavioral regulation was also important, but primarily so for children who tended to react with intense, negative emotions such as anger or anxiety. When children high in negative emotionality were able to control their behavior, they were regarded as more socially appropriate and gained higher social status.

Because children shape their environments as well as react to them, they may also become increasingly effective in their social interactions by understanding the emotions they are likely to experience in a given situation and subsequently trying either to minimize or maximize their participation in that situation (Eisenberg, 2001). For example, during competitive sports, a 4th grader may become withdrawn because he or she does not like the competitive nature of the activity. As a child's understanding of this reaction grows, he or she may increasingly select activities and friends that make competitive sports play less likely for that child.

Rydell, Hagekull, and Bohlin (1997) conducted a study of 121 Swedish children in grades 1–3, their parents, and their teachers. The authors reported that children's social competence was reflected by two overall factors, prosocial orientation and social initiative, as derived from teacher ratings. Prosocial orientation captured personality qualities such as generosity, empathy, understanding of others, conflict resolution, and helpfulness. Teachers rated social initiative on the basis of the extent to which children took the initiative in social interactions, for example, by being leaders in play activities as opposed to withdrawing from social interactions. Each of the measured factors discriminated between popular and rejected children, and each related to observations of children's positive peer behavior in school. Even though rejected children may have friends of their own, those relationships are typically not as supportive as are the friendships of socially competent children; they seem to offer less personal validation, effective conflict resolution, and help than do the friendships of competent children (Ladd, 1999).

Even though the Rydell and associates (1997) study involved children in grades 1–3, its relevance for middle childhood lies in how these earlier patterns of greater or lesser social competence strongly influence children's current and subsequent social relationships in middle childhood and adolescence. Again, early patterns do not predict subsequent ones with *certainty*, but considerable stability exists in the relationship effects of social competence. For example, Haselager, Cillessen, Van Lieshout, Riksen-Walraven, and Hartup (2002) followed a sample of Dutch children from kindergarten and grade 1 through grades 5 and 6, examining developmental trends in peer acceptance and rejection, which the studies in this chapter show are related to social competence. One-third of children's trajectories varied, but two-thirds were stable. Children who had been rejected in early childhood tended to stay rejected in middle childhood, and the same stability over time characterized children who had been accepted by peers in early childhood.

Of course, social competence at any age does not refer solely to effective interactions with age-mates or peers, but also includes interactions with both younger and older people. Hartup (1992) observed that child-to-child interactions are "essentially egalitarian" (p. 257). There may be status differences among same-age playmates or friends, but typically those peer relationships reflect equality of power, whereas child-adult relationships are clearly marked by enormous differences in power, talents, and resources. Socially competent children must successfully navigate both kinds of relationships. Evidence suggests that different skills may be involved in each type of relationship: social competence in dealing with peers involves more relationship-building behaviors, and competence in relationships with adults emphasizes cooperation, behavioral control, and obedience (Greener & Crick, 1999).

We measure five social-competencies assets in middle childhood. Peaceful conflict resolution is measured with a single item, and resistance skills has a low reliability (below .60). But field test results show that Search Institute's *Me and My World* (MMW) survey measures the remaining three social-competencies assets at the .70 level of internal consistency reliability or above (see Appendix).

Table 14. The Social-Competencies Assets	
Planning and decision making	Child thinks about decisions and is usually happy with the results of her or his decisions.
Interpersonal competence	Child cares about and is affected by other people's feelings, enjoys making friends, and, when frustrated or angry, tries to calm her- or himself.
Cultural competence	Child knows and is comfortable with people of different racial, ethnic, and cultural backgrounds and with her or his own cultural identity.
Resistance skills	Child can stay away from people who are likely to get her or him in trouble and is able to say no to doing wrong or dangerous things.
Peaceful conflict resolution	Child attempts to resolve conflict nonviolently.

Summary of the Research:
The Social-Competencies Assets in Middle Childhood

Childhood social competence research is abundant and extraordinarily well documented. Although the support assets may perhaps be the most "foundational" of all asset categories throughout childhood and adolescence (see Chapter 1), the sheer volume and depth of studies conducted on the social-competencies assets suggest the critical value of this asset category to positive development. In particular, many researchers have investigated relationships among the interpersonal and self-regulatory dynamics of social competence and a variety of indicators and outcomes in middle childhood (for review, see Ladd, 1999). Research indicates that peer acceptance, friendship-making ability, empathy, and self-control are essential resources for healthy development in middle childhood, especially since children increasingly move outside the realm of the family and into that of the peer group during these years (Eccles, 1999).

Despite evidence regarding the positive impact of social competencies in middle childhood, investigations into the specific assets of planning and decision making, cultural competence, and resistance skills (as Search Institute defines them) are underrepresented in the literature. The lack of research on planning, decision making, and resistance skills in children, for example, may be a reflection of their lesser developmental salience compared to the importance of these competencies for youth in the middle and high school years, among whom research is more widespread. As we have mentioned throughout this book, middle childhood marks a period in which children coregulate many aspects of their lives with help and guidance from parents and other adults. Independently planning activities and making decisions for themselves, along with resisting negative peer pressure, indeed occur less frequently in middle childhood relative to adolescence, perhaps resulting in little research emphasis and support.

Cultural competence research in middle childhood, on the other hand, deals primarily with the impact of ethnic identity, personal awareness, and/or level of contact between multiracial groups, and focuses less on interracial or intercultural sensitivity. It is likely that this research gap is due more to issues of measurement difficulty or to the relatively new or untapped state of cultural sensitivity research than to a conclusion that intercultural sensitivity among 4th through 6th graders is considered developmentally unimportant. Although it is sensible to speculate that the social-competencies assets can play important roles in fostering healthy development in developed societies that are increasingly multicultural, the relative handful of existing studies suggests caution in generalizing those links too broadly.

Planning and Decision Making

Children's planning and decision-making abilities have been less well studied than other interpersonal competencies, but remain important assets for children to develop on their path toward eventual self-regulation. For example, 3rd graders' ability to systematically solve school-based tasks and their ability to efficiently organize and allocate their time during the school day significantly predict school grades, independent of IQ (Cohen, Bronson, & Casey, 1995). Planning and decision making have been associated, directly or indirectly, with:

Academic Outcomes

- **Better grades** (Cohen et al., 1995).

Mental and Behavioral Health Outcomes

- **Decreased alcohol use** (Milgram, 1996); **lessened use of tobacco** (Gersick, Grady, & Snow, 1988); and **greater sense of autonomy** (Helwig & Kim, 1999).

Planning can be thought of as encompassing skills such as setting goals, forming mental representations, anticipating consequences, carrying out logical steps, regulating one's reactions to the effects of those steps, and varying goals as necessary. Each process informs every other in a continuous cycle of evaluation and revision (Parilla, Das, & Dash, 1996). Children as young as 12 months have been found to exhibit some level of planning ability (Gauvain & Huard, 1998), and the evidence increases for children in the later preschool years. Because of their limited language and cognitive skills, however, those 4- and 5-year-old preschoolers can rarely articulate their plans, leading to underestimates of the capacity of even young children to form simple plans (Prevost, Bronson, & Casey, 1995).

An intriguing study illustrates children's capacity to make informed decisions while in preadolescence. Using a sample of 96 participants ages 9, 14, 18, and 21, Weithorn and Campbell (1982) examined differences in youth's competency in making informed decisions about treatment for four hypothetical medical dilemmas (diabetes, epilepsy, depression, and enuresis). They found that while 9-year-olds differed significantly from the 18- and 21-year-old young adults in their ability to understand and reason about the treatment information provided, no significant differences were reported between the two groups regarding their treatment preferences. The researchers concluded that despite their inability to fully understand the treatment process, children as young as 9 can maintain a mature enough mental capacity to warrant their meaningful involvement in personal health-care decision making.

Children's early experiences in helping to make family plans may vary as a function of the parenting relationship and other environmental factors. For example, Parent, Gosselin, and Moss (2000) studied relationships of French Canadian 4- to 7-year-olds and their mothers, and reported that children with more secure attachments to their mothers were more likely to share in the planning of a laboratory task. In addition, in dyads marked by greater family adversity (including father absence, low maternal education, or low income), less sharing of planning was also observed between mother and child.

In the earlier discussion of empowerment (see Chapter 2), we noted that as children move through preadolescence to adolescence, they increasingly prefer to be involved in decision-making opportunities in the classroom, although they feel they are granted fewer of these opportunities as they get older (see Midgley & Feldlaufer, 1987). Not surprisingly, this desire is reflected in the family decision-making literature as well. Even very young children participate in family decision making at the level of asserting wants and desires, such as asking, or even demanding, to be taken out for ice cream. One longitudinal study found that children initiate more planning-related family discussions as they grow older, and children's initiations of those discussions occurred less often in strict, directive, authoritarian families than in families employing other parenting styles (Gauvain & Huard, 1999).

As Gauvain and Huard (1998, p. 35) describe it, planning in the family "emerges from the social situation as individuals coordinate their needs and actions, and jointly attempt to direct their behavior toward future goals." This observation captures both the cognitive and the socioemotional aspects of planning and decision making. Thus, depending on the child's situation, the asset of planning and decision making may or may not be bound intricately with the other social-competencies assets. Planning an organized approach to homework assignments or devising a savings plan for a desired toy or clothing item involves some qualitatively different elements than offering input to family vacation plans or making decisions with friends about whom to spend time with and what activities to engage in.

Of course, parental beliefs about the kinds of planning and decision-making roles in which their children should participate bear an important relation to the actual kinds of developmental planning and decision-making opportunities children experience. Savage and Gauvain (1998), for example, studied European American and Latino children ages 5 through 12 and their parents. The authors found that culture, child age, acculturation, and child gender all affected parents' beliefs about when the "average" child would be able to perform various planning activities, ranging from doing regular chores around the house to making decisions concerning sports team participation. Parents were also asked at what age their own child had done, or would be able to do, these tasks. Less acculturated Latino parents generally expected the average child to plan and make such decisions at later ages than did European American parents, and reported their own children actually did so at older ages. More highly acculturated Latino parents' responses were similar to those of European American parents in that they expected children to plan and make decisions regarding their activities at younger ages, and in reporting younger ages for their own child's participation in planning and decision-making processes. Girls, in general, were expected to make these decisions at older ages than were boys, especially decisions about "nonorganized after-school activities," such as deciding how to spend allowance, choosing what TV shows to watch, and deciding what to do in the evening before bedtime.

Another study also illustrates the increasing jockeying in which children and parents engage to define their roles in family decision making over the middle childhood years. Vuchinich, Angelelli, and Gatherum (1996) conducted a two-year longitudinal study of 63 intact families with 4th grade children whose average age was 9½ years. In this laboratory study, families were asked to choose topics on which they would be observed having a problem-solving discussion in their home (e.g., clothing choices, bedroom cleaning, behavior problems). The findings were instructive. The quality of family decision making grew worse over the two-year period as the children advanced from 4th grade to 6th grade, largely because both fathers and preadolescents became more negative in the problem-solving discussion. It is important to note that at both observation times, the quality of family decision making was much better when the *children* selected the topic for discussion; if the parents selected the discussion topic, negative problem-solving processes were especially apparent during the second scheduled family observation (at time 2, when the children averaged 11½ years old).

Interpersonal Competence

The interpersonal-competence asset includes three components: empathy, friendship, and positive self-control. We consider those dimensions together because of their close conceptual and empirical association (i.e., children who are more sensitive to others' feelings and demonstrate positive self-control are more likely to satisfactorily make and maintain friendships with peers and adults). Empathy and friendship have been extensively examined in the literature on children's social competence skills and development. The research shows that children who are able to take the perspective of others (e.g., to feel sad when a peer is hurt) and form and maintain significant, lasting relationships with peers are less aggressive, more prosocial, scholastically more competent, and less negative about their friendship expectations.

Most of the studies we found that examine positive self-control in children include broad definitions of self-control, such as the ability to regulate, maintain, and shift attention, emotional reactivity and expression, and subsequent positive behavioral responses (see Eisenberg et al., 1997). Our conception of positive self-control is narrower—we define it as the ability to regulate and minimize negative behavioral displays and to behave in an appropriate manner when frustrated, angry, or excited. Nevertheless, we can draw parallel inferences between the broad definition of positive self-control and our own conceptualization due to conceptual overlap among the various ways of describing positive self-control.

Empathy in children has been associated, directly or indirectly, with:

Mental and Behavioral Health Outcomes

- **Fewer direct aggressive behaviors in school** (e.g., physical aggression, verbal intimidation), as rated by peers in a sample of Finnish children (Kaukiainen et al., 1999); and **decreased behavior problems** (Hastings, Zahn-Walker, Robinson, Usher, & Bridges, 2000).

Social Outcomes

- **Higher level of agreeableness** for girls but not for boys (Sneed, 2002); and **prosocial behavior** (e.g., helpfulness, sharing, cooperation, and positive responsiveness to peers' distress) (Bengtsson & Johnson, 1992 [for boys only in a Swedish sample]; Garner, 1996; Litvack-Miller, McDougal, & Romney, 1997; Roberts & Strayer, 1996 [stronger for boys than girls]).

Friendship in children has been associated, directly or indirectly, with:

Academic Outcomes

- **Increased academic achievement** (Chen, Rubin, & Li, 1997 [among Chinese children and adolescents]; Morison & Masten, 1991 [in adolescence]); and **increased standardized test scores** and **academic competence**, especially for teacher ratings of children's social skills (Malecki & Elliot, 2002).

Mental and Behavioral Health Outcomes

- **Decreased internalizing behaviors** (Cillessen & Bellmore, 1999 [for children with higher social preference scores]; Morison & Masten, 1991 [in adolescence]); **fewer feelings of loneliness** (Cillessen & Bellmore, 1999 [for children with higher social preference scores]; Parker & Asher, 1993 [for children who reported having best friends]); **less anxiety** (Fordham & Stevenson-Hinde, 1999); **decreased externalizing behaviors** (Morison & Masten, 1991 [in adolescence]; Mott & Krane, 1994); **less negative emotionality** (Eisenberg et al., 1996); **increased sense of self-worth** (Fordham & Stevenson-Hinde, 1999; Morison & Masten, 1991 [later in adolescence]); **increased positive self-perceptions of competence in social, work, and athletic/activity environments** in adolescence (Morison & Masten, 1991); and **increased problem-solving ability** (Chen et al., 1997 [among Chinese children and adolescents]; Mott & Krane, 1994).

Social Outcomes

- **Increased positive perceptions of friendship-making ability** and **decreased perceptions of friends' deviant behavior** in adolescence (Barry & Wigfield, 2002); **greater support from friends** (Fordham & Stevenson-Hinde, 1999; Phillipsen, 1999 [for well-accepted peers]); and **more positive enjoyment expectations and greater perceptions of closeness** (Strough, Swenson, & Cheng, 2001 [among children who report a high degree of friendship with peers during task collaboration exercises, especially for same-gender dyads]; Phillipsen, 1999 [for well-accepted peers]).

Positive self-control in children has been associated, directly or indirectly, with:

Academic Outcomes

- **Increased academic achievement** (Malecki & Elliot, 2002).

Mental and Behavioral Health Outcomes

- **Fewer internalizing and externalizing behaviors and more internalizing well-being** (Lengua, 2002); **more sympathetic feelings toward others** (for review, see Eisenberg, Wentzel, & Harris, 1998); **higher self-esteem** (Musser & Browne, 1991); and **increased likelihood of being employed in adulthood** (Kokko & Pulkkinen, 2000).

Social Outcomes

- **Increased social competence** (Lengua, 2002); and **increased popularity with peers** (Musser & Browne, 1991).

Litvack-Miller and colleagues (1997) studied nearly 500 Canadian children in grades 2, 4, and 6. They reported that prosocial behaviors such as sharing, helping, and comforting others were significantly predicted by children's ability to be empathetic toward others (that is, showing concern for the distress of others) and to adopt another perspective and understand what others might be feeling. Girls were more empathetic than boys, and older children were more empathetic than younger children. Litvack-Miller and associates suggested that the increased empathy of 6th graders, in comparison to observed levels of empathy in the younger children, was related to how 6th graders' better cognitive abilities enabled them to regulate their emotional responses to various situations.

Other research has suggested that, for girls in grade 4, caring, sharing, and helping behaviors are moderately correlated to each other and represent a coherent structure of prosocial behavior; for boys, however, those dimensions remain relatively independent (Larrieu & Mussen, 1987). In other words, girls who express caring toward others are also more likely to share and help others than are boys.

The ability to make friends in middle childhood is clearly important, not only for positive experiences in middle childhood, but also for positive outcomes later in adolescence. Barry and Wigfield (2002), for example, studied 430 children in grades 3, 4, and 6, and again 5 years later when they were in grades 8, 9, and 11. The authors found that children's perceptions that they made friends easily in middle childhood, along with the value children attached to having friends and the frequency of their interactions with friends, all predicted having positive perceptions of their friend-making abilities 5 years later. Moreover, adolescents who 5 years earlier had been highly affiliated children perceived in adolescence that their friends engaged less often in deviant behavior, such as fighting or encouraging the adolescent to try dangerous behaviors.

The importance of making friends easily throughout these years should not be underestimated, since children's friendship networks change often. Even "best friendships" in childhood and adolescence rarely have been found to last 2 years; most last only a few months, so that children must regularly cultivate new friendships (Berndt, 1998).

Children's ability to establish good relationships does not hinge solely on competencies such as helping and sharing, although these two have received most of the attention in research on prosocial disposition and behavior. In two studies involving nearly 900 students in grades 3 through 6, Greener and Crick (1999) elicited boys' and girls' definitions of "prosocial" behavior by asking them separately, "What do boys (girls) do when they want to be nice to someone?" Greener and Crick found that children (both boys and girls) defined "being nice" more by behaviors such as showing interest in another person or by letting a child play in the established group than by sharing and helping behaviors.

As grade level increased, children's definitions of "being nice" depended even less on traditional prosocial behaviors. For same-sex interactions, older girls especially valued behaviors that established one-on-one relationships, such as invitations to eat lunch together, while boys were more likely to name inclusion in group activities as evidence of being nice. These trends described the most common same-sex interactions in middle childhood. For opposite-sex interactions, the children named sharing and helping behaviors more often as defining "being nice" (and about 10% of the definitions involved "romantic" behaviors such as flirting or sending love letters).

It is noteworthy that the children emphasized traditional prosocial behaviors as defining "niceness" more often in opposite-sex encounters. In an observational study of more than 500 children ages 8, 10, and 12, Underwood, Schockner, and Hurley (2001) reported that both genders responded to provocation from a peer of the opposite sex with more negative facial expressions, gestures, and remarks than they did to a same-sex peer. Children tried less hard to get along with the person of the opposite sex and reported liking the person less than when the same provocation came from a same-sex peer. The researchers interpreted their results as consistent with the body of research showing that children from preschool even into early adolescence strongly prefer interactions with peers of the same gender. Greener and Crick's (1999) data on 3rd through 6th graders' definitions of "nice" opposite-sex interactions as a function of prosocial helping and sharing behaviors suggest that children in these years may recognize that opposite-sex encounters call for more attentive and sensitive behaviors than do interactions with same-sex peers, a more subtle social competence skill than is captured by these assets.

Research suggests that interpersonal factors that affect children's exercise of positive self-control may come into play during middle childhood. Through research on children's emotional and behavioral regulation during their responses to provocation, Underwood and colleagues (Underwood, Coie, & Herbsman, 1992; Underwood, Hurley, Johanson, & Mosley, 1999) suggest that children may oftentimes choose to control their emotions out of fear of embarrassment and/or rejection. In addition, an implicit belief for many in Western cultures is that overt expressions of anger or sadness are taboo, and that such "coarse" emotions should be internalized and hidden. Such assertions are not surprising, as it is well established in the developmental literature that children who frequently express anger or emotional outbursts often have a harder time making friends. Because the ability to form and maintain friendships is an integral developmental hallmark of middle childhood, the relative lack of positive self-control can have serious social consequences for children.

Further, the long-term consequences of poor emotional self-control can be profound. A longitudinal study of several hundred Finnish 8-year-olds who were followed until age 36 found that children who had been aggressive in middle childhood were more likely to be unemployed 28 years later. The mechanism appeared to be that children's early aggressiveness was related to poorer school adjustment at age 14 and that school maladjustment was both directly and indirectly related to long-term unemployment by age 36 (Kokko & Pulkkinen, 2000).

Rothbart, Ahadi, Hershey, and Fisher (2001) found that what they called "effortful control," a childhood personality trait akin to what has been called "constraint" or "superego strength" in adults, appeared as one of the major factors in children's personalities as early as ages 3 to 7. Effortful control included constructs such as being able to focus attention, regulate or inhibit behavior, be soothed or calmed down, smile and laugh, experience "low intensity pleasure" (not "sensation-seeking"), and be sensitive to perceptual cues. The researchers showed that effortful control had a similar structure across samples of White American, Chinese, and Japanese children.

Typically, although not always (see Rodkin et al., 2000), children whose personalities reflect lower levels of effortful control are liable to enter a cycle of peer rejection that begins early in formal schooling. For example, in an observational study, Hubbard (2001) found that among African American 2nd graders, the rejected children, regardless of gender, expressed more verbal and facial anger than did nonrejected children. Similar to reports of other research, boys also expressed anger of all kinds more often than girls.

Analysis of data from the National Longitudinal Survey of Children and Youth, involving more than 13,000 children ages 4 to 11 and their parents, suggests that the origin of low self-control may involve a mix of individual characteristics, such as child hyperactivity, and family processes, such as hostile parenting (Brannigan, Gemmell, Pevalin, & Wade, 2002). Low self-control, when coupled with single-parent status, male gender of the child, and lower levels of prosocial behavior, strongly predicted misconduct and aggression.

Resistance Skills

The resistance-skills asset is a good example of both developmental continuity and stage uniqueness. We conceptualize resistance skills for adolescents as the abilities to stay away from troublemaking people and to say no when invited to do things that are wrong or dangerous. This is an important developmental asset at the adolescent stage of life because it is during adolescence that many, if not most, young people experience a significant increase in opportunities to engage in high-risk behaviors such as alcohol or other illegal drug use and early and/or unprotected sexual intercourse. A young person's ability to minimize such engagement through the exercise of personal choice may act directly as a powerful protective influence and may indirectly increase the chances of positive, thriving behavior by steering her or him instead toward association with more responsible peers and caring adults.

The ability to say no is obviously important to younger children, too, and thus reflects developmental continuity to some extent, but this ability may also be manifested in differing ways. For example, we teach younger children to say no to inappropriate touching and other indications of physical or sexual abuse from strangers or family. But at least some already have "boyfriends" and "girlfriends" in the upper elementary years, and may then increasingly have to deal with reconciling the healthy acceptance of their sexuality with resisting pressures to act in more overtly sexual ways. They also have to deal with whether they will exclude someone on the playground or in the lunchroom, watch an inappropriate movie, or visit an inappropriate Web site. These certainly speak to the need for resistance skills.

During the high school years, the majority of young people engage at least once in risky behaviors such as alcohol consumption or other illegal drug use and sexual experimentation. Such behaviors are normative at some point in adolescence, and the great majority of adolescents have had to decide whether to use resistance skills when confronted with such choices. Knowing how to make appropriate choices about such issues is thus an important part of the increasingly sophisticated array of developmental assets that adolescents should accrue on their journey toward greater self-regulation.

Although such risk behaviors and choices are far less common during middle childhood, they do occur among preadolescents (see review, Finke & Bowman, 1997). Thus, we ask about resistance skills in the MMW survey, although in a slightly different way than was done for adolescents. We do ask children whether "most of the time" they are able to stay away from people who are likely to get them into trouble. But we also conceptualize resistance skills in middle childhood as still more in development than they are in adolescence, with one significant source of support being parents' teachings. For that reason, we ask children if their parents *tell* them it is important to say no when people want them to do things they know are wrong or dangerous.

Most research on resistance skills has been conducted as part of evaluations of alcohol and other drug abuse prevention programs, and although 4th and 5th graders are sometimes included, the predominant samples in these studies are of middle and high school students. In a review of 16 such studies of resistance skills training programs, Gorman (1995) reported that the majority of programs had "little or no" impact on participants, or that positive effects were found only for subgroups. Gorman attributed these findings in part to the focus of most resistance skills training on only peer pressure and media influence, and not on other factors (e.g., low self-concept, poor parenting, community disorganization) that might place students at risk of alcohol and other drug use. Perhaps the most significant of these studies that involved students in middle childhood was a metaevaluation of eight studies of the Project DARE program (Ennett, Tobler, Ringwalt, & Flewelling, 1994). The average size of the program effect across those studies was so small as to be practically negligible.

Donaldson, Graham, Piccinin, and Hansen (1995) conducted a study of nearly 12,000 students in grades 5 through 8 that sheds light on the processes by which resistance skills programs may operate best. They reported that an alcohol use prevention program was most effective when students believed that using alcohol was wrong and that the prevalence of alcohol use among their peers was relatively low. In contrast, if students thought alcohol use was acceptable and thought "a lot" of peers in their school offered alcohol to their friends, a negative effect was observed: Under those conditions, refusal skills training in 5th and 7th grades was associated with greater alcohol use in 8th grade.

Thus, resistance or refusal skills are multidimensional, involving personal attitudes and beliefs about the behavior in question, awareness of and efficacy in applying strategies for saying no, and perceptions about how much the behavior is a social norm among one's peers. This brief discussion also suggests that resistance skills may be difficult to measure globally; because attitudes, social perceptions, and situational influences are involved, it may be necessary to examine separately young people's ability to say no to alcohol and other drugs, sexual behaviors, opportunities to steal or cheat, and so on. In our MMW survey, we tap students' ability to say no to doing "wrong or dangerous" things, but not these other components of a broader definition of resistance skills.

Resistance skills have been associated, directly or indirectly, with:

Mental and Behavioral Health Outcomes

- **Decreased problem behaviors such as alcohol and other substance use** (Caplan et al., 1992; Donaldson et al., 1995 [if students believed alcohol use was wrong and that the use among their peers was relatively low]; Rohrbach, Graham, Hansen, Flay, & Johnson, 1987).

Social Outcomes

- **Increased autonomy** (Steinberg & Silverberg, 1986); and **improved social competence skills** (Caplan et al., 1992).

Cultural Competence

Research into cultural competence generally involves the study of ethnic identification and preferences when studying young children, and ethnic identity formation when looking at adolescents (Spencer & Markstrom-Adams, 1990) and preadolescents (Simons et al., 2002). We do include pride in one's own cultural heritage as part of this asset, but unfortunately, scant research exists on the *effects* on children's development of another important aspect of cultural competence, as Search Institute defines it—the child knows and feels comfortable with people of different cultural, racial, and ethnic backgrounds. In the few studies we identified, children who were more culturally sensitive reported more diverse friendships, were friendlier, and were more accepting of peers of different races and cultures.

Compelling contributions to our discussion of cultural competence are made, however, by studies investigating bilingual education programs and intergroup relations among children (by means of intervention programs geared at enhancing cultural sensitivity and decreasing prejudice through cooperative learning groups). For example, Slavin and Cooper (1999) reviewed the research regarding eight cooperative learning procedures used in elementary and secondary schools. They found that children involved in cooperative learning groups that encourage positive interactions among students of diverse racial and ethnic backgrounds showed evidence of stronger interracial friendships and a greater reduction in stereotyping, discrimination, and prejudice than did children in the control groups. Cultural competence development is not always an explicit goal of cooperative learning groups or bilingual education. But research shows that providing children of diverse backgrounds with opportunities to work together to achieve common goals allows children to understand, accept, and celebrate cultural and racial differences among themselves and others, while simultaneously fostering an understanding of similarities and an appreciation of one's own cultural heritage.

Cultural competence in children has been associated, directly or indirectly, with:

Mental and Behavioral Health Outcomes

- **Fewer depressive symptoms** for children who identified with and took pride in their community ethnic group (Simons et al., 2002).

Social Outcomes

- **Less rejection of minority friendships** and **more diverse social networks** (Genesee & Gándara, 1999 [children involved in bilingual education programs]; Hunter & Elias, 2000 [for girls]; Slavin & Cooper, 1999); **reduction in prejudice, discrimination, and stereotyping** (Aboud & Fenwick, 1999; Genesee & Gándara, 1999 [children involved in bilingual education programs]; Levy, 1999; Slavin & Cooper, 1999); **more sociability toward peers** (Hunter & Elias, 2000 [for girls]); and **increased leadership skills** (Hunter & Elias, 2000 [for girls]).

Research shows that children become less prejudiced and more positive in their attitudes toward other-race peers across elementary school (Aboud & Mendelson, 1998), perhaps because of an increasing cognitive ability to deal simultaneously with multiple dimensions of the people and situations they encounter (Bigler, 1999). However, Grant and Haynes (1995) suggested that children in middle childhood might best be described more as developing cultural "sensitivity" than cultural "competence." That is, in middle childhood they are becoming less stereotyped in their thinking and behavior and more open to accepting differences in others, although they may not necessarily value those different people, feel highly empathetic toward them, or act to promote social equality and change.

There is conflicting evidence, however, about whether children engage in more positive cross-race interactions as they develop across the elementary years. For example, Howes and Wu (1990) reported that 3rd graders had more cross-ethnic friendships than kindergartners, and Doyle and Aboud (1995) found that 9-year-olds were less racially prejudiced than 6-year-olds. However, in Hallinan and Teixeira's earlier (1987a) longitudinal study of children in grades 4 through 7, the researchers found that as the children got older, they formed *fewer* cross-race friendships.

Rather than being in conflict, these different results suggest that the relation between age/grade and cross-race friendships might be curvilinear. Children's increasing social competencies in the early childhood years may contribute to increasing their pool of friends who are different from them. But as children go through middle childhood and early adolescence, with increasing clique formation and awareness of how one compares in a variety of ways with peers, stronger pressures may be experienced to identify and affiliate with children more "like" oneself.

In another study of the same sample of 4th–7th graders, Hallinan and Teixeira (1987b) also suggested that classroom and status issues may account for differing cross-race friendship patterns as much as or more than students' racial attitudes. White students were most resistant to cross-race friendships, but in classrooms in which standardized tests and grades were relatively less emphasized, and Black and White students were assigned together to the same ability groups, White children were more likely to have cross-race friendships. Nevertheless, Bigler (1999) argued that, in the elementary years, children's racial knowledge, attitudes, and behavior are only weakly associated, underscoring the comprehensive nature needed from interventions intended to combat racism.

What is functional or competent culturally in one setting, for one type of child, may differ from what is adaptive for another child in the same setting. For example, Rodkin and colleagues (2000) found that in racially integrated elementary schools in which African Americans comprised a distinct minority, popular boys perceived as "tough" were disproportionately African American; popular White boys were perceived disproportionately as "model" students. However, in schools with almost a 100% African American student body, popular boys were only marginally more likely to be considered "tough" rather than "model." The researchers interpreted these results as suggesting that tough behavior adopted by African American boys attending a predominantly White school could be viewed as a strategy for maintaining positive identity in the face of negative stereotypes and discrimination.

Cultural competence may be more immediately salient for some students, depending on the setting and their racial and ethnic background. For example, DuBois and Hirsch (1990) studied African American and White children who attended a racially integrated junior high school. They reported that the African American students were more likely than the White students to form interracial friendships that extended beyond school to neighborhood and community activities. Hallinan and Teixeira (1987b) also reported that the African American 4th through 7th graders in their sample were "basically friendlier" than White children toward peers of the other race (p. 1370). It may be that, even in integrated settings, cultural competence dispositions and skills are functionally more important for cultural minority children, whose social competencies are critical as they learn to forge and maintain a distinct cultural identity at the same time as being successful in navigating within the majority culture in order to access resources.

Of course, children from different cultural backgrounds may also bring differing values and preferences to their peer and nonpeer interactions. "Cultural competence" implies that children have the ability to understand and react to such differences in socially adaptive ways. However, variables such as culture, age, and gender interact in a complex manner to influence each interpersonal encounter somewhat differently. For example, in a study of Brazilian and European American children averaging 7 years old, researchers examined whether, after playing a game, children would allocate more rewards to themselves or share rewards equally between themselves and a playmate (Carlo, Roesch, Knight, & Koller, 2001). In the study, Brazilian children preferred cooperative solutions, while European American children preferred competitive solutions. For both groups, however, cooperative solutions increased with age. Moreover, gender differences were minimal within the American sample, but quite strong among the Brazilian children, with boys favoring much more competitive solutions. In any given situation, the way in which culture interacts with individual and contextual variables may create ambiguous or conflictual situations that many children must deal with.

Cultural differences may also affect not only relationships among children of different cultural backgrounds but also the way in which they relate to other "different" children. For example, Crystal, Watanabe, and Chin (1997) studied more than 900 5th, 8th, and 11th graders in the United States, Japan, and China. They examined how children from different cultures accepted "atypical" children (such as those who were aggressive, withdrawn, nonathletic, or poor). The authors also looked at how tolerance varied depending upon whether the responding child would have to be friends with the atypical child. In other words, they asked children, hypothetically, whether it was likely they would be friends with such a "different" child or would just merely work together on a project with that atypical child. Overall, 5th and 8th graders across the three surveyed cultures were less tolerant of atypical children than were 11th graders, suggesting this aspect of cultural competence may increase with age. The researchers also found numerous cultural differences in children's responses to the study. Japanese children were more tolerant of having an aggressive child as either a friend or coworker in a group than were Chinese or American children. More American and Japanese children were intolerant of poor children in either situation than were Chinese children.

Children's cultural competence levels may reflect gender differences, as well as differences in the degree to which contact with children from other racial and ethnic backgrounds affects the quality of interracial friendships. For example, Hunter and Elias (2000) reported that in a racially and ethnically diverse sample of students in grade 5, girls whose peers considered them sociable, non-aggressive, and having leadership qualities had more "high-quality" interracial friendships (i.e., the children reported higher levels of support and satisfaction derived from the friendships). Their racial attitudes, sociability characteristics, and interracial friendship patterns were all linked. No such relations were reported for boys. These results led the researchers to suggest that girls' overall attitudes about children from other backgrounds may benefit from favorable interracial friendship interactions, but that boys may retain negative orientations toward different cultural groups even when they have some high-quality interracial friendships.

We do include as part of the cultural-competence asset an item measuring whether the child's parents tell her or him it is important to be proud of their own cultural heritage. The research suggests that ethnic identity may be a more salient issue for adolescents than for children in middle childhood, and may be more an element of positive identity, in any case, than it is a dimension of the social-competencies assets (see review in Scales & Leffert, 1999). Nevertheless, a consistent message to children in middle childhood from their parents about the importance of having a positive cultural identity is likely to contribute to the gradual development of such an identity component in adolescence.

Peaceful Conflict Resolution

In the discussion of empowerment (see Chapter 2), we noted that a wealth of literature exists on the inherent power of giving children opportunities to mediate conflicts within the school environment (for review, see Johnson & Johnson, 1996). Many other studies have corroborated this evidence by showing that children who use less aggressive, more peaceful conflict resolution strategies are more likely to be better self-regulated and psychologically healthy, have better friendships, and feel safer. Peaceful conflict resolution tendencies and beliefs in children have been associated, directly or indirectly, with:

Academic Outcomes

- **Increased academic achievement** (Johnson & Johnson, 1996); **improved critical thinking skills** (Stomfay-Stitz, 1994); **more positive perceptions of school climate** (Johnson & Johnson, 1996); and **decreased early school withdrawal** (Kupersmidt & Coie, 1990).

Mental and Behavioral Health Outcomes

- **Self-responsibility and self-regulation** (Johnson & Johnson, 1994, 1996); **lower levels of depression** (Goodman, Gravitt, & Kaslow, 1995 [moderated the relationship between negative life events and depression]); **better self-esteem** (Johnson & Johnson, 1996); **less aggression,** especially for girls in a Finnish sample of children (Keltikangas-Jarvinen & Pakaslahti, 1999); **more positive perceptions of the value of conflicts** (Johnson & Johnson, 1996); **better self-regulation skills** (Maxwell, 1989); **fewer conflict problems referred to teachers and the principal** (Johnson, Johnson, Dudley, & Ackigoz, 1994); and **decreased use of alcohol and other substances** (O'Donnell, Hawkins, & Abbott, 1995).

Social Outcomes

- **Greater appreciation of maintaining equality and positive relationships with peers** (Delveaux & Daniels, 2000); and **decreased antisocial behavior** (Kupersmidt & Coie, 1990).

A recent meta-analysis of 31 research reports on peer conflict resolution concluded that coercion was the most common strategy among children 2 to 10 years old, and that negotiation increases with age (Laursen, Finkelstein, & Betts, 2001). Peaceful conflict resolution may traditionally have been seen as a greater developmental need for boys. Recent research suggests, however, that girls may be as likely as boys to exhibit aggressive behavior, but they do so covertly and relationally, avoiding overt and physical confrontation by using instead behaviors like talking meanly about someone behind her or his back (Brendgen, Vitaro, Bukowski, Doyle, & Markiewicz, 2001). A study of several hundred 4th graders illustrates these more recent findings. Delveaux and Daniels (2000) reported that boys were more likely than girls to endorse physical strategies for resolving conflict, and girls were more likely to endorse prosocial solutions. But both genders equally endorsed relational aggression, such as excluding a child from a play group or intentionally withdrawing friendship in order to hurt them. Relational aggressors were more likely to have as goals staying out of trouble or maintaining the peer group, whereas physical aggressors pursued self-interest and control goals.

Other factors appear to affect children's use of aggressive conflict resolution strategies. Guerra, Huesmann, Tolan, Van Acker, and Eron (1995) conducted a comprehensive longitudinal study on a racially and ethnically diverse sample of 1,935 students in grades 1, 2, and 4 that examined the predictive value of economic disadvantage, stressful events, and individual beliefs on children's subsequent risk for aggression. They found that children from more disadvantaged environments displayed relatively higher levels of aggression than did the less disadvantaged cohort. More specifically, the results showed that for children across all ethnic groups in the sample (White, African American, and Hispanic), both stress and positive beliefs about aggression significantly predicted children's later aggression. However, poverty, a more distal factor, was significantly predictive of aggression only for White children.

Peaceful conflict resolution is not entirely independent of the interpersonal-competence asset, with its dimensions of empathy, friendship, and self-control. For example, research has consistently reported that children display both more positive, supportive behavior and *negative, conflictual* behavior with their friends than with their nonfriends (Simpkins & Parke, 2002). Thus, resolving conflicts peacefully is not simply a strategy for avoiding harm to self and others, but is, developmentally, an important aspect of maintaining friendships. Empathetic children can better understand the feelings of others, including in situations in which negative behavior is directed toward them. Children who exhibit positive self-control likely can also manage their emotional reactions more effectively as well. Those skills may help them reduce the level of conflict and tension in ambiguous, potentially provocative encounters (Sneed, 2002).

The Social-Competencies Assets across the Early Childhood-Adolescence Life Span

At the beginning of the early elementary years, children undergo a dramatic shift in their social ecology. Social competencies learned and honed during the preschool years become increasingly important as both the frequency and quantity of peer relations increase at the outset of formal schooling (Ladd, 1996).

The importance of empathy, friendship, and self-control strategies to children's social development is clear at very young ages, as are gender differences favoring girls' skills in these areas. In a longitudinal study of 4- to 5-year-olds followed until they were 9 to 10 years old, Hastings and colleagues (2000) found that, whether part of a subgroup showing clinical behavior problems or not, girls at each of the studied ages demonstrated greater empathy and concern for others than did boys. The importance of those gender differences is reflected in the longitudinal finding that greater empathy in all children at the ages of 4 and 5 years predicted less prevalent and severe behavior problems at ages 6 and 7, and greater levels of empathy at ages 6 and 7 predicted decreases in behavior problems by ages 9 and 10. Likewise, another study of 1st through

4th graders also reported that greater prosocial skills predicted fewer behavior problems (Vinnick & Erickson, 1992).

The kinds of interpersonal experiences detailed in this chapter center on a number of ways in which children interact positively with others. These experiences are intimately related to the manner in which young children are able to adjust their actions and emotions in social settings (Eisenberg et al., 2000). Thus, for children in the early elementary grades, regulation and self-control seem to set the tone for interpersonal experiences.

A small longitudinal study of 40 children followed from infancy through middle adolescence (Englund, Levy, Hyson, & Sroufe, 2001) shows how early social competence and attachment to parents may contribute to positive social outcomes many years later. Children who were self-confident and socially competent in preschool and middle childhood (at age 10) were also significantly more likely to be socially competent and leaders at ages 15 and 16 than were less socially competent children. And adolescents who had been securely attached to parents in infancy were more likely to be leaders and to have social confidence and competence than were adolescents with less secure infant attachments to parents.

The research suggests that one mechanism through which these long-term effects may have occurred is that early secure relationships with parents may facilitate the development of regulation and self-control. Eisenberg and her colleagues distinguish between *emotional regulation* and *behavioral regulation,* and argue that these two kinds of regulatory abilities are integral to children's social functioning (Eisenberg et al., 2000). Emotional regulation refers to the child's ability to control the intensity and/or duration of her or his internal states. For example, a child who is able to view a negative experience in a positive way is said to exhibit emotional regulation. Eisenberg and colleagues also often refer to this as "attentional regulation," in that the ability to shift and refocus one's attention in order to decrease negative emotions is a part of emotional regulation. Related to, and often a consequence of, emotional regulation is behavioral regulation, the child's ability to control her or his behaviors and actions in the face of emotional excitement. Eisenberg and colleagues also have examined how these regulatory capabilities interact to influence the kinds of positive peer experiences children have with their classmates, as well as the kinds of positive social behaviors children display with their peers, such as helping, sharing, and perspective taking (Eisenberg et al., 1995).

Eisenberg and others suggest that these self-control qualities are important for positive social experiences because of the nature of children's peer groups. As explained by Maszk, Eisenberg, and Guthrie (1999), peer interactions involve intricate social rules calling for the child's ability to handle conflict and disruption, as well as to deal with heightened levels of excitement. Children who can adjust both their emotions and behaviors during peer play are more likely to interact positively with their age-mates than are children who do not possess such self-control.

Empirical analyses support these hypothesized relations between self-control and social competencies such as the ability to make friends and engage in prosocial behaviors. Eisenberg and colleagues (1997) have reported that emotional regulation and behavioral regulation were related to social status and socially appropriate behaviors in a group of children in kindergarten through 3rd grade, although through different pathways for older and younger children. The effect of emotional regulation on both social status and socially appropriate behaviors was mediated by the degree to which a child was able to adapt flexibly in the face of stress, a quality Eisenberg and colleagues (1997) labeled "resiliency"; this finding was especially strong for children who were prone to react with intensity to negative emotions. Behavioral regulation, on the other hand, was directly related to socially appropriate behaviors *only for* children who were rated high in negative emotionality (the tendency to react with strong negative emotions like anger or fear). However, if children were low in negative emotionality, their ability to regulate their behavior was unrelated to displaying socially appropriate behaviors or to their social status.

Furthermore, these self-control constructs seem to predict social status and positive social competencies more so than the reverse. Maszk and associates (1999) conducted an academic-year (fall to spring) longitudinal study of preschoolers and kindergartners to examine the temporal relations between regulation and children's social status. Regression analyses indicated that when a child's social status in the fall was controlled, levels of emotionality and self-regulation predicted social status the following spring. Social status itself predicted only low levels of emotionality and regulation over the same time period. This result suggests that the degree to which a child was able to competently regulate her or his emotions and behaviors was related to positive *changes* in social status—these children became *more* popular over the course of the school year. Of course, the converse is also true: Those children who had self-regulation difficulties in the fall became *less* well liked from fall to spring.

The significance of "starting off on the right foot" with regard to peer relations cannot be overstated, as voluminous theory and research publications implicate problematic peer relations as a major risk factor for later life problems. A widely held two-step model of peer influence and socialization indicates that children tend to congregate in peer groups according to behavioral preferences. Thus, children who exhibit socially appropriate behaviors associate with other children who are also socially competent; children who show problems in the ways in which they interact with others tend to befriend others who are not very socially competent (Hartup, 1999; Urberg, 1999). In the context of these relationships, children grow more like their peer associates, becoming either more socially skilled or reinforcing and learning less socially competent ways of interacting. This process, while most often studied among children and adolescents (Berndt, Hawkins, & Jiao, 1999; Dishion, Andrews, & Crosby, 1995), is also seen in children as young as preschool age. Even at that young age, youngsters who are socially skilled choose their playmates based on positive social consequences encountered in social situations with these other children (Snyder, West, Stockemer, Gibbons, & Almquist-Parks, 1996).

Another body of literature regarding children's social competencies involves the way in which they are able to handle conflicts both with friends and with acquaintances. In a now-classic study, Nelson and Aboud (1985) found that when a child encountered a conflict with a friend, children in grades 3 and 4 were more likely to communicate more explanations of their positions in the conflict, as well as articulate more criticisms of their partners. An important finding from this study was that friends engaged in conflict more frequently than did nonfriends. This result suggests that there is something unique to a friendship that makes conflictual situations less avoidable and indicates that there may be some developmental significance to engaging in conflict within the context of a supportive, mostly positive relationship. Subsequent empirical research (Hartup, French, Laursen, Johnston, & Ogawa, 1993; Hartup, Laursen, Stewart, & Eastenson, 1988) and the aforementioned meta-analysis (Laursen et al., 2001) support Nelson and Aboud's (1985) initial findings that younger children tend to negotiate and use coercion with their friends in conflict situations. Children tend not to use a disengagement strategy or engage in more frequent but less intense conflicts with friends. It remains to be seen whether conflict with friends is developmentally significant and helps promote more skilled conflict resolution strategies or simply reflects social cognitive maturity.

Measuring the Social-Competencies Assets in Middle Childhood

In Search Institute's MMW field tests with 4th–6th graders in Nevada, California, and New York, a majority of the children surveyed describe themselves as experiencing resistance skills, cultural competence, and peaceful conflict resolution (see Table 15). Generally, a minority of children say they experience planning and decision making and interpersonal competence.

Few if any meaningful differences in these assets arose across the field test sites, and, for the most part, the two pilot sites' results were consistent with these trends. However, with regard to peaceful conflict resolution, considerable differences exist when comparing the responses of the three field-test sites and the more affluent, university community pilot site in Norman, Oklahoma, with the less affluent, urban Oklahoma City pilot site. Whereas about 80% of children in the other four sites said they peacefully resolved conflicts, only 54% of the Oklahoma City children did. This suggests that the conflict-resolution asset may be particularly sensitive to differences across communities and that, therefore, averages resulting from aggregating many communities may mask important variations in children's experience of that asset.

There is some evidence that 3rd graders' self-reports may be less valid than parental ratings when it comes to children's social competence, but that self-ratings may be acceptable among 7th graders (Byrne & Bazana, 1996). However, in our pilot results of children who are between those grades (i.e., in grades 4 through 6), children described favorably their experiences of three of the five social-competencies assets (describing the other two unfavorably). This suggests reasonable variation across the social-competencies assets, and that the children did not respond with either a consistently positive or consistently negative bias. It may be that it is during these upper elementary years that a transition occurs during which children become more valid reporters of their own social competencies.

Levels of cognitive and emotional development vary widely among children in the upper elementary years. Given the relationship of planning and decision-making skills to cognitive and emotional development, as well as parents' and other adults' roles in children's planning and decision making, it is perhaps understandable, and not an alarming result, that a majority of children did not report experiencing this asset. In addition, our questions measure global self-

Table 15. Proportion of Field Test Study 4th–6th Graders Who Report Experiencing the Social-Competencies Assets			
Asset	**% Who Report Experiencing Asset**		
	Nevada	**California**	**New York**
Planning and decision making	52	48	47
Interpersonal competence	44	37	43
Empathy	73	71	72
Friendship	40	34	43
Positive self-control	47	40	41
Cultural competence	77	74	74
Resistance skills	82	82	86
Peaceful conflict resolution	77	71	82
From field tests in 2003; N = 1,294.			

reports, not children's specific abilities in concrete examples of planning and decision making. This, too, may also account for the relatively lower levels of this asset in the children's reports.

In contrast, the research reviewed here shows clearly how important friendship and empathy are, and the key role that positive self-control plays in establishing and maintaining satisfying relationships, especially with peers. Hence, low levels of the interpersonal-competence asset are cause for concern. Future research with the MMW survey is needed to determine whether children continue to report relatively lower levels of the interpersonal-competence asset, or whether these results were an anomaly of the pilot and field test studies. Unfortunately, however, the relative consistency of the trends across five different pilot and field test communities leads us to think the results are not serendipitous, but meaningful.

References

Aboud, F. E., & Fenwick, V. (1999). Exploring and evaluating school-based interventions to reduce prejudice. *Journal of Social Issues, 55,* 767–786.

Aboud, F. E., & Mendelson, M. J. (1998). Determinants of friendship selection and quality: Developmental perspectives. In W. M. Bukowski, A. F. Newcomb, & W. W. Hartup (Eds.), *The company they keep: Friendship in childhood and adolescence* (pp. 87–112). Cambridge: Cambridge University Press.

Barry, C. M., & Wigfield, A. (2002). Self-perceptions of friendship-making ability and perceptions of friends' deviant behavior: Childhood to adolescence. *Journal of Early Adolescence, 22,* 143–172.

Bengtsson, H., & Johnson, L. (1992). Perspective taking, empathy, and prosocial behavior in late childhood. *Child Study Journal, 22,* 11–22.

Berndt, T. J. (1998). Exploring the effects of friendship quality on social development. In W. M. Bukowski, A. F. Newcomb, & W. W. Hartup (Eds.), *The company they keep: Friendship in childhood and adolescence* (pp. 346–365). Cambridge: Cambridge University Press.

Berndt, T. J., Hawkins, J. A., & Jiao, Z. (1999). Influences of friends and friendships on adjustment to junior high school. *Merrill-Palmer Quarterly, 45,* 13–41.

Bigler, R. S. (1999). The use of multicultural curricula and materials to counter racism in children. *Journal of Social Issues, 55,* 687–705.

Bolger, K. E., & Patterson, C. J. (2001). Developmental pathways from child maltreatment to peer rejection. *Child Development, 72,* 549–568.

Brannigan, A., Gemmell, W., Pevalin, D. J., & Wade, T. J. (2002). Self-control and social control in childhood misconduct and aggression: The role of family structure, hyperactivity, and hostile parenting. *Canadian Journal of Criminology, 44,* 119–143.

Brendgen, M., Vitaro, F., Bukowski, W. M., Doyle, A. B., & Markiewicz, D. (2001). Developmental profiles of peer social preference over the course of elementary school: Associations with trajectories of externalizing and internalizing behavior. *Developmental Psychology, 37,* 308–320.

Byrne, B. M., & Bazana, P. G. (1996). Investigating the measurement of social and academic competencies for early/late preadolescents and adolescents: A multitrait-multimethod analysis. *Applied Measurement in Education, 9,* 113–132.

Caplan, M., Weissberg, R. P., Grober, J. S., Sivo, P. J., Grady, K., & Jacoby, C. (1992). Social competence promotion with inner-city and suburban young adolescents: Effects on social adjustment and alcohol use. *Journal of Consulting and Clinical Psychology, 60,* 56–63.

Carlo, G., Roesch, S. C., Knight, G. P., & Koller, S. H. (2001). Between- or within-culture variation? Culture group as a moderator of the relations between individual differences and resource allocation preferences. *Applied Developmental Psychology, 22,* 559–579.

Chen, X., Rubin, K. H., & Li, D. (1997). Relation between academic achievement and social adjustment: Evidence from Chinese children. *Developmental Psychology, 33,* 518–525.

Cillessen, A. H., & Bellmore, A. M. (1999). Accuracy of social self-perceptions and peer competence in middle childhood. *Merrill-Palmer Quarterly, 45,* 650–676.

Cohen, G. N., Bronson, M. B., & Casey, M. B. (1995). Planning as a factor in school achievement. *Journal of Applied Developmental Psychology, 16,* 405–428.

Crystal, D. S., Watanabe, H., & Chin, W. (1997). Intolerance of human differences: A cross-cultural and developmental study of American, Japanese, and Chinese children. *Journal of Applied Developmental Psychology, 18,* 149–167.

Delveaux, K. D., & Daniels, T. (2000). Children's social cognitions: Physically and relationally aggressive strategies and children's goals in peer conflict situations. *Merrill-Palmer Quarterly, 46,* 672–691.

Dishion, T. J., Andrews, D. W., & Crosby, L. (1995). Anti-social boys and their friends in early adolescence: Relationship characteristics, quality, and interactional process. *Child Development, 66,* 139–151.

Donaldson, S. I., Graham, J. W., Piccinin, A. M., & Hansen, W. B. (1995). Resistance-skills training and onset of alcohol use: Evidence for beneficial and potentially harmful effects in public schools and private Catholic schools. *Health Psychology, 14,* 291–300.

Doyle, A. B., & Aboud, F. E. (1995). A longitudinal study of white children's racial prejudice as a social cognitive development. *Merrill-Palmer Quarterly, 41,* 209–228.

DuBois, D. L., & Hirsch, B. J. (1990). School and neighborhood friendship patterns of Blacks and whites in early adolescence. *Child Development, 61,* 524–536.

Eccles, J. S. (1999). The development of children ages 6–14. *The Future of Children, 9,* 30–44.

Eisenberg, N. (2001). The core and correlates of affective social competence. *Social Development, 10,* 120–124.

Eisenberg, N., Fabes, R. A., Karbon, M., Murphy, B. C., Wosinksi, M., Polassi, L., Carlo, G., & Juhnke, C. (1996). The relations of children's dispositional prosocial behavior to emotionality, regulation, and social functioning. *Child Development, 67,* 974–992.

Eisenberg, N., Fabes, R. A., Murphy, B. C., Maszk, P., Smith, M., & Karbon, M. (1995). The role of emotionality and regulation in children's social functioning: A longitudinal study. *Child Development, 66,* 1360–1384.

Eisenberg, N., Guthrie, I. K., Fabes, R. A., Reiser, M., Murphy, B. C., Holgren, R., Maszk, P., & Losoya, S. (1997). The relations of regulation and emotionality to resiliency and competent social functioning in elementary school children. *Child Development, 68,* 295–311.

Eisenberg, N., Guthrie, I. K., Fabes, R. A., Shepard, S., Losoya, S., Murphy, B. C., Jones, S., Poulin, R., & Reiser, M. (2000). Prediction of elementary school children's externalizing problem behaviors from attentional and behavioral regulation and negative emotionality. *Child Development, 71,* 1367–1382.

Eisenberg, N., Wentzel, N. M., & Harris, J. D. (1998). The role of emotionality and regulation in empathy related responding. *School Psychology Review, 27,* 506–521.

Englund, M. M., Levy, A. K., Hyson, D. M., & Sroufe, L. A. (2001). Adolescent social competence: Effectiveness in a group setting. *Child Development, 71,* 1049–1060.

Ennett, S. T., Tobler, N. S., Ringwalt, C. L., & Flewelling, R. L. (1994). How effective is drug abuse resistance education? A meta-analysis of Project DARE outcome evaluations. *American Journal of Public Health, 84,* 1394–1401.

Finke, L. M., & Bowman, A. C. (1997). Factors in childhood drug and alcohol use: A review of literature. *Journal of Child and Adolescent Psychiatry, 10,* 29–34.

Fordham, K., & Stevenson-Hinde, J. (1999). Shyness, friendship quality, and adjustment during middle childhood. *Journal of Child Psychology and Psychiatry, 40,* 757–768.

Garner, P. W. (1996). The relations of emotional role-taking, affective/moral attributions, and emotional display rule knowledge to low-income school-age children's social competence. *Journal of Applied Developmental Psychology, 17,* 19–36.

Gauvain, M., & Huard, R. D. (1998). The role of the family in the development of competence in planning. In A. Colby & J. B. James (Eds.), *Competence and character through life* (pp. 31–55). Chicago: University of Chicago Press.

Gauvain, M., & Huard, R. D. (1999). Family interaction, parenting style, and the development of planning: A longitudinal analysis using archival data. *Journal of Family Psychology, 13,* 75–92.

Genesee, F. & Gándara, P., (1999). Bilingual education programs: A cross-national perspective. *Journal of Social Issues, 55,* 665–685.

Gersick, K. E., Grady, K., & Snow, D. L. (1988). Social-cognitive skill development with sixth graders and its initial impact of substance use. *Journal of Drug Education, 18,* 55–70.

Goleman, D. (1995). *Emotional intelligence: Why it can matter more than IQ.* New York: Bantam.

Goodman, S. H., Gravitt, G. W., & Kaslow, N. J. (1995). Social problem solving: A moderator of the relation between negative life stress and depression symptoms in children. *Journal of Abnormal Child Psychology, 23,* 473–485.

Gorman, D. M. (1995). Are school-based resistance skills training programs effective in preventing alcohol misuse? *Journal of Alcohol and Drug Education, 41,* 74–98.

Grant, D., & Haynes, D. (1995). A developmental framework for cultural competence training with children. *Social Work in Education, 17,* 171–182.

Greener, S., & Crick, N. R. (1999). Normative beliefs about prosocial behavior in middle childhood: What does it mean to be nice? *Social Development, 8,* 349–365.

Guerra, N. G., Huesmann, L. R., Tolan, P. H., Van Acker, R., & Eron, L. D. (1995). Stressful events and individual beliefs as correlates of economic disadvantage and aggression among urban children. *Journal of Consulting and Clinical Psychology, 62,* 518–528.

Hagekull, B., & Bohlin, G. (1998). Preschool temperament and environmental factors related to the five-factor model of personality in middle childhood. *Merrill-Palmer Quarterly, 44,* 194–215.

Halberstadt, A. G., Denham, S. A., & Dunsmore, J. C. (2001). Affective social competence. *Social Development, 10,* 79–119.

Hallinan, M. T., & Teixeira, R. A. (1987a). Student's interracial friendships: Individual characteristics, structural effects, and racial differences. *American Journal of Education, 95,* 563–583.

Hallinan, M. T., & Teixeira, R. A. (1987b). Opportunities and constraints: Black-white differences in the formation of interracial friendships. *Child Development, 58,* 1358–1371.

Hartup, W. W. (1992). Peer relations in early and middle childhood. In V. B. Van Hasselt & M. Herson (Eds.), *Handbook of social development: A lifespan perspective* (pp. 257–281). New York: Plenum.

Hartup, W. W. (1999). Constraints on peer socialization: Let me count the ways. *Merrill-Palmer Quarterly, 45,* 172–183.

Hartup, W. W., French, D. C., Laursen, B., Johnston, M. K., & Ogawa, J. R. (1993). Conflict and friendship relations in middle childhood: Behavior in a closed-field setting. *Child Development, 64,* 445–454.

Hartup, W. W., Laursen, B., Stewart, M. I., & Eastenson, A. (1988). Conflict and the friendship relations of young children. *Child Development, 59,* 1590–1600.

Haselager, G. J. T., Cillessen, A. H. N., Van Lieshout, C. F. M., Riksen-Walraven, J. M. A., & Hartup, W. W. (2002). Heterogeneity among peer-rejected boys across middle childhood: Developmental pathways of social behavior. *Developmental Psychology, 38,* 446–456.

Hastings, P. D., Zahn-Walker, C., Robinson, J., Usher, B., & Bridges, D. (2000). The development of concern for others in children with behavior problems. *Developmental Psychology, 36,* 531–546.

Helwig, C. C., & Kim, S. (1999). Children's evaluation of decision-making procedures in peer, family, and school contexts. *Child Development, 70,* 502–512.

Howes, C., & Wu, F. (1990). Peer interactions and friendships in an ethnically diverse school setting. *Child Development, 61,* 537–541.

Hubbard, J. A. (2001). Emotion expression processes in children's peer interaction: The role of peer rejection, aggression, and gender. *Child Development, 72,* 1426–1438.

Hunter, L., & Elias, M. J. (2000). Interracial friendships, multicultural sensitivity, and social competence: How are they related? *Journal of Applied Developmental Psychology, 20,* 551–573.

John, K. (2001). Measuring children's social functioning. *Social Development, 10,* 181–187.

Johnson, D. W., & Johnson, R. T. (1994). Constructive conflict in the schools. *Journal of Social Issues, 50,* 117–138.

Johnson, D. W., & Johnson, R. T. (1996). Conflict resolution and peer mediation programs in elementary and secondary schools: A review of the research. *Review of Educational Research, 66,* 459–506.

Johnson, D. W., Johnson, R., Dudley, B., & Ackigoz, K. (1994). Effects of conflict resolution training on elementary school students. *Journal of Social Psychology, 134,* 803–817.

Kaukiainen, A., Bjorkqvist, K., Lagerspetz, K., Osterman, K., Salmivalli, C., Rothberg, S., & Ahlbom, A. (1999). The relationships between social intelligence, empathy, and three types of aggression. *Aggressive Behavior, 25,* 81–89.

Keltikangas-Jarvinen, L., & Pakaslahti, L. (1999). Development of social problem-solving strategies and changes in aggressive behavior: A 7-year follow-up from childhood to late adolescence. *Aggressive Behavior, 25,* 269–279.

Kokko, K., & Pulkkinen, L. (2000). Aggression in childhood and long-term unemployment in adulthood: A cycle of maladaptation and some protective factors. *Developmental Psychology, 36,* 463–472.

Krishnakumar, A., & Black, M. M. (2002). Longitudinal predictors of competence among African American children: The role of distal and proximal risk factors. *Applied Developmental Psychology, 23,* 237–266.

Kupersmidt, J. B., & Coie, J. D. (1990). Preadolescent peer status, aggression, and school adjustment as predictors of externalizing problems in adolescence. *Child Development, 61,* 1350–1362.

Ladd, G. W. (1996). Shifting ecologies during the 5–7 year period: Predicting children's adjustment during the transition to grade school. In A. J. Sameroff & M. M. Haith (Eds.), *The five to seven year shift: The age of reason and responsibility* (pp. 363–386). Chicago: University of Chicago Press.

Ladd, G. W. (1999). Peer relationships and social competence during early and middle childhood. *Annual Review of Psychology, 50,* 333–359.

Larrieu, J., & Mussen, P. (1987). Some personality and motivational correlates of children's prosocial behavior. *Journal of Genetic Psychology, 147,* 529–542.

Laursen, B., Finkelstein, B. D., & Betts, N. T. (2001). A developmental meta-analysis of peer conflict resolution. *Developmental Review, 21,* 423–449.

Lengua, L. J. (2002). The contribution of emotionality and self-regulation to the understanding of children's response to multiple risks. *Child Development, 73,* 144–61.

Levy, S. R. (1999). Reducing prejudice: Lessons from social-cognitive factors underlying perceiver differences in prejudice. *Journal of Social Issues, 55,* 745–765.

Litvack-Miller, W., McDougal, D., & Romney, D. M. (1997). The structure of empathy during middle childhood and its relationship to prosocial behavior. *Genetic, Social, and General Psychology Monographs, 123,* 303–324.

Malecki, C. K., & Elliot, S. N. (2002). Children's social behaviors as predictors of academic achievement: A longitudinal analysis. *School Psychology Quarterly, 17,* 1–23.

Masten, A. S., Coatsworth, J. D., Neemann, J., Gest, S. D., Tellegen, A., & Garmezy, N. (1995). The structure and coherence of competence from childhood through adolescence. *Child Development, 66,* 1635–1659.

Maszk, P., Eisenberg, N., & Guthrie, I. K. (1999). Relations of children's social status to their emotionality and regulation: A short-term longitudinal study. *Merrill-Palmer Quarterly, 45,* 468–492.

Maxwell, J. (1989). Mediation in the schools: Self-regulation, self-esteem, and self-discipline. *Mediation Quarterly, 7,* 149–155.

Meisel, C. J. (1989). Interpersonal problem solving and children's social competence: Are current measures valid? *Psychology in the Schools, 26,* 37–47.

Midgley, C., & Feldlaufer, H. (1987). Students' and teachers' decision-making fit before and after the transition to junior high school. *Journal of Early Adolescence, 7,* 225–241.

Milgram, G. G. (1996). Responsible decision making regarding alcohol: A re-emerging prevention/education strategy for the 1990s. *Journal of Drug Education, 26,* 357–365.

Mistry, R. S., Vandewater, E. A., Huston, A. C., & McLoyd, V. C. (2002). Economic well-being and children's social adjustment: The role of family processes in an ethnically diverse low-income sample. *Child Development, 73,* 935–951.

Morison, P., & Masten, A. S. (1991). Peer reputation in middle childhood as a predictor of adaptation in adolescence: A seven-year follow-up. *Child Development, 62,* 991–1007.

Mott, P., & Krane, A. (1994). Interpersonal cognitive problem-solving and childhood social competence. *Cognitive Therapy and Research, 18,* 127–141.

Musser, L. M., & Browne, B. A. (1991). Self-monitoring in middle childhood: Personality and social correlates. *Developmental Psychology, 27,* 994–999.

Nelson, J., & Aboud, F. E. (1985). The resolution of social conflict between friends. *Child Development, 6,* 1009–1017.

O'Connor, T. G. (2002). Annotation: The "effects" of parenting reconsidered: Findings, challenges, and applications. *Journal of Child Psychology and Psychiatry, 43,* 555–572.

O'Donnell, J., Hawkins, J. D., & Abbott, R. D. (1995). Predicting serious delinquency and substance abuse among aggressive boys. *Journal of Consulting and Clinical Psychology, 63,* 529–537.

Parent, S., Gosselin, C., & Moss, E. (2000). From mother-regulated to child-regulated joint planning activity: A look at familial adversity and attachment. *Journal of Applied Developmental Psychology, 21,* 447–470.

Parilla, R. K., Das, J. P., & Dash, U. N. (1996). Development of planning and its relation to other cognitive processes. *Journal of Applied Developmental Psychology, 17,* 597–624.

Parker, J. G., & Asher, S. R. (1993). Friendship and friendship quality in middle childhood: Links with peer group acceptance and feelings of loneliness and social dissatisfaction. *Developmental Psychology, 29,* 611–621.

Phillipsen, L. C. (1999). Associations between age, gender, and group acceptance and three components of friendship quality. *Journal of Early Adolescence, 19,* 438–464.

Plybon, L. E., & Kliewer, W. (2001). Neighborhood types and externalizing behavior in urban school-age children: Tests of direct, mediated, and moderated effects. *Journal of Child and Family Studies, 10,* 419–437.

Prevost, R. A., Bronson, M. B., & Casey, M. B. (1995). Planning processes in pre-school children. *Journal of Applied Developmental Psychology, 16,* 505–527.

Prinstein, M. J., & LaGreca, A. M. (2002). Peer crowd affiliation and internalizing distress in childhood and adolescence: A longitudinal follow-back study. *Journal of Research on Adolescence, 12,* 325–351.

Roberts, W., & Strayer, J. (1996). Empathy, emotional expressiveness, and prosocial behavior. *Child Development, 67,* 449–470.

Rodkin, P. C., Farmer, T. W., Pearl, R., & Van Acker, R. (2000). Heterogeneity of popular boys: Antisocial and prosocial configurations. *Developmental Psychology, 36,* 14–24.

Rohrbach, L. A., Graham, J. W., Hansen, W. B., Flay, B. R., & Johnson, C. A. (1987). Evaluation of resistance skills training using multitrait-multimethod role play skill assessments. *Health Education Research, 2,* 401–407.

Rothbart, M. K., Ahadi, S. A., Hershey, K. L., & Fisher, P. (2001). Investigations of temperament at three to seven years: The Children's Behavior Questionnaire. *Child Development, 72,* 1394–1408.

Rydell, A., Hagekull, B., & Bohlin, G. (1997). Measurement of two social competence aspects in middle childhood. *Developmental Psychology, 33,* 824–833.

Savage, S. L., & Gauvain, M. (1998). Parental beliefs and children's everyday planning in European-American and Latino families. *Journal of Applied Developmental Psychology, 19,* 319–340.

Scales, P. C., & Leffert, N. (1999). *Developmental assets: A synthesis of the scientific research on adolescent development.* Minneapolis: Search Institute.

Simons, R. L., Murry, V., McLoyd, V., Lin, K., Cutrona, C., & Conger, R. (2002). Discrimination, crime, ethnic identity, and parenting as correlates of depressive symptoms among African American children: A multilevel analysis. *Development and Psychopathology, 14,* 371–393.

Simpkins, S. D., & Parke, R. D. (2002). Do friends and nonfriends behave differently? A social relations analysis of children's behavior. *Merrill-Palmer Quarterly, 48,* 263–283.

Slavin, R. E., & Cooper, R. (1999). Improving intergroup relations: Lessons learned from cooperative learning programs. *Journal of Social Issues, 55,* 647–663.

Sneed, C. D. (2002). Correlates and implications for agreeableness in children. *Journal of Psychology, 136,* 59–67.

Snyder, J., West, L., Stockemer, V., Gibbons, S., & Almquist-Parks, L. (1996). A social learning model of peer choice in the natural environment. *Journal of Applied Developmental Psychology, 17,* 215–237.

Spencer, M. B., & Markstrom-Adams, C. (1990). Identity processes among racial and ethnic minority children in America. *Child Development, 61,* 290–310.

Steinberg, L., & Silverberg, S. B. (1986). The vicissitudes of autonomy in early adolescence. *Child Development, 57,* 841–851.

Stomfay-Stitz, A. M. (1994). Conflict resolution and peer mediation: Pathways to safer schools. *Childhood Education, 70,* 279–283.

Strough, J., Swenson, L. M., & Cheng, S. (2001). Friendship, gender, and preadolescents' representations of peer collaboration. *Merrill-Palmer Quarterly, 47,* 475–499.

Underwood, M. K., Coie, J. D., & Herbsman, C. K. (1992). Display rules for anger and aggression in school-age children. *Child Development, 63,* 366–380.

Underwood, M. K., Hurley, J. C., Johanson, C. A., & Mosley, J. E. (1999). An experimental, observational investigation of children's responses to peer provocation: Developmental and gender differences in middle childhood. *Child Development, 70,* 1428–1446.

Underwood, M. K., Schockner, A. E., & Hurley, J. C. (2001). Children's responses to same- and other-gender peers: An experimental investigation with 8-, 10-, and 12-year-olds. *Developmental Psychology, 37,* 362–372.

Urberg, K. A. (1999). Introduction: Some thoughts about studying the influence of peers on children and adolescents. *Merrill-Palmer Quarterly, 45,* 1–12.

Vinnick, L. A., & Erickson, M. T. (1992). Relationships among accumulated lifetime life events, prosocial skills, and behavior problems in elementary school children. *Journal of Child and Family Studies, 1,* 141–154.

Vuchinich, S., Angelelli, J., & Gatherum, A. (1996). Context and development in family problem solving with preadolescent children. *Child Development, 67,* 1276–1288.

Walsh, M., Parke, R. D., Widaman, K., & O'Neil, R. (2001). Linkages between children's social and academic competence: A longitudinal analysis. *Journal of School Psychology, 39,* 463–481.

Weithorn, L. A., & Campbell, S. B. (1982). The competency of children and adolescents to make informed treatment decisions. *Child Development, 53,* 1589–1598.

Developing a sense of confidence, worth, and a positive outlook, and beginning to think about life's meaning, are important developmental "building blocks" as children construct their personal identity.

8

The Positive-Identity Assets

Why Is Positive Identity Important?

Throughout their development, children generally fare better when they are confident in their ability to make desired events happen, optimistic about what the future holds for them, and happy with the total person they are and are becoming. Children who enjoy such assets usually, although not always, exhibit fewer emotional and behavioral problems, have better mental health, are more resilient, and are more successful in a number of ways than are children who are less confident, optimistic, and happy. These elements of self-esteem, competence, and optimism are neither conceptually nor statistically completely independent of each other (Robins, Hendin, & Trzesniewski, (2001). Each may, at a particular point in time, become the single most salient dimension affecting the developmental outcomes in a particular context or under specific circumstances. The *collective* importance of these identity traits has been repeatedly demonstrated, however. Indeed, Masten (2001) noted that a small set of factors has consistently been found to be associated with resilience. Among them are "connections to competent and caring adults in the family and community, cognitive and self-regulation skills, *positive views of self*, and motivation to be effective in the environment" (p. 234, emphasis added).

In his treatment of identity development throughout childhood and youth, Erikson (1968) described the significant identity "crisis" of middle childhood as one of achieving a sense of "industry" instead of "inferiority." Middle childhood is the stage when learning to do things, from behaving and achieving in school to interacting effectively with peers and adults inside and outside of the family, takes on particular developmental importance. The inevitable result when children confront the task of developing academic, social, and behavioral competencies is a refinement of their self-image and their sense of life's possibilities.

Studies have generally concluded that children's self-concepts become less concrete, more abstract, and more differentiated as they age from preschool through early childhood to middle childhood (Anderson, 1992; Byrne, 1996). Although the self-concept becomes *more* differentiated across childhood, there is evidence that even young children have significantly differentiated self-structures. Marsh, Craven, and Debus (1991) studied a sample of children in kindergarten through grade 2 and reported that the children distinguished well between what they thought of themselves in general, and what they thought of themselves within specific contexts involving physical ability, physical appearance, peer relationships, parent relationships, and academic areas such as reading, math, and general relationship to school.

Van den Bergh and Van Ranst (1998) reported similar results from a study of 758 Dutch students in grades 4 through 6, finding that the dimensions of children's self-structures become more distinct across these years. For example, correlations between scholastic competence and behavioral conduct, and between social acceptance and physical appearance, are significantly stronger for children in 4th grade than for children in 6th grade. Using a personal interview approach, Marsh, Ellis, and Craven (2002) reported that even 4- and 5-year-olds can identify physical, peer, verbal, and mathematical self-concepts.

Cole and associates (2001) followed two cohorts totaling nearly 2,000 children from 3rd grade through 11th grade in order to investigate aspects of self-concept. They found that, in perceived academic competence, sports competence, and social acceptance, both boys and girls appeared to recover during grades 3 through 6 from the typical declines in self-concept observed in earlier years. During those same middle childhood years, however, both genders reported less favorable impressions of their behavioral conduct (boys' reports were significantly worse). Girls also reported declines in their sense of personal physical attractiveness. Cole et al. (2001) noted that these gender differences were present among even the youngest 3rd-grade children in the study, and their impressions remained stable over time. In fact, the overall conclusion they drew was that, over the course of middle childhood, the self-concept becomes both more stable and more differentiated (or "domain-specific"). Other research has also found that girls' body image (which seems to develop concurrently with global self-esteem) becomes more negative than boys' body image between the ages of 8 and 10 (Ricciardelli & McCabe, 2001).

Much of the previous discussion concerns the descriptive and evaluative aspects of self-concept generally thought of as self-esteem, or how one feels about oneself as a person (Burnett, 1994). Self-esteem "involves an evaluation *of* oneself followed by an emotional reaction *towards* oneself" (Wang & Ollendick, 2001, p. 255). Another important aspect of children's positive identity is their sense of self-efficacy, of being an effective "agent" who is able to make desired things happen in their own lives (i.e., believing that one has some control or influence over one's life course).

As Bandura (2001) described it, the core features of agency include performing actions intentionally, with forethought; having the ability to motivate and regulate oneself; and being able to examine, reflect on, and create meaning out of one's functioning. The degree to which children feel capable or efficacious influences the goals they set, their motivation, how they evaluate themselves, and their overall sense of optimism or pessimism. Prilleltensky, Nelson, and Peirson (2001) also observed that self-efficacy is an important component of power and control, both of which have significant relationships with wellness and resilience. One of the operative mechanisms for these associations, they argued, may be that children with adequate levels of self-efficacy have more opportunities for participation in family, school, and community, affording them greater access to valued resources for healthy development.

Another mechanism may be *plasticity*, children's growing ability to adapt to differing or changing circumstances, as well as to challenges and opportunities. Children with adequate levels of self-efficacy may have access to more motivational and problem-solving resources and be better able to flexibly adjust to and help shape the environments they live in. Clearly, children in the upper elementary years reach a critical developmental juncture in becoming agents who increasingly put a personal stamp on their own lives. In Bandura's words: "Through agentic action, people devise ways of adapting flexibly to remarkably diverse geographic, climatic, and social environments; they figure out ways to circumvent physical and environmental constraints, redesign and construct environments to their liking, create styles of behavior that enable them to realize desired outcomes, and pass on the effective ones to others by social modeling and other experiential modes of influence" (2001, p. 22).

This increasing psychological and social flexibility may also be related to a gradually increasing internal locus of control among children in middle childhood (Richaud de Minzi, 1991), such that they feel more responsible for both their successes and failures, rather than attributing failure, especially, to external forces. By increasingly perceiving that they have influence over events in their lives, children may be more open to exploring ways of adapting to situations than if they feel nothing can be done to change events that are "external."

A review of the literature on aggressive children reveals that flexibility in the components of identity is an important adaptational mechanism of children. Edens (1999) reported that the research suggests that most aggressive children seem either too globally positive or too negative in assessing their personal competencies and the degree to which they are esteemed by others. Aggressive children are more at risk for behavior problems than are nonaggressive children, most of whom seem to have a more balanced, flexible view of themselves. In fact, overestimation of these positive identity elements appears to put aggressive children at even greater risk for behavior problems than aggressive children who accurately identify and understand their weaknesses.

Evidence shows that self-efficacy is probably not an exclusively global characteristic of children, but can also be domain-specific. For example, Skinner (1990) reported that children ages 7 to 12 had different senses of perceived control over their school performance and friendships. They believed that effort was relatively more important to school success than to friendship, whereas powerful others, luck, or personal attributes like niceness were more important determinants of friendship. With increasing age, however, personal attributes such as ability were considered the most important contributors to outcomes. Thus, although we measure a kind of self-efficacy in the asset of personal power, it is a global construct that may not fully reflect the actual processes that children experience as they come to appreciate their competency and efficacy in *specific* domains or situations.

The positive-identity assets reflect the general dimensions of self-efficacy, self-worth, and senses of meaning and hopefulness. As the previous discussion implies, these dimensions are related to each other, but each is also important in its own right. Children's identities are also influenced by other constructs we do not measure, such as ethnic identity, gender identity, and body esteem. For example, in a study of nearly 200 children in grades 4 through 8, Egan and Perry (2001) found that children who felt content with their biological sex, or felt that they were a typical member of their sex, reported higher levels of self-esteem and peer acceptance than children who reported less positive gender identities.

In the cultural competence asset, we do not ask about pride in one's own cultural heritage, but this is not a sufficiently comprehensive measure to be called "ethnic identity." Regarding children's ethnic identity, in a large study of African American families living in Iowa and Georgia, researchers did not find that the ethnic identification of individual 10- to 12-year-olds protected them from depression. The researchers speculated that even a strong ethnic identification at this age was insufficient to protect children from depression if they also perceived considerable racial discrimination in their lives (Simons et al., 2002). However, if the children's *community* espoused a strong community-level ethnic identification or racial pride, this ethnic identification served as a protective influence for the children surveyed, probably because such a community fosters "a sense of meaning, belonging, and optimism" (p. 388) that may be especially supportive when racial discrimination is commonly experienced. Community ethnic identification was derived by averaging the individual ethnic identity scores of children from the same community. This result suggests that elements of an individual's positive identity may become activated as meaningful assets only if the environment features a critical mass of individuals who have similarly strong positive identities.

Likewise, Hughes and Johnson (2001) reported that African American parents transmitted more messages about discrimination to their 3rd- to 5th-grade children when those children showed an interest in and exploration of their ethnic identity. The study could not distinguish whether a discussion of discrimination came first, subsequently influencing ethnic identity exploration, or whether the order was reversed. However, these studies do show that issues such as discrimination, ethnic identity, parent-child communication, and the prevailing ethos of ethnic pride in a community likely interact to influence identity processes among cultural minority children.

Cultural considerations also make it challenging to accurately interpret cross-cultural differences in the various dimensions of positive identity. For example, within the Chinese vocabulary there is no word for self-esteem. Although increasing access to Western culture is expected to bring some changes to the mainland Chinese cultural backdrop for child development, the situating of "self" as a concept largely experienced in relationship to significant others and in groups, not individually, is likely to remain a strong characteristic of Chinese culture and child rearing (Wang & Ollendick, 2001).

In Search Institute's *Me and My World* field test surveys of young people in Nevada, California, and New York, each of the positive-identity assets is measured at what we term "promising" levels of internal consistency, with reliabilities most often in the .60s (see Appendix). The earlier pilot studies with 800 students in two Oklahoma communities yielded higher reliabilities, in the .70s. Thus, although there appears to be reasonable internal consistency in these positive-identity asset measures, the range across samples may be more than in the other asset categories, ranging from promising to acceptable levels.

Table 16. The Positive-Identity Assets	
Personal power	Child feels he or she has some influence over things that happen in her or his life.
Self-esteem	Child likes and is proud to be the person he or she is.
Sense of purpose	Child sometimes thinks about what life means and whether there is a purpose for her or his life.
Positive view of personal future	Child is optimistic about her or his personal future.

Summary of the Research: The Positive-Identity Assets in Middle Childhood

Investigations concerning locus of control, self-concept, self-efficacy, self-esteem, self-competence, and optimism comprise the bulk of research studies related to what Search Institute calls the positive-identity assets. In many of the studies, aspects of two or more of these concepts are interwoven and, thus, studied together; rarely are individual effects separated from the whole. This suggests that the positive-identity assets are both intricately related and overlapping in nature. Underlying most of the positive-identity research in middle childhood, although treated in distinctly different ways in different studies, are children's perceptions and emotional reactions to their abilities. These include the ability to exercise control over events and decisions in one's life (personal power), satisfaction with one's strengths and abilities (self-esteem), and one's outlook on future opportunities and abilities (positive view of personal future).

Indeed, the central importance of the association between a child's abilities and her or his positive identity in middle childhood is elucidated in Erikson's widely accepted notion of the crucial developmental "crisis" of this life stage: The child develops either a sense of industry or a sense of inferiority during this period (Erikson, 1968). The child who feels capable and efficacious in carrying out tasks and responsibilities, who recognizes her or his strengths, and understands that past successes bring hope for the future is more likely to be guided by a sense of accomplishment and agency, which in turn influences positive identity formation. It is not surprising, then, that the research identified in our literature review indicates that personal power, self-esteem, and a positive view of the future are of central importance for overall well-being in middle childhood. The sense-of-purpose asset is far less represented by empirical studies. During middle childhood, sense of purpose may not yet be differentiated well from the other three positive-identity assets. However, we do discuss it here as an increasingly important indication, not so much that the child at this stage "has" a sense of purpose, but more that he or she sometimes reflects on the meaning of life and her or his unique role in the world.

Personal Power

The literature supporting the positive impact and developmental significance of a sense of personal power in preadolescence largely involves plentiful research on self-efficacy and locus of control. Research consistently shows that an internal sense of control and efficacy over one's life in middle childhood is related to better school outcomes, emotional adjustment, social competence, and healthy behaviors. Specifically, personal power has been associated, directly or indirectly, with:

Academic Outcomes

- **Better school attendance and increased grades and standardized test scores** (Connell, Spencer, & Aber, 1994 [via engagement in school]; Skinner, Wellborn, & Connell, 1990); **increased school engagement** (Connell et al., 1994; Skinner et al., 1990); and **better problem-solving skills** (Adalbjarnardottir, 1995).

Mental and Behavioral Health Outcomes

- **Better socioemotional adjustment** for children experiencing high levels of stress (Seifer, Sameroff, Baldwin, & Baldwin, 1992; Wyman, Cowen, Work, & Kerley, 1993); **increased positive adjustment and self-esteem across the junior high school/middle school transition** (Lord, Eccles, & McCarthy, 1994); **decreased substance use and abuse** (Dielman, Campanelli, Shope, & Butchart, 1987); and **decreased at-risk status** (Browne & Rife, 1991).

Social Outcomes

- **Improved peer status among initially rejected children** (Sandstrom & Coie, 1999).

The concept of locus of control is closely related to self-efficacy and personal power. Children who feel they have more control over what happens in their lives have been found to have more positive attitudes toward school (Browne & Rife, 1991), have less risk of emotional or conduct problems (Siefer et al., 1992), and negotiate more effectively when resolving hypothetical interpersonal conflicts (Adalbjarnardottir, 1995). A study of 364 families with daughters in grades 3 and 4 found that parents who held less gender-stereotyped attitudes—in a measure of such indicators as whether parents held greater beliefs in equality of power between men and women, and control over household tasks and child-rearing practices—had daughters with high internal locus of control scores, better coping skills, and, among middle-class girls, higher achievement scores (Hoffman & Kloska, 1995).

In a study of more than 200 children ages 9 to 12, Skinner and colleagues (1990) showed that the degree to which children thought they could influence their school success or failure was related to their engagement with school, which in turn positively affected their school performance. Students who felt more personal control were more engaged. Teachers were also found to contribute to children's perceptions of personal control when they provided clear and consistent guidelines and feedback, and showed an interest in the child.

Self-Esteem

Of the four positive-identity assets identified for children in middle childhood, research studies are most abundant with regard to self-esteem. The literature on the relation of self-esteem to positive developmental outcomes is inconsistent, however, in part because of widely varying definitions and instruments used to measure self-esteem (Haney & Durlak, 1998). High levels of self-esteem, while not invariably associated with positive outcomes, do tend to be associated more often than not with positive development, whether in studies of adolescents (see review in Scales & Leffert, 1999) or younger children (e.g., Haney & Durlak, 1998; Young, Werch, & Bakema, 1989). The evidence suggests that positive self-esteem is associated, directly or indirectly, with:

Academic Outcomes

- **Better school attendance and increased grades and standardized test scores** for African American children (Connell et al., 1994 [via engagement in school]); and **increased school engagement** (Connell et al., 1994).

Mental and Behavioral Health Outcomes

- **Fewer emotional and behavioral problems** (DuBois et al., 2002); **increased positive adjustment during the junior high school transition** (Lord et al., 1994); **decreased current and expected substance use and abuse** (Dielman et al., 1987; Young et al., 1989 [for home and school, but not peer, self-esteem]); **decreased likelihood of smoking** (Abernathy, Massad, & Romano-Dwyer, 1995 [for girls only]; Kawabata, Cross, Nishioka, & Shimai, 1999 [for

Japanese youth]); and **better physical fitness habits** (Overbay & Purath, 1997).

Of course, parental practices play a major role in the development of children's self-esteem. Warm and firm parenting experienced early in life sets the stage for children to feel accepted, capable, and confident. Research has found that, in the middle childhood years, 11- and 12-year-old children of critical, overcontrolling parents report lower and less stable levels of self-esteem than peers who experience more positive parenting styles (see Chapter 1 for more on positive parenting practices) (Kernis, Brown, & Brody, 2000).

Similarly, 9- to 12-year-old children who claim a strong attachment to their mothers and fathers have been reported to exhibit greater global self-worth than children whose attachment to their parents is less secure (Doyle, Markiewicz, Brendgen, Lieberman, & Voss, 2000). Young and colleagues (1989) also reported that, among students surveyed in grades 4 through 9, those who scored higher on "home" self-esteem (i.e., who felt good about the warmth and supportiveness of their home environments) were less likely to report current or intended alcohol, nicotine, or other drug use.

Adults other than parents are also potentially important influences on children's developing self-esteem. For example, DuBois and colleagues (2002) reported, in a study of 350 Midwestern 5th through 8th graders, that behavioral adjustment in young people was related to their having a balance of peer- and adult-oriented (school and adult family mentors) sources for social support and self-esteem development. Young people whose support and esteem came to a greater degree from their peers tended to exhibit more behavioral problems over the 2-year longitudinal study. During late middle childhood, children's levels of social support seemed to contribute to their levels of self-esteem, which in turn affected behavioral adjustment.

Research has shown a complicated relationship between self-worth and eating disorders among children, with the findings varying depending on children's gender, age, and ethnicity. For example, girls ages 6 to 12 years generally show a greater link between low self-worth and dieting concerns, although when race and ethnicity are taken into account, the effect seems to occur predominantly among White rather than African American girls (Ricciardelli & McCabe, 2001).

In a small study of children in grades 1 through 8, Overby and Purath (1997) investigated self-concept and physical fitness, using an instrument that correlated well with other self-esteem measures. They found that children who had more positive self-concepts also reported exercising more regularly than their peers with more negative self-concepts. Although the direction of effect could not be determined from their study, the authors noted that other research suggests a bidirectional effect, with positive self-concept contributing to physical fitness, and fitness contributing to positive self-concept. Another study of children ages 6 to 11 also found that normal-weight children had a higher level of physical self-concept than did overweight children (Stein, Bracken, Haddock, & Shadish, 1998). In their study of children ages 5 to 7, Davison and Birch (2002) suggested, too, that peer teasing and parental criticism of overweight girls mediated the relation between being overweight and having a lower self-concept, such that overweight girls were more likely to have lower self-concepts if they also were the subject of teasing and criticism because of their weight.

Sense of Purpose

Sense of purpose represents an asset present across boundaries of age and developmental stage. One task in which all human beings engage at some level of awareness, after meeting their minimum survival needs, is to arrive at an inner sense of what their lives mean and why they are here (in other words, their purpose for being). In a sense, the journey to discover purpose and create meaning in one's life reflects developmental continuity across the life span. But at what developmental stage do we expect people to have even an inchoate sense of what that purpose is for their life?

It is fair to suggest that some, perhaps many, adults do not feel a genuine, firm sense of purpose in their lives. But as part of their identity exploration, most adolescents should be developmentally involved in thinking, at least occasionally, about the meaning of life and their place in it. To what degree, however, is such exploration developmentally even possible for elementary school children, given their common levels of cognitive, emotional, moral, and social maturity?

We consider it unreasonable in developmental terms to expect most 4th and 5th graders, and even most 6th graders, to "have" a solid sense of their mission in life or to "have" a real idea of their "purpose." So sense of purpose must reflect a somewhat different developmental "nutrient" at this stage than at adolescence.

Certainly, almost all children, from their earliest moments of self-awareness as beings separate from their parents, and well before the upper elementary years, do at least occasionally think about the kind of person they are and want to be. They have to do the work of all growing persons, to come to terms with common events such as the death of a pet, rejection by a friend, parental divorce and remarriage, and illness, as well as uncommon events, such as the September 2001 terrorist attacks on the United States. (Unfortunately, although drive-by shootings and other kinds of violence are uncommon occurrences for most

American children, they are all-too-common parts of development for too many children in poor urban areas.) More prosaically, they start liking and noticing their talents or lack thereof in particular kinds of music, art, sports, and social interactions with others, all of which add "meaning" to their lives. Some children also may have a more firmly rooted sense than other children of religious faith or spirituality that heightens their understanding of what "purpose" signifies and what their life's purpose might be.

So it is not unreasonable to expect that most children will be engaging in some level of meaning making about their lives. Thus, we suggest that a more developmentally nuanced expression of "sense of purpose" for middle childhood is not whether children "have" a sense of purpose, but whether they report being sometimes engaged in thinking about what their life means and whether there is a purpose for their lives.

Unfortunately, few studies deal primarily with children ages 8–12. Of the studies we report here, only the upper end of middle childhood (age 11) is represented. This research suggests that a sense of purpose or meaning ascribed to life is associated with better mental health, personal control, and less participation in risky activities. A meaningful sense of purpose is associated, directly or indirectly, with:

Mental and Behavioral Health Outcomes

- **Decreased emotional or behavioral problems such as depression and sexual risk taking** (DuRant, Getts, Cadenhead, Emans, & Woods, 1995); **fewer symptoms of depression and anxiety** among Chinese youth (Shek, 1992); **reduced violence** (DuRant, Cadenhead, Pendergrast, Slavens, & Linder, 1994); **internal locus of control** (Shek, 2001 [among Chinese youth]; Showalter & Wagener, 2000).

Positive View of Personal Future

The literature suggests, in particular, that children who experience tremendous life stress (e.g., economic hardship, discrimination, dangerous neighborhoods) appear especially to benefit from a positive view of the future. For example, Seligman, Reivich, Jaycox, and Gillham (1995) examined 70 5th and 6th graders who participated in the Penn Prevention Program, an innovative intervention for children and adolescents at risk for depression. The program aimed to challenge children's pessimistic explanatory styles and teach them more positive coping strategies. After a 2-year follow-up, the researchers found that the enrolled children were only half as likely as the control group to exhibit moderate to severe depressive symptoms. In addition, an optimistic outlook during middle childhood on one's future possibilities has been linked to many positive outcomes, such as a sense of personal control, better school-related behaviors, and satisfaction with one's life and general abilities. A positive future orientation has been associated, directly or indirectly, with:

Academic Outcomes

- **Increased reading achievement** (Wyman et al., 1993 [for children experiencing high levels of stress]); and **greater interest in school and motivation in studying** (Koizumi, 1995 [Japanese youth]; Wyman et al., 1993 [for children experiencing high levels of stress]).

Mental and Behavioral Health Outcomes

- **Greater self-esteem** (Fischer & Leitenberg, 1986); **lessened anxiety, depression, or both** (Seligman et al., 1995; Wyman et al., 1993 [for children experiencing high levels of stress]; Yu & Seligman, 2002 [for Chinese children]); **better socioemotional adjustment** (Wyman et al., 1993 [for children experiencing high levels of stress]); **greater internal locus of control** (Wyman et al., 1993 [for children experiencing high levels of stress]); **decreased teacher-rated behavior problems** (Wyman et al., 1993); **increased ability to develop competently in high-risk, high-stress environments** (Wyman et al., 1999; Wyman, Cowen, Work, & Parker, 1991; Wyman et al., 1992).

Social Outcomes

- **Better peer relationships** (Koizumi, 1995 [Japanese youth]).

One study of nearly 3,000 young people from Africa, Asia, Australia, and the United States reported that African children generally had the most positive overall self-concept, but cultural differences regarding individualism and collectivism were not sufficient to explain the results (Wastlund, Norlander, & Archer, 2001). The researchers speculated that the differences in self-concept were at least partly attributable to variations in levels of hope and optimism across cultures, with African children experiencing greater levels of learned resourcefulness and optimism and lower levels of hopelessness. The young adolescents in this study averaged 13 years of age; therefore, these findings may not be as applicable to children in middle childhood, but they do raise the possibility for younger children as well that a sense of optimism may be an important element of one's overall positive identity.

However, Fischer and Leitenberg (1986) reported that the relation of optimism to self-esteem may not be simple. In their study of 9- to 13-year-olds, the authors found that optimism and pessimism did not lie on opposite ends of the same continuum, but represented separate constructs. A stronger association existed between pessimism and lower self-esteem than between optimism and higher self-esteem. Nevertheless, studies have generally found that children's reported optimism and positive expectations for their futures are associated with positive outcomes, such as relative resilience to life stress (Wyman et al., 1992) and being more engaged academically (Koizumi, 1995).

In addition, how *parents* view a child's future possibilities may provide important resources for children. In a study of more than 300 urban 4th- through 6th-grade children and their parents, Wyman and colleagues (1991) found that stress-resilient children were distinguished from stress-affected children by their easygoing temperaments and their parents' reports of both a close parent-child relationship and more supportive family and community resources. In addition, parents of stress-resilient children held more hope for their children's futures than did the parents of children affected adversely by life stress.

The Positive-Identity Assets
across the Early Childhood-Adolescence Life Span

One of the sweet, endearing traits of many young children is their generally unflagging belief in themselves and their expressions of high self-confidence and self-esteem (Harter, 1998). More sophisticated conceptual and methodological investigations of children's self-concepts have shown that young children do possess multidimensional and multifaceted self-concept structures (Marsh et al., 2002). Those studies also report, however, that young children approximately 4 to 5 years old hold fairly optimistic beliefs in their self-esteem and competencies relative to older children (7 years old to adolescence) (Harter, 1998). These early positive beliefs are due, in part, to the manifestly behavioral nature of children's self-attributes; that is, most young children tend to base their beliefs about their identity on things they can do, and in particular, on the things they can do well (Harter, 1998).

With age, however, self-descriptions and beliefs become increasingly based on the *interpersonal*, in that relationships with others take on a greater role in the development of the self. This idea—that the self is inherently constructed relationally—has its roots in the symbolic interactionist perspective espoused by Cooley (1902) and Mead (1934) in the early part of the 20th century. This perspective asserts that individuals define themselves as a function of their relationships, since it is through these experiences that one learns about her- or himself; Cooley (1902) called this process the "looking glass self."

As we stated earlier, parents and other adults play major roles in children's construction of their self-esteem. During the early elementary period, necessary relational conditions for fostering the development of positive self-esteem include supportive, nurturing, fair, and consistent discipline from parents and others close to the child (Davison & Birch 2002; Harter, 1998). As children grow older, they experience an increase in the significance of peer relationships in the molding of their self-beliefs. Sullivan developed a theory around the idea that a child's "chumships" provide a unique, enduring influence on whether that child suffers from loneliness or develops positive, healthy self-esteem (1953). Indeed, many studies of the developmental significance of child and adolescent friendships include self-esteem as an outcome, given the rich theoretical and empirical literature linking these two constructs (Berndt, Hawkins, & Jiao, 1999; Hartup, 1996).

While related to self-concept, the asset construct of personal power may have deeper developmental roots than other self-beliefs. This construct is hypothesized to have its origins in early caregiver-child interactions, where a history of emotional availability and responsiveness leads to, among other things, children's beliefs that they have some influence on the behaviors of their caregivers and, subsequently, over their environment (Sroufe, Egeland, & Carlson, 1999). This belief, which Bandura has called "the essence of humanness" (2001, p. 1), is a central node around which many of the other constructs discussed in this book—self-esteem, self-worth, persistence, and motivation—orbit (Sroufe, 1983). The converse of this idea is that of "learned helplessness"—in which the child's sense of meaningfulness and participation *within* the environment becomes distorted.

In an elegantly designed longitudinal study, Kistner, Ziegert, Castro, and Robertson (2001) addressed the relative influences of self-worth and learned helplessness (the converse of which can be considered agency) on indexes of children's well-being both during kindergarten and in grade 5. In kindergarten, children engaged in solving a series of four puzzles, the first three of which were actually unsolvable. The investigators then assessed a number of indicators of children's sense of helplessness, including affect, expectations of future success, and attributions for success or failure in the puzzle tasks. Additionally, measures of children's sense of self-worth, self-reported levels of depression, and teacher ratings of anxiety and/or depression were collected at both the kindergarten and grade 5 time points.

No significant relation was found between the degree to which children displayed agency and their perceptions of self-worth in kindergarten, indicating that helplessness was not an indicator of a general tendency to report negatively about oneself (see also Dweck, 1999). Kistner and colleagues (2001) found that the students' levels of helplessness in kindergarten predicted their levels of depression, global self-worth, and teacher ratings of anxiety and depression in grade 5, but children's kindergarten self-perceptions were *not* related to these indexes of well-being.

The authors speculated that because younger children's self-concepts are more global, tend to be relatively optimistic, and are constrained by their cognitive limitations (which do not allow for the kinds of social comparisons that more accurately reflect a child's abilities), these self-concepts may have low predictive utility. As discussed earlier, learned helplessness and its converse, agency, are thought to be intimately related to the interpersonal history of the child's relationship with primary caregivers (Sroufe et al., 1999). That is, agency and helplessness are natural outgrowths of the quality of relationships that children experience and, as such, are not as heavily influenced by children's relatively unsophisticated cognitive processing abilities. Thus, this study poses an interesting developmental question regarding the positive-identity assets: If personal power (agency) develops earlier and is a more reliable predictor of later functioning than are self-concepts in the early elementary years, in what ways does a child's sense of agency contribute to her or his ongoing development of a sense of self? Unfortunately, Kistner and associates (2001) did not report the predictive significance of kindergarten helplessness on 5th graders' self-concept. As Search Institute's work continues on developmental assets present in the first decade of life, it will be interesting to track the development not only of individual assets but also of *how* assets that develop relatively early in life influence or affect the trajectory of other assets.

Measuring the Positive-Identity Assets in Middle Childhood

The results of Search Institute's *Me and My World* survey field tests suggest that a majority of children in grades 4 through 6 (roughly 60% to 70%) may experience each of three positive-identity assets (the fourth asset, sense of purpose, was added after the field tests—see Table 17). Although welcome, this finding means, of course, that a considerable minority of children, perhaps 30% to 40%, do *not* experience developmentally adequate levels of personal power, self-esteem, or a positive view of their personal future.

In middle childhood, children are engaged in ongoing development of a

Table 17. Proportion of Field Test 4th–6th Graders Who Report Experiencing the Positive-Identity Assets			
Asset	**% Who Report Experiencing Asset**		
	Nevada	**California**	**New York**
Personal power	66	60	66
Self-esteem	72	59	75
Sense of purpose[a]	–	–	–
Positive view of personal future	62	62	57

From field tests in 2003; N = 1,294.
[a] Measure added after field tests; no data available.

number of dimensions or elements of the self that eventually will reflect a mature personal identity. From this perspective, identity during middle childhood is emergent; therefore, it is not surprising if considerable proportions of children say they do not experience positive "identity." In middle childhood, children are also less able to reflect on their inner self-perceptions than they will be later in adolescence, and so considerable proportions of them may indeed "have" a positive identity but not capture that reality well in responding to questions.

Nor is it particularly surprising that the least commonly experienced positive-identity asset may be that of personal power. As Bandura (2001) described it, the sense that one can have some measure of influence over one's world, and can draw confidence from that realization, may be only incipient in early childhood and beginning to take shape in middle childhood, through repeated intentional acts of human agency and reflection. Personal power may also be quite domain specific, leaving cognitively less mature upper elementary children less able than adolescents, for example, to infer a general pattern of whether they "have" or "don't have" personal power.

References

Abernathy, T. J., Massad, L., & Romano-Dwyer, L. (1995). The relationship between smoking and self-esteem. *Adolescence, 30*, 899–907.

Adalbjarnardottir, S. (1995). How schoolchildren propose to negotiate: The role of social withdrawal, social anxiety, and locus of control. *Child Development, 66*, 1739–1751.

Anderson, K. M. (1992). Self-complexity and self-esteem in middle childhood. In R. P. Lipka & T. M. Brinthaupt (Eds.), *Self-perspectives across the life span* (pp. 11–52). Albany: State University of New York Press.

Bandura, A. (2001). Social cognitive theory: An agentic perspective. *Annual Review of Psychology, 51,* 1-26.

Berndt, T. J., Hawkins, J. A., & Jiao, Z. (1999). Influences of friends and friendships on adjustment to junior high school. *Merrill-Palmer Quarterly, 45,* 13-41.

Browne, C. S., & Rife, J. (1991). Social, personality, and gender differences in at-risk and not-at-risk sixth-grade students. *Journal of Early Adolescence, 11,* 482-495.

Burnett, P. C. (1994). Self-concept and self-esteem in elementary school children. *Psychology in the Schools, 31,* 164-171.

Byrne, B. M. (1996). *Measuring self-concept across the life span: Issues and instrumentation* (pp. 85-124). Washington, DC: American Psychological Association.

Cole, D. A., Maxwell, S. E., Martin, J. M., Peeke, L. G., Seroczynski, A. D., Tram, J. M., Hoffman, K. B., Ruiz, M. D., Jacquez, F., & Maschman, T. (2001). The development of multiple domains of child and adolescent self-concept: A cohort sequential longitudinal design. *Child Development, 72,* 1723-1746.

Connell, J. P., Spencer, M. B., & Aber, J. L. (1994). Educational risk and resilience in African-American youth: Context, self, action, and outcome in school. *Child Development, 65,* 493-506.

Cooley, C. H. (1902). *Human nature and social order.* New York: Charles Scribner's Sons.

Davison, K. K., & Birch, L. L. (2002). Processes linking weight status and self-concept among girls from ages 5 to 7 years. *Developmental Psychology, 38,* 735-748.

Dielman, T. E., Campanelli, P. C., Shope, J. T., & Butchart, A. T. (1987). Susceptibility to peer pressure, self-esteem, and healthy locus of control as correlates of adolescent substance abuse. *Health Education Quarterly, 14,* 207-221.

Doyle, A. B., Markiewicz, D., Brendgen, M., Lieberman, M., & Voss, K. (2000). Child attachment security and self-concept: Associations with mother and father attachment style and marital quality. *Merrill-Palmer Quarterly, 46,* 514-539.

DuBois, D. L., Burk-Braxton, C., Swenson, L. P., Tevendale, H. D., Lockerd, E. M., & Moran, B. L. (2002). Getting by with a little help from self and others: Self-esteem and social support as resources during early adolescence. *Developmental Psychology, 38,* 822-839.

DuRant, R. H., Cadenhead, C., Pendergrast, R. A., Slavens, G., & Linder, C. W. (1994). Factors associated with the use of violence among urban Black adolescents. *American Journal of Public Health, 84,* 612-617.

DuRant, R. H., Getts, A., Cadenhead, C., Emans, S. J., & Woods, E. (1995). Exposure to violence and victimization and depression, hopelessness, and purpose in life among adolescents living in and around public housing. *Journal of Developmental and Behavioral Pediatrics, 16,* 233-237.

Dweck, C. S. (1999). *Self-theories: Their role in motivation, personality, and development.* Philadelphia: Psychology Press.

Edens, J. F. (1999). Aggressive children's self-systems and the quality of their relationships with significant others. *Aggression and Violent Behavior, 4,* 151-177.

Egan, S. K., & Perry, D. G. (2001). Gender identity: A multidimensional analysis with implications for psychological adjustment. *Developmental Psychology, 37,* 451-463.

Erikson, E. (1968). *Identity, youth and crisis.* New York: W. W. Norton.

Fischer, M., & Leitenberg, H. (1986). Optimism and pessimism in elementary school-aged children. *Child Development, 57,* 241-248.

Haney, P., & Durlak, J. A. (1998). Changing self-esteem in children and adolescents: A meta-analytic review. *Journal of Clinical Child Psychology, 27,* 423–433.

Harter, S. (1998). The development of self-representations. In W. Damon (Series Ed.) & N. Eisenberg (Vol. Ed.), *Handbook of Child Psychology: Vol. 3. Social, emotional, and personality development* (5th ed., pp. 553–617). New York: John Wiley & Sons.

Hartup, W. W. (1996). The company they keep: Friendships and their developmental significance. *Child Development, 67,* 1–13.

Hoffman, L. W., & Kloska, D. D. (1995). Parents' gender-based attitudes toward marital roles and child rearing: Development and validation of new measures. *Sex Roles, 32,* 273–295.

Hughes, D., & Johnson, D. (2001). Correlates in children's experiences of parents' racial socialization practices. *Journal of Marriage and the Family, 63,* 981–995.

Kawabata, T., Cross, D., Nishioka, N., & Shimai, S. (1999). Relationships between self-esteem and smoking behavior among Japanese early adolescents: Initial results from a three-year study. *Journal of School Health, 69,* 280–284.

Kernis, M. H., Brown, A. C., & Brody, G. H. (2000). Fragile self-esteem in children and its associations with perceived patterns of parent-child communication. *Journal of Personality, 68,* 225–252.

Kistner, J. A., Ziegert, D. I., Castro, R., & Robertson, B. (2001). Helplessness in early childhood: Prediction of symptoms associated with depression and negative self-worth. *Merrill-Palmer Quarterly, 47,* 336–354.

Koizumi, R. (1995). Feelings of optimism and pessimism in Japanese students' transition to junior high school. *Journal of Early Adolescence, 15,* 42–428.

Lord, S. E., Eccles, J. S., & McCarthy, K. A. (1994). Surviving the junior high transition: Family processes and self-perceptions as protective and risk factors. *Journal of Early Adolescence, 14,* 162–199.

Marsh, H. W., Craven, R. G., & Debus, R. (1991). Self-concepts of young children 5 to 8 years of age: Measurement and multidimensional structure. *Journal of Educational Psychology, 83,* 377–392.

Marsh, H. W., Ellis, L. A., & Craven, R. G. (2002). How do preschool children feel about themselves? Unraveling measurement and multidimensional self-concept structure. *Developmental Psychology, 38,* 376–393.

Masten, A. S. (2001). Ordinary magic: Resilience processes in development. *American Psychologist, 56,* 227–238.

Mead, G. H. (1934). *Mind, self, and society from the standpoint of a social behaviorist.* Chicago: University of Chicago Press.

Overbay, J. D., & Purath, J. (1997). Self-concept and health status in elementary-school-aged children. *Issues in Comprehensive Pediatric Nursing, 20,* 89–101.

Prilleltensky, I., Nelson, G., & Peirson, L. (2001). The role of power and control in children's lives: An ecological analysis of pathways toward wellness, resilience, and problems. *Journal of Community and Applied Social Psychology, 11,* 143–158.

Ricciardelli, L. A., & McCabe, M. P. (2001). Children's body image concerns and eating disturbance: A review of the literature. *Clinical Psychology Review, 21,* 325–344.

Richaud de Minzi, M. C. (1991). Age changes in children's beliefs of internal and external control. *Journal of Genetic Psychology, 152,* 217–224.

Robins, R. W., Hendin, H. M., & Trzesniewski, K. H. (2001). Measuring global self-esteem: Construct validation of a single-item measure and the Rosenberg Self-Esteem Scale. *Personality and Social Psychology Bulletin, 27,* 151–161.

Sandstrom, M. J., & Coie, J. D. (1999). A developmental perspective on peer rejection: Mechanisms of stability and change. *Child Development, 70,* 955–966.

Scales, P. C., & Leffert, N. (1999). *Developmental assets: A synthesis of the scientific research on adolescent development.* Minneapolis: Search Institute.

Seligman, M. E. P., Reivich, K., Jaycox, L., & Gillham, J. (1995). *The Optimistic Child.* New York: Houghton Mifflin.

Shek, D. T. (1992). Meaning in life and psychological well-being: An empirical study using the Chinese version of the Purpose in Life Questionnaire. *Journal of Genetic Psychology, 153,* 185–200.

Shek, D. T. (2001). Meaning in life and sense of mastery in Chinese adolescents with economic disadvantage. *Psychological Reports, 88,* 711–712.

Showalter, S. M., & Wagener, L. M. (2000). Adolescents' meaning in life: A replication of DeVogler and Ebersole (1983). *Psychological Reports, 87,* 115–126.

Siefer, R., Sameroff, A. J., Baldwin, C. P., & Baldwin, A. (1992). Child and family factors that ameliorate risk between 4 and 13 years of age. *Journal of the American Academy of Child and Adolescent Psychiatry, 31,* 893–903.

Simons, R. L., Murry, V., McLoyd, V., Lin, K., Cutrona, C., & Conger, R. (2002). Discrimination, crime, ethnic identity, and parenting as correlates of depressive symptoms among African American children: A multilevel analysis. *Development and Psychopathology, 14,* 371–393.

Skinner, E. A. (1990). What causes success and failure in school and friendship? Developmental differentiation of children's beliefs across middle childhood. *International Journal of Behavioral Development, 13,* 157–176.

Skinner, E. A., Wellborn, J. G., & Connell, J. P. (1990). What it takes to do well in school and whether I've got it: A process model of perceived control and children's engagement and achievement in school. *Journal of Educational Psychology, 82,* 22–32.

Sroufe, L. A. (1983). Infant-caregiver attachment and patterns of adaptation in preschool: The roots of maladaptation and competence. In M. Perlmutter (Ed.), *Minnesota symposia on child psychology: Vol. 16. Development and policy concerning children with special needs* (pp. 41–83). Hillsdale, NJ: Lawrence Erlbaum.

Sroufe, L. A., Egeland, B., & Carlson, E. A. (1999). One social world: The integrated development of parent-child and peer relationships. In W. A. Collins & B. Laursen (Eds.), *Minnesota symposia on child psychology: Vol. 29. Relationships as developmental context* (pp. 241–261). Hillsdale, NJ: Lawrence Erlbaum.

Stein, R. J., Bracken, B. A., Haddock, C. K., & Shadish, W. R. (1998). Preliminary development of the Children's Physical Self-Concept Scale. *Developmental and Behavioral Pediatrics, 19,* 1–8.

Sullivan, H. S. (1953). *The interpersonal theory of psychiatry.* New York: Norton.

Van den Bergh, B. R. H., & Van Ranst, N. (1998). Self-concept in children: Equivalence of measurement and structure across gender and grade of Harter's Self-Perception Profile for Children. *Journal of Personality Assessment, 70,* 564–582.

Wang, Y., & Ollendick, T. H. (2001). A cross-cultural and developmental analysis of self-esteem in Chinese and Western children. *Clinical Child and Family Psychology Review, 4,* 253–271.

Wastlund, E., Norlander, T., & Archer, T. (2001). Exploring cross-cultural differences in self-concept: A meta-analysis of the Self-Description Questionnaire-1. *Cross-Cultural Research, 35,* 280–302.

Wyman, P. A., Cowen, E. L., Work, W. C., Hoyt-Meyers, L., Magnus, K. B., & Fagen, D. B. (1999). Caregiving and developmental factors differentiating young at-risk urban children showing resilient versus stress-affected outcomes: A replication and extension. *Child Development, 70,* 645–659.

Wyman, P. A., Cowen, E. L., Work, W. C., & Kerley, J. H. (1993). The role of children's future expectations in self-system functioning and adjustment to life stress: A prospective study of urban at-risk children. *Development and Psychopathology, 5,* 649–661.

Wyman, P. A., Cowen, E. L., Work, W. C., & Parker, G. R. (1991). Developmental and family milieu correlates of resilience in urban children who have experienced major life stress. *American Journal of Community Psychology, 19,* 405–426.

Wyman, P. A., Cowen, E. L., Work, W. C., Raoof, B. A., Gribble, P. A., Parker, G. R., & Wannon, M. (1992). Interviews with children who experienced major life stress: Family and child attributes that predict resilient outcomes. *Journal of the American Academy of Child and Adolescent Psychiatry, 31,* 904–910.

Young, M., Werch, C. E., & Bakema, D. (1989). Area specific self-esteem scales and substance use among elementary and middle school children. *Journal of School Health, 59,* 251–254.

Yu, D. L., & Seligman, M. E. P. (2002, May 2). Preventing depressive symptoms in Chinese children. *Prevention and Treatment, 5,* Article 9. Retrieved May 2, 2003, from journals.apa.org/prevention/volume5/pre0050009a.html.

Summary and Conclusions:
Developmental Assets in Middle Childhood

In this book, we have reviewed a wide range of scientific studies bearing on positive development in middle childhood. From this review, we can draw two classes of conclusions: (1) lessons learned about the developmental asset categories, and (2) insights into the overall role of developmental assets and the utility of the assets framework in middle childhood. In this chapter, we discuss each of those classes of conclusions.

Lessons Learned about the Categories of Developmental Assets

The Internal Asset Categories: Commitment to Learning, Positive Values, Social Competencies, and Positive Identity

If a child were a boat, the internal asset categories would represent her or his compass and rudder. They focus mostly on values and self-perceptions, and secondarily on skills. Although skills can be directly taught and rehearsed even by very young children, values and self-perceptions, as we have suggested throughout this book, are slipperier creatures in middle childhood and earlier.

In that observation, the field test data are encouraging. These early studies suggest that the great majority—70% to 90%—of the 4th–6th graders studied experience most of the internal assets. They are especially likely to say their parents teach them the importance of the various positive values, and that they feel engaged in learning in and outside of school, feel close to adults at school, and exercise resistance skills, cultural competence, and skill at resolving conflicts peacefully. A smaller proportion—40% to 60%—say they are skilled at planning and decision making or that they experience interpersonal competence or the various positive-identity assets.

These results are obviously encouraging because even the least commonly reported internal assets are reportedly experienced by around half of the 4th–6th graders we studied, and most of them are reportedly far more common. In addition, the comparable asset data for adolescents suggests (Benson, Scales, Leffert, & Roehlkepartain, 1999; *Developmental assets: A profile of your youth,* 2001) that the majority of the internal assets, like the external ones, decrease over grades 6 through 12 (the exception is the positive-identity assets, which are either stable or increase). Thus, the more these internal assets can be built during middle childhood, the better the start young people are given as they head into adolescence.

But there is also reason to be cautious. First, children in grades 4 through 6 may tend to overestimate many of the internal assets. Precisely because the internal assets are predominantly values and self-perceptions, they are very much in development and not nearly as consistent during middle childhood as they are likely to be in adolescence. And as we have noted, children in the upper elementary years, although beginning to become more self-critical, are still for the most part characterized as optimistic, and their cognitive and psychological capacities for self-reflection are still at a relatively immature stage of development.

A more important caution, however, may be that most of the internal assets cannot *directly* be "built" in quite the same way as can most of the external assets. For example, parents can build family support by saying "I love you" to their children more often. A neighbor can build neighborhood caring and boundaries by calling a child by name and admonishing her or him to wear a bicycle helmet. And a child can build the creative-activities asset simply by spending a few hours per week in artistic, musical, or dramatic pursuits. In contrast, rather than being built, it is more accurate to say that most of the internal assets can be *grown* or *nurtured.* An immediate, direct action can often positively influence an external asset fairly quickly. But to be grown and nurtured, most of the internal assets take time and may develop out of indirect paths. Those paths may include partial contributions from high levels of external assets, particular aspects of a child's temperament, other developmental strengths that the asset framework does not capture (such as a sense of humor, courage, respect, or humility), the cultural identification of a child and the degree of discrimination he or she experiences, and circumstances of history and place, such as war, flooding, and economic boom or bust times.

These qualifications notwithstanding, the research strongly supports the positive impact on child development of the internal assets, especially the commitment-to-learning and the social-competencies assets; indeed, studies consistently suggest those two categories of developmental strengths are particularly linked in middle childhood. Socially competent children are also better liked and considered more academically competent by peers and teachers. This apparently encourages teachers to think of them and treat them as more competent than less socially adept students. Not surprisingly, then, studies show that those students psychologically feel more academically competent, work harder, and end up getting better grades. Within these categories, research is less common on the impact of homework, reading for pleasure, cultural competence, and resistance skills (except for resisting alcohol and other drugs), but the overall categories are robustly validated in the literature.

In contrast, the research on the positive-values and, to a lesser extent, the positive-identity assets in middle childhood, although still quite supportive of their developmental importance, is both less voluminous and, because of the nature of those assets, less capable of clear interpretation. We have argued that both of these asset categories represent beliefs and self-perceptions that during middle childhood are increasingly well formed, but not yet stable. Thus, it may be more difficult for researchers to link them to specific outcomes than to do so for the other internal assets or for the external assets categories. The exceptions to these comments are self-esteem and personal power or self-efficacy, both of which are represented by a considerable literature supporting their links to numerous positive outcomes in middle childhood.

The External Asset Categories: Support, Empowerment, Boundaries and Expectations, and Constructive Use of Time

We have suggested that the *internal* assets are more accurately seen as being grown or nurtured than directly built. In that light, we can better appreciate that the special importance of the *external* assets is that they are generally the ones that can directly be provided by parents, other adults, and a child's peers. But successfully building these assets also calls for a rather remarkable balancing act. The prototype for positive external influences in middle childhood is authoritative parenting that offers a mix of warmth and control calibrated to each child, while simultaneously promoting children's capacity to have and express ideas of their own, develop their talents and interests, and exercise choices. The ideal developmentally attentive community is one in which teachers, classmates, neighbors, and other adults provide a comparably balanced menu of developmental nourishment for all children.

Thus, the asset category of support, in the sense of a child's being loved and cared for, cannot be well understood in the absence of considering the category of boundaries and expectations. Nor can either be fully appreciated without reference to empowerment, whether a child is growing in her or his sense of being valued and playing meaningful roles, and whether the child is using her or his time in constructive ways. The developmentally appropriate mix of all these external assets varies for each individual child, but all children need a balance that is, like Goldilocks's sampling of the bears' porridge, personally "just right." Too much support and help, and some children can feel incompetent; too little and they can feel alone. Too much boundary setting, and some children can feel suffocated; too little and they can become undisciplined or even injured. Too much empowerment, and children can become self-centered; too little and they can feel disconnected and useless. Too much structured time and children can become exhausted and unimaginative; too little and they may squander talents, become directionless, and increase the risks in their lives.

What the external assets collectively provide during middle childhood are safe relationships and opportunities that enable children to develop academic and social competence, and grow in their ability to coregulate themselves with the guidance of parents and other caregivers. They deliver for those in middle childhood the knowledge that they are loved, accepted, valued, and protected— embraced not just by family but by neighbors, teachers, coaches, religious leaders, and others. Those external assets hold out for children the expectation that they meet certain societal standards of behavior and striving, as well as develop their personal talents and gifts so that they flourish to be the best people they can be.

The result of these effects is to provide simultaneously the safety and fulfillment of feeling connected to others, with the encouragement to put one's individual stamp on life. That combination of promoting group membership and individuation is especially meaningful in middle childhood, a time when children's environments are rapidly expanding in complexity and demand. Children at this stage can either feel increasingly capable of coming into their own or instead head on a path toward a less confident, connected, and contributing adolescence.

We are struck by how much the level of success in this developmental endeavor in middle childhood is conditioned on the theme of consistency, congruence, and connection among the adults in a child's life in providing the external assets, so that multiple contexts are favorably affected simultaneously. As we have seen in Chapters 1–4, children who have parents who are involved in their schooling and a caring school climate, and whose parents and teachers have similar styles, achieve at higher levels than children who have only one of those assets. Children who experience both nurturant parenting and collective socialization in their neighborhoods are less likely than other children to have deviant friends. Children are more likely to experience caring "other adult" relationships if their parents explicitly encourage or "give permission" to other adults to engage positively with their kids, and so on.

The importance of these adult connections crosses contexts, but strengthens children's developmental experiences *within* contexts as well. For example, we have noted that the better the marital or partner relationship parents have, the more they may be able intentionally to create and sustain a family life that builds assets for and with their children. Moreover, they may be better able to influence their children's choices of friends, time management, and connection to other asset-building adults, programs, and resources. And in schools, the more teachers believe that working *together* they can be effective educators for all children, the better children's achievement, compared to schools in which teachers feel less collectively efficacious as educators.

Thus, the external assets are not merely relationships and opportunities adults *provide* for children: They are developmental outgrowths of the very connections adults have *among themselves*.

And what having these external assets reflects and reinforces—apart from the lists of positive academic, mental and behavioral health, and social outcomes we have noted accrue to children from experiencing the external assets—is less quantifiable: children's connection to institutions and ideas larger than themselves, such as family, school, congregation, neighborhood, community, society.

Do they feel nurtured and cared for everywhere they turn? Are they asked to help out and join with adults in meaningful conversations and tasks? Are they given chances to volunteer, and are they exposed to multiple adults who do so? Are they encouraged in spiritual pursuits or a religious tradition that encourages them to make meaning in their lives? The answer to those questions affects the quality of children's lives and the nature of civil society, for it is during middle childhood that children's orientations toward or away from connection and contribution to larger units of society, while still malleable, are solidifying.

Children at this stage become both more interested in societal problems and challenges, and capable of participating with adolescents and adults in dealing with those issues. It is no exaggeration to suggest that their tendency toward civic engagement can be given a meaningful boost, or that opportunity to promote civil society squandered, depending on adults' resolve to support and empower children, to set expectations and model for them, and to occupy children's time constructively.

In that light, children's reports of these external assets in middle childhood as gleaned from our field tests in Nevada, California, and New York (echoing for the most part the earlier pilot study results in Oklahoma) are both reassuring and troubling:

- The great majority of 4th–6th graders seems to experience support from their parents and teachers, though far less from their peers and neighborhood.
- The great majority feels safe, but far fewer feel valued, useful, or that they contribute to community betterment.
- Most seem to experience clear rules and expectations in their families and schools, but far fewer experience neighborhood boundaries or positive adult role models, especially outside the family.
- And although a majority occupy their time constructively in structured programs and in being connected to religious community, it is a slim majority, with especially wide variations related to socioeconomic status in children's participation in structured child development programs.

These are field test data from a new survey, of course, and only the accumulation of a larger and more comprehensive database can confirm these observations. But they come from nearly 1,300 children across three demographically different communities (and nearly another 800 from two demographically different pilot study communities), and so merit consideration if only to generate hypotheses for further investigation about the state of these external assets among upper elementary children. From that perspective, a great deal more effort in communities is needed around the five action strategies mentioned in the Introduction (pp. 2–3) to ensure that all young people are valued and thrive: Engage adults, mobilize young people, activate sectors, invigorate programs, and influence civic decisions.

Insights into the Role of Assets and Utility of the Asset Framework

Several conclusions are apparent as we try to sum up the insights that research offers into the role of developmental assets in middle childhood development, and into the utility of the asset framework as an organizing principle for understanding this stage of life.

1. **The essence of the contribution made by developmental assets to children's healthy development in the middle childhood years appears to be the broad promotion of academic and social competencies, and the shifting of regulatory processes toward a model of coregulation among child and caring adults.**
    Most of the middle childhood assets identified by Search In-

stitute appear to be related to one or both of the fundamental processes of developing competencies and effective regulation. The flourishing of these processes cannot be imagined without children also continuing to make progress in developing their values and sense of themselves and their place in the world.

Children's assessments of their own competencies, as well as the assessments of them by their teachers, family, and friends, "firm up" during the middle childhood years. If children *are*—and *feel*—academically and socially competent, they are more successful in middle childhood and later on as well. The emergence of better defined competencies and coregulation also contributes to children's ongoing identity formation, as they increasingly make meaning of their lives. And the shift in how children are emotionally and behaviorally regulated, as they play a greater role in governing themselves with adult guidance, compared to the early childhood years, strengthens the foundation for emergent self-regulation in adolescence. The challenge for parents, teachers, neighbors, and other caring adults present in children's lives during middle childhood is to find the right balance of other regulation, coregulation, and self-regulation for each child.

2. The assets in middle childhood are interdependent.

It is unlikely that the development of various competencies and a growing coregulation are independent processes, nor are the assets that promote them. Parents and other adults likely cede more regulatory influence, negotiate more, and make exceptions to rules more often when children display the kinds of academic, emotional, social, and behavioral competencies discussed in this book. Children shape their environments, even as their environments shape them. For example, children whose parents and other caregivers employ an authoritative style likely already display components of interpersonal competence such as positive self-control and empathy skills. They also subsequently benefit from those social competencies and from supportive caregiving, as well as from the reciprocal effect that encourages parents and other adults to provide them with still more nurturing.

Similarly, children in middle childhood who are engaged in learning at school and emotionally connected to adults at school enjoy better peer relationships. The combination of those assets likely contributes to positive dimensions of self-efficacy, which in turn help young people feel more capable in both of those contexts (school and peer), as well as leading to other positive associations.

None of the 40 assets in the middle childhood developmental asset framework operates as a factor fully independent of the other assets and the nested contexts in which they are experienced. Thus, as we concluded in reviewing the research relevant to assets in adolescence (Scales & Leffert, 1999), the search for the handful of "most important" developmental assets in middle childhood is not the most appropriate strategy for understanding complex developmental processes as they actually occur.

3. **Tremendous variability exists, both between and within individuals, in how important each asset is in promoting particular developmental outcomes, both concurrently and longitudinally.**

Although we draw general conclusions about average or group trends by citing numerous specific studies in this book, our descriptions of the average relationships the assets have with various outcomes often mask enormous inter- and, over time, intraindividual variability in developmental processes and trajectories. For example, we describe in Chapter 5 how, even among elementary students achieving at above-average levels, differing degrees of student perceptions of their own abilities and of how much their teachers tried to control them produced very different constellations of motivations and connections to school (Miserandino, 1996). Some students succeed because of their positive perceptions of their own abilities and a good fit between the autonomy they need and the autonomy their teachers provide, whereas other students succeed despite less positive self-perceptions and less responsive teacher relationships.

In our synthesis of the asset-relevant literature in adolescence, we wrote, "How the assets 'work' is a function of the characteristics of the individual adolescent and how he or she is embedded in multiple nested and interacting worlds of family, school, friends, and community" (Scales & Leffert, 1999, p. 220). That assessment is just as apt when considering children in grades 4 through 6 and the developmental assets framework for middle childhood.

For example, as we reported in Chapter 2, poor children exposed to violence report greater levels of anxiety and depression than do poor children with less exposure to violence. However, the most adversely affected are those children who *also* have low levels of parent support and can't talk with their parents about violence they witness or experience (Kliewar, Lepore, Oskin, & Johnson, 1998). No child should be exposed to violence, but children who feel that their parents love and care for them and who can talk about uncomfortable topics with their parents are spared some of the worst effects of violence.

4. **The research suggests that the middle childhood developmental assets reflect much of what children need for healthy growth across a variety of physical, cognitive, behavioral, social, emotional, and moral dimensions. However, the asset framework and *Me and My World* survey have some limitations; several key constructs identified in the literature are not represented among the 40 assets we conceptualize and measure in middle childhood.**

For example, the research suggests that personal power (or self-efficacy) and even self-esteem are at least as well captured, if not more than adequately so, by examining personal power and self-esteem, not only globally, but also within specific contexts or domains. In order to measure many assets in one survey, however, our positive-identity measures are necessarily global, thus perhaps sacrificing some construct validity.

Similarly, the developmental assets framework for middle childhood and Search Institute's *Me and My World* (MMW) survey cover the positive influence peers can have on children, and children's affiliation or friendship-making skills, two assets that have important relations with a variety of developmental outcomes. During middle childhood, children's peer groups and their "best friendships" become more differentiated and appear to have differing effects for each child, as individual friends sometimes play the more important role in a child's development, while at other times, the peer group assumes the more important role. Our middle childhood assets framework and survey do not tease out to a large degree the differences in how children's social worlds are constructed and how they subsequently affect children's development. While we also cover a number of important positive values, there are a number of other values, from spirituality to interdependence to humility, that we do not cover and that may be equally important for some or even all children.

Then, too, our MMW survey covers achievement motivation and learning engagement but does not address broader societal issues. For example, do children actually attend high-quality schools, live in poverty, have access to sufficient health care, or experience racial discrimination? Similar observations can be made about most of the asset categories: Much is included, but plenty is missing, too. The 40 developmental assets for middle childhood, like the same 40 assets for adolescence, appear to be very well represented in the scientific literature as positive developmental influences, and they tell much, although not all, of the story of the pathways children take to growth and maturation.

Finally, some of the asset categories and individual assets within them are much less common in the empirical literature on middle childhood. Quite comparable to the distribution of studies we reported in our earlier review of the scientific research on adolescent development (Scales & Leffert, 1999), the support, commitment-to-learning, and social-competencies asset categories offer the greatest range and depth of studies from which to understand these developmental influences. Less, but still plentiful, research exists on the boundaries-and-expectations, constructive-use-of-time, and positive-identity asset categories for middle childhood. As for adolescents, however, the empowerment and positive-values assets appear to be the least well-researched categories of assets reported in the middle childhood years, certainly in terms of the impact that "having" those assets has on children's development. Thus, although the literature supports our description of how those assets may affect development, the related interpretations should be regarded as more speculative than our treatment of the assets that are grounded in a more substantial research base.

5. **Nevertheless, the developmental assets framework generally has broad application to children in the upper elementary years.**

Studies consistently provide evidence that the constructs reflected in the developmental assets framework, and in Search Institute's MMW survey measuring those assets among 4th through 6th graders, are important correlates of, and often contributors to, young people's positive growth and development. The asset framework is somewhat different in conceptualization and measurement for middle childhood than for adolescence, as detailed in the Introduction, because we have tried to construct a framework that is sensitive to key developmental differences between the two stages.

Search Institute's general finding that the framework for middle childhood is well grounded in the scientific literature echoes the broad conclusions about the content validity of the asset framework that we reached previously in synthesizing the research on adolescent development (Scales & Leffert, 1999). This affirmation means that practitioners and policy makers seeking to strengthen formal and informal positive developmental influences on children—trying to create developmentally attentive communities (Benson, Scales, & Mannes, 2002)—are on solid empirical ground in drawing applied lessons from the developmental assets framework for middle childhood.

6. **The developmental assets framework has utility for describing and explaining developmental processes and outcomes among children across a wide range of diversities.**

There may be divergent *mechanisms* by which the experience of some assets operates to promote particular outcomes among some groups of children more so than among others, but the framework itself appears to be well reflected in studies of young people who represent a wide array of diversities.

For example, time spent in religious community seems valuable for children across racial/ethnic groups, but may be a particularly important source of strength for African American children. All groups of children benefit from positive structured activities, but unstructured time spent outdoors may be less a negative influence on African American children's academic and emotional adjustment than it is for European American children. Being socially competent is important for all groups of children, but may make more of a difference for boys. Similarly, the impact of a number of the asset constructs on various adjustment outcomes seems to be moderated by variations in children's degree of vulnerability. All children generally seem to benefit from experiencing the developmental assets, but vulnerable children, such as those experiencing poverty or violence, benefit *more* than less vulnerable children.

7. **Despite utility across diversities, it is unlikely that the developmental assets for middle childhood "work" equally well**

for all groups of children in order to explain developmental outcomes.

Previous research with large samples of adolescents, for example, has suggested two broad hypotheses about assets and diversity that are not contradictory but do suggest caution: (1) The framework may "work" reasonably well across diversities in describing the developmental nourishment young people experience or do not; and (2) there may be some differences in *how* the assets work to explain particular outcomes for particular groups of youth. For example, studies have found few differences in the absolute levels of assets that youth in different racial/ethnic groups, family situations, and economic circumstances report, and somewhat more but still not pervasive differences in levels of particular assets experienced (Benson et al., 1999). In short, these differences are generally less notable than the similarity of assets experienced across diversities.

These samples are diverse, but not representative within the U.S., and so it is unclear whether there would be greater differences in a truly nationally representative sample. Moreover, because the assets and their definitions have emerged from United States cultural contexts, it is likely that there would be more differences in the experience of the assets as reported by representative samples of children from other countries, especially those not sharing either a similar "Western" heritage or highly developed economic status. One study did suggest that the asset framework for adolescents may explain somewhat more of particular developmental outcomes for some racial/ethnic groups of youth than it does for others, at least for indicators of thriving (Scales, Benson, Leffert, & Blyth, 2000). Again, however, those data came from a large but not necessarily representative sample, so it is unclear how robust those results would be using different samples of youth. In addition, girls consistently report experiencing more assets than boys, but that may be not because boys actually "have" fewer assets but because some developmental strengths that boys might experience more often have not been studied (see discussion in Scales & Leffert, 1999).

Our field test data suggest similar gender and grade trends in reported assets in middle childhood as those seen for adolescents. However, much more research needs to be conducted with the MMW survey to be able to draw conclusions about other kinds of group similarities or differences. The field test data are best used to generate hypotheses for future studies on the variation in middle childhood assets across diversities. However, caution urges us to consider that such gender, racial, and ethnic differences may well be observed as the developmental assets database for middle childhood grows. Thus, although the basic structure of positive development appears to be similar within the lives of diverse children, the explanatory power of the assets framework and *how* the assets come to make their contributions surely vary across many differing child-context combinations.

8. **Our pilot and field test data on children's experience of these assets are limited, but early trends are consistent with what we know about adolescents.**

Our two pilot studies and three field tests of the MMW survey collectively involved about 2,000 4th- through 6th-grade students, approximately 40% non-White, and reflecting significant socio-economic diversity as well. Although ongoing data collection will both broaden and deepen the database beyond these five samples, it appears that the developmental assets pilot and field test data are fairly consistent with trends observed for older students in middle and high school.

For example, in both age groups, the great majority of children say they experience family support, but far fewer children report positive family communication. In both age groups, most children say they experience most of the positive-values assets, although greater proportions of elementary-age children report them. However, in neither age group does a majority say they experience the empowerment assets of feeling valued by the community or being given useful roles. Elementary children report higher levels of assets, such as other adult relationships and adult role models, than do middle or high school–age youth, but more than 40% of the elementary children surveyed say that adults outside the family do not provide them the experience of those two essentials of development.

Across all 40 assets, while the majority of children participating in our middle childhood pilot and field test studies said they experienced an asset, a substantial 25% to nearly 50% said they *did not*. Thus, although the database on the experience of developmental assets in middle childhood is still limited, these early pilot and field test survey results suggest considerable weakness in the developmental attentiveness experienced by preadolescents in the United States. They may fare better than middle and high school–age youth in experiencing a developmentally rich, positive environment, but not by a large margin.

Nor is there an equal experience of developmental attentiveness within families, schools, peer groups, and community settings across different groups of children. Although we generally have not reported subgroup data in this book, it does appear from our pilot and field test results that girls report the experience of more assets than boys do, and that 4th and 5th graders report more assets than 6th graders. Adolescent girls also generally report more assets than do adolescent boys, and 6th through 8th graders generally report more developmental assets than do high school youth (Benson et al., 1999; *Developmental assets: A profile of your youth*, 2001). Thus, these preliminary gender and grade trends in the middle childhood assets data are consistent with the gender and grade differences we see in the adolescent data.

These differing results by gender and grade level, found over many years and across adolescent geographies, have held quite steady. Similar emergent data among our initial pilot and field-test samples of upper elementary children suggest, at the least, that girls and younger children may experience quite different levels of developmental attentiveness than do boys and older children.

Implications for the Future

This review has suggested that the developmental assets framework for middle childhood, like its counterpart framework for adolescents, has considerable content validity from a research standpoint and significant practical implications for families, schools, congregations, child and youth organizations, and community residents. More research is needed into the effects of children's experiences with the empowerment and positive-values asset categories, and on neighborhood influences, as well as on specific assets such as cultural competence. However, the general research base is plentiful and points to the usefulness of the asset framework both for understanding development in middle childhood and for suggesting individual and collective actions that can promote more developmentally attentive communities for children in the upper elementary years.

Children in middle childhood need parents who raise them with a combination of loving firmness, growing democracy, and coregulation as children contribute more and more to choices and decisions. They need safe schools filled with caring teachers, students, and other adults whose rules, expectations, modeling, and support converge to connect children emotionally to the adults at school and engage them in the excitement and joy of learning, both inside and outside of school. Children in the upper elementary years need to experience widening circles of caring, watchful adults in their neighborhoods, congregations, after-school programs, and other community settings who explicitly guide them and give them opportunities to develop positive values, social competencies, and a sense of personal possibilities.

The research is compelling: Children who lack these positive relationships and opportunities simply do not develop as positively as children who have them.

To a significant extent, these dynamics are reciprocal and recursive: Children enjoy more positive relationships and opportunities when they already bring easygoing temperaments, positive self-perceptions, and competent behaviors to their interactions with adults and peers. Those positive relationships and opportunities further enhance the personal qualities and skills they use to shape their future contexts.

But the past is not inevitably prologue: At nearly every point in this complex geometry of development, the "social dance" children engage in (Hart & Risley, 1995) as they interact with their contexts, their parents and caregivers, other adults, and peers holds both formal and informal opportunities to positively affect children's developmental trajectories. These opportunities can keep children on track for a hopeful future or propel them onto a hopeful path they had not previously occupied. Even, and perhaps especially, the most vulnerable children experiencing great challenges in their lives, from poverty to violence, can gain a foothold on that more hopeful pathway if they also experience a sufficient breadth and depth of the developmental assets.

We end this book with what the John D. and Catherine T. MacArthur Foundation Research Network on Successful Pathways through Middle Childhood described as their beginning, once again illustrating the recursive, neverending blurring of cause and effect that is the essence of developmental processes. This network of scholars said that to understand development in middle childhood, "we begin with the perceptions, thoughts, behaviors and feelings of children themselves, with the meanings they attach to their interactions and relationships with their families, peers, teachers and others, and with their own sense of who they are as active agents in their own development" (John D. and Catherine T. MacArthur Foundation, n.d). This seems to be an apt description of what we mean when we say that experiencing these assets during middle childhood can significantly help children "come into their own."

265

The 40 assets we have described for middle childhood are not a panacea for all childhood ills, to be sure. Collectively, though, the evidence is that the developmental assets in middle childhood positively contribute to shaping each child's unique emerging self, protecting children from harm, promoting their resilience, enabling them to thrive and become the best they can be. Experiencing the developmental assets can help children develop a solid sense of their own emerging capacities and a growing ability to make their way in the world. They can help children come into their own as aware, strong, and sensitive people, constructing nourishing relationships and taking advantage of exciting opportunities, confident in their ability to make a difference for themselves and others. All children deserve no less.

References

Benson, P. L., Scales, P. C., Leffert, N., & Roehlkepartain, E. C. (1999). *A fragile foundation: The state of developmental assets among American youth.* Minneapolis: Search Institute.

Benson, P. L., Scales, P. C., & Mannes, M. (2002). Developmental strengths and their sources: Implications for the study and practice of community-building. In R. M. Lerner, F. Jacobs, & D. Wertlieb (Eds.), *Handbook of applied developmental science: Vol. 1. Applying developmental science for youth and families: Historical and theoretical foundations* (pp. 369–406). Thousand Oaks, CA: Sage.

Developmental assets: A profile of your youth. (2001). Minneapolis: Search Institute (1999–2000 school year aggregate database).

John D. and Catherine T. MacArthur Foundation Research Network on Successful Pathways through Middle Childhood (n.d.). Retrieved March 12, 2003, from middlechildhood.org/mission/index.htm.

Hart, B., & Risley, T.R. (1995). *Meaningful differences in the everyday experience of young American children.* Baltimore: Paul H. Brookes.

Kliewar, W., Lepore, S. J., Oskin, D., & Johnson, P. D. (1998). The role of social and cognitive processes in children's adjustment to community violence. *Journal of Consulting and Clinical Psychology, 66,* 199–209.

Miserandino, M. (1996). Children who do well in school: Individual differences in perceived competence and autonomy in above-average children. *Journal of Educational Psychology, 88,* 203–214.

Scales, P. C., Benson, P. L., Leffert, N., & Blyth, D. A. (2000). Contribution of developmental assets to the prediction of thriving among adolescents. *Applied Developmental Science, 4,* 27–46.

Scales, P. C., & Leffert, N. (1999). *Developmental assets: A synthesis of the scientific research on adolescent development.* Minneapolis: Search Institute.

Appendix

Pilot and Field Tests of Search Institute's *Me and My World* Survey

Below we display the developmental assets framework for middle childhood, which is measured by the *Me and My World* (MMW) survey, the internal consistency reliabilities for each asset measure found across the survey's three field test samples, and the percentages of students reporting each asset with the field test samples aggregated.

After an initial prepilot study in the St. Paul suburb of New Brighton, Minnesota, the MMW survey was pilot-tested with a total of 781 4th–6th graders in Norman and Oklahoma City, Oklahoma. Those studies suggested numerous revisions to the survey, which was then field-tested with a total of 1,294 4th–6th graders in Yucca Loma, California; Douglas County, Nevada; and Amherst, New York. Analysis of those field test data suggested a small number of final revisions to the survey items. Students who participated had received active parent permission to do so. Across the pilot and field test samples, about 41% of students received parental permission to participate.

The collective pilot and field test samples were quite diverse. Fifty-one percent of the aggregate sample was White, with multiracial, Hispanic, and African Americans the largest groups in the remaining 49%. The samples averaged 55% female and 45% male students, and the grade breakdown was 35% each for grades 4 and 5, and 30% for grade 6. As is often done with samples of young people, we used their parents' education levels as a proxy for family socio-economic status. About half of all parents (46% of fathers and 54% of mothers) were described as having at least some college, with 17% of fathers and 18% of mothers having a high school education or less. However, 37% of children did not know their father's education level, and 28% did not know their mother's.

We describe the aggregated pilot and field test sample to demonstrate the considerable diversity of the samples from which the MMW survey was developed. The data presented here and in the rest of this book, however, are based only on the field test samples, which were somewhat less diverse. This is because the wording of items on the field test surveys was the most refined and current, having been improved over the earlier pilot test versions.

Table 18. MMW Asset Measures: Asset Names and Definitions, Alpha Reliability, and Percentage Reporting Asset		
Assets Measured on MMW Survey	Internal Consistency Reliability across Three Field Tests	Percentage (%) Reporting Asset across Three Field Test Sites
External Assets		
Support		
1. Family support Family life provides high levels of love and support.	.71–.78	89
2. Positive family communication Parent(s) and child communicate positively. Child feels comfortable seeking advice and counsel from parent(s).	.63–.74	58
3. Other adult relationships Child receives support from adults other than her or his parent(s).	.72–.74	61
4. Caring neighborhood Child experiences caring neighbors.	.68–.75	55
5. Caring school climate Relationships with teachers and peers provide a caring, encouraging school environment.	.77–.82	60
6. Parent involvement in schooling Parent(s) are actively involved in helping the child succeed in school.	.69–.76	53

Table 18. MMW Asset Measures: Asset Names and Definitions, Alpha Reliability, and Percentage Reporting Asset (cont.)		
Assets Measured on MMW Survey	**Internal Consistency Reliability across Three Field Tests**	**Percentage (%) Reporting Asset across Three Field Test Sites**
Empowerment		
7. Community values children Child feels valued and appreciated by adults in the community.	.82–.84	36
8. Children as resources Child is included in decisions at home and in the community.	.29–.40	46
9. Service to others Child has opportunities to help others in the community.	n.a.	38
10. Safety[a] Child feels safe at home, at school, and in her or his neighborhood.	.23–.37	60
Boundaries and Expectations		
11. Family boundaries Family has clear and consistent rules and consequences and monitors the child's whereabouts.	.72–.74	58
12. School boundaries School provides clear rules and consequences.	n.a.	86
13. Neighborhood boundaries Neighbors take responsibility for monitoring the child's behavior.	.66–.72	59
14. Adult role models Parent(s) and other adults in the child's family, as well as nonfamily adults, model positive, responsible behavior.	.87–.88	57
15. Positive peer influence Child's closest friends model positive, responsible behavior.	.58–.64	90
16. High expectations Parent(s) and teachers expect the child to do her or his best at school and in other activities.	.47–.63	91

Table 18. MMW Asset Measures: Asset Names and Definitions, Alpha Reliability, and Percentage Reporting Asset (cont.)		
Assets Measured on MMW Survey	**Internal Consistency Reliability across Three Field Tests**	**Percentage (%) Reporting Asset across Three Field Test Sites**
Constructive Use of Time		
17. Creative activities[a] Child participates in music, art, drama, or creative writing two or more times per week.	n.a.	64
18. Child programs[b] Child participates two or more times per week in cocurricular school activities or structured community programs for children.	n.a.	58
19. Religious community[a] Child attends religious programs or services one or more times per week.	n.a.	60
20. Time at home[b] Child spends some time most days both in high-quality interaction with parent(s) and doing things at home other than watching TV or playing video games.	—	—
Internal Assets		
Commitment to Learning		
21. Achievement motivation Child is motivated and strives to do well in school.	.72–.75	79
22. Learning engagement[c] Child is responsive, attentive, and actively engaged in learning at school and enjoys participating in learning activities outside of school.	.75–.84	54
23. Homework[b] Child usually hands in homework on time.	—	—
24. Bonding to adults at school Child cares about teachers and other adults at school.	.50–.68	80
25. Reading for pleasure[a] Child enjoys and engages in reading for fun most days of the week.	n.a.	56

Table 18. MMW Asset Measures: Asset Names and Definitions, Alpha Reliability, and Percentage Reporting Asset (cont.)

Assets Measured on MMW Survey	Internal Consistency Reliability across Three Field Tests	Percentage (%) Reporting Asset across Three Field Test Sites
Positive Values		
26. Caring Parent(s) tell the child it is important to help other people.	n.a.	88
27. Equality and social justice Parent(s) tell the child it is important to speak up for equal rights for all people.	n.a.	69
28. Integrity Parent(s) tell the child it is important to stand up for one's beliefs.	n.a.	88
29. Honesty Parent(s) tell the child it is important to tell the truth.	n.a.	88
30. Responsibility Parent(s) tell the child it is important to accept personal responsibility for behavior.	n.a.	84
31. Healthy lifestyle[a] Parent(s) tell the child it is important to have good health habits and an understanding of healthy sexuality.	.57–71	86
Social Competencies		
32. Planning and decision making Child thinks about decisions and is usually happy with the results of her or his decisions.	.65–.73	49
33. Interpersonal competence Child cares about and is affected by other people's feelings, enjoys making friends, and, when frustrated or angry, tries to calm her or himself.	.77–.83	41
34. Cultural competence Child knows and is comfortable with people of different racial, ethnic, and cultural backgrounds and with her or his own cultural identity.	.79–.84	75

Table 18. MMW Asset Measures: Asset Names and Definitions, Alpha Reliability, and Percentage Reporting Asset (cont.)		
Assets Measured on MMW Survey	**Internal Consistency Reliability across Three Field Tests**	**Percentage (%) Reporting Asset across Three Field Test Sites**
35. Resistance skills[a] Child can stay away from people who are likely to get her or him in trouble and is able to say no to doing wrong or dangerous things.	.44–.55	83
36. Peaceful conflict resolution Child attempts to resolve conflict nonviolently.	n.a.	77
Positive Identity		
37. Personal power Child feels he or she has some influence over things that happen in her or his life.	.55–.64	64
38. Self-esteem Child likes and is proud to be the person he or she is.	.60–.72	69
39. Sense of purpose[b] Child sometimes thinks about what life means and whether there is a purpose for her or his life.	—	—
40. Positive view of personal future Child is optimistic about her or his personal future.	.63–.65	60

Note: *Most items are measured on a five-point scale (1 = Strongly Disagree to 5 = Strongly Agree). n.a. = Alpha coefficients cannot be computed on one-item scales.*

[a] *Survey items for this asset were revised or added after field test.*

[b] *Items for this asset were added after field test.*

[c] *After field tests, engagement in learning at school, and enjoyment of learning outside school—two separate measures—were combined to learning engagement. Reliabilities given refer to range for the two separate measures.*

Index

Academic success: and child programs, 117, 119, 122–24, 135, 137; and high expectations, 100, 106; and social competencies, 197; and teacher efficacy, 102. *See also* Achievement motivation; School

Achievement motivation, 147, 150–52, 169–70, 231; and peer influence, 98; and positive outcomes, 156–57

Action strategies for community change, 2–3

Adult-child relationships, 14–15, 122–23, 200, 231; and commitment to learning, 167–68. *See also* Mentors; Teachers

Adult role models, 23, 86, 93, 104–05; and positive/negative outcomes, 92–96. *See also* Mentors; Other adult relationships; Teachers

After-school programs. *See* Child programs

Aggression/aggressiveness: and peer influence, 97, 98; and positive identity, 234; and social competencies, 198, 205; and violence, 68–69. *See also* Peaceful conflict resolution

Alcohol use/abuse: and adult modeling, 93–94. *See also* Substance use/abuse

Anxiety: and self-esteem, 244–45; and social competencies, 197–98; and values, 189; and violence, 68–69

Autonomy, 19, 38, 82; as fundamental need, 45–46

Bonding to adults at school, 89, 147–48, 169–70; and positive outcomes, 160–63. *See also* Caring school climate

Boundaries and expectations, 11, 13, 81–107, 253–56, 260; and empowerment, 68; family, 86–88; internalization of, 102–03; measurement of, in middle childhood, 106–07; school, 89–90, 104; and support, 81–82. *See also specific assets*; Neighborhood; Peers and peer relationships; School

Bullying, 74; effects of, by gender, 69–70

Caring, 182, 188, 207

Caring neighborhood, 48–49; and positive outcomes, 40–41. *See also* Neighborhood

Caring school climate, 23, 43–44. *See also* School; Teachers

Child programs, 116, 120; access to, 126–27; and positive/negative outcomes, 116–19; quality of, 122–23. *See also* Sports

About the Authors

Peter C. Scales, Ph.D., is Senior Fellow in the Office of the President at Search Institute. A developmental psychologist, he has been for more than 25 years recognized as one of the nation's leading authorities on children, youth, and families; adolescent health and sexuality education; effective schools; and healthy communities. Among his honors, Dr. Scales received a 1988 U.S. Administration for Children, Youth, and Families' Commissioner Award for "outstanding efforts in child abuse prevention and a spirit which is an inspiration to others." He has authored or co-authored more than 250 articles, chapters, and books, including *The Sexual Adolescent: Communicating with Teenagers about Sex, Great Places to Learn: How Asset-Building Schools Help Students Succeed,* and *Developmental Assets: A Synthesis of the Scientific Research on Adolescent Development.* His latest book is *Other People's Kids: Social Expectations and American Adults' Involvement with Children and Adolescents* (Kluwer/Plenum).

Arturo Sesma, Jr., is an applied developmental researcher at Search Institute. He earned his bachelor's degree in psychology from the University of Illinois at Urbana-Champaign and his doctorate from the Institute of Child Development at the University of Minnesota.

Brent Bolstrom, a research assistant at Search Institute, earned his bachelor of arts degree with honors in psychology from St. Olaf College. Mr. Bolstrom's research interests lie around the contexts that contribute to healthy youth development, various indicators of resilience in development, and the protective factors that buffer against adversity and stress during childhood and adolescence. Other scientific work he is involved in at Search Institute includes multiple facets of the development of *Me and My World: A Search Institute Survey of Developmental Assets in Grades 4–6,* and two multi-year projects, *Positive Youth Development: Advancing the Field's Intellectual and Scientific Foundations,* and *Exploring the Science and Theology of Spiritual Development During Childhood and Adolescence.*